SEEING RED

Graham Poll

SEEING RED

HarperSport
An imprint of HarperCollins*Publishers*

HarperCollinsPublishers
77–85 Fulham Palace Road,
Hammersmith, London W6 8JB

www.harpercollins.co.uk

First published in 2007 by HarperSport
an imprint of HarperCollins London
First published in paperback in 2008

1 3 5 7 9 10 8 6 4 2

A CIP catalogue record for this book
is available from the British Library

ISBN 13 978-0-00-726283-0
ISBN 10 0-00-726283-3

Printed and bound in Great Britain by
Clays Ltd, St Ives plc

All photographs supplied courtesy of Graham Poll with the exception of the following: Action Images 7 (top right), 8 (top left); Empics/PA Photos 7 (top left), 7 (bottom); Getty Images 7 (centre); Reuters 6 (bottom left); Tracey Murrell (www.tracey-murrell.com) 8 (bottom).

For Julia,
Gemma, Josie and Harry

Contents

'Roman Abramovich is rich enough to have bought Chelsea and, if he wanted, he could select himself to play at centre-forward. But he could not referee a Premiership match, because that is something you can't buy'

G Poll

'If it doesn't kill you, it will make you stronger'

Craig Mahoney,
referees' sports psychologist

FOREWORD

By Sir Alex Ferguson

Referees have football's poisoned chalice. Obviously the game needs refereeing and yet very few people want to do it. So the likes of Graham Poll, who get involved at a young age at grassroots level, deserve enormous credit and the thanks of all of us who care about the game of football. Perhaps – no disrespect, Graham! – they are not the greatest footballers but they want to be involved in football because they love the game, and that is a very good thing.

Then, if they work their way up to professional level and the very serious stuff, they become the focus of an enormous amount of scrutiny. It is not just me, and all the other managers, watching their every move and being very demanding. It is not just the players and the fans who are focused on everything they do. It is, of course, all the television cameras. If a referee makes the smallest mistake, a television analyst will tell the world, 'That mistake cost this team a goal.' It is incredibly difficult to have the confidence to make decisions in those circumstances. Big brother is watching you all the time.

That is why, when the discussions were going on about referees becoming full-time professionals a few years ago, I was against the move. At a meeting in London about the subject I said that it didn't matter how much referees were paid and how often they trained, some of them would still not be able to make decisions. I said that it would not matter if we paid referees £300,000 a week and got them training every day; some of them would still not be able to make decisions.

I think I have been proved right about that. Some of our professional referees still cannot make decisions. That is a human characteristic which you will find in every walk of life. It is not confined to refereeing. You can either make a decision or you can't and I have worked with people, and known people, who just cannot.

My summary of Graham Poll is quite simple. He can make decisions. Without question, in my time in England, he has been the referee who has been easily the best decision-maker of all. He has been able to deport himself throughout his whole career with a confidence, and with expression, which has never been diluted by the presence of dozens of TV cameras watching him.

That view is supported by sound evidence, because it is not just me who thinks Graham has been a good decision-maker. That is what many others have said. That praise has enabled him to go into games with a certain confidence, but he had to have the gift for decision-making in the first place and had to earn the praise that came his way.

I am not saying that he gave decisions I approved of, or which favoured my club. He has taken some of our big games, and he has been hopeless in some of them! But now, as Graham is retiring, I am not assessing his career on the basis of some decision he made ten years ago or something like that. I am appraising him on the basis of the whole career and, as I say, he was never afraid to make decisions. When, as a manager, you take your team to places like Arsenal or Chelsea or Liverpool for really big games, you want a strong referee and that is why, for those huge fixtures, I was generally pleased to see the referee's name listed as 'Graham Poll'.

The other aspect of his character which struck me, as well as his ability and readiness to make decisions, was that he smiled when he refereed. I noted that the very first time he refereed a Manchester United game – against Queens Park Rangers in 1994. I remember that, in my match report to the authorities about the referee, I wrote that Graham was the first referee I had seen since arriving in England who I thought had a chance of being very good. I made that comment because I had seen him smiling.

With some referees, if they smile you get worried because you think they are about to do something to hurt you! But lots of them are too uptight to smile at all during the ninety minutes. Over the years, I came to know that when Graham smiled during a game, it meant he was relaxed and enjoying himself and enjoying the game. He was delighted to be on the pitch with great players and able to express his individuality.

I get asked to talk about a lot of people in football. I get approached to do a lot of forewords to books but I turn down many of these. I have to assess whether the person concerned has made a genuine contribution to football, and I am happy to introduce Graham's book because he has passed that test in my mind. He has, indeed, made a real contribution to football with his ability and his personality.

If he is retiring because of any disillusionment, I am sorry about that, but I know he has not fallen out of love with football itself. In what proved to be his last season he was still able to smile – a genuine, warm smile – during games. He is right to get out before he stops smiling.

CHAPTER ONE

Alone in the Middle

I stood in the centre-circle of the almost empty stadium in Stuttgart, fearful and very tearful. It was an hour and a quarter after the game and I craved a private moment at the scene of my public humiliation. The only place where I could be sure of being alone was out there on the pitch, where, in one sense, a referee is always alone.

The Gottlieb-Daimler Stadion had been revamped for the World Cup. It held 52,000 spectators and boasted the two biggest video screens in Europe, apparently. Cleaners were threading their way along the rows of seats and there were some lights on desks high up in one stand where journalists were still working on their reports. They were writing about the shocking mistake I had made but were probably too preoccupied to look at the forlorn figure in the middle of the pitch.

I was certainly preoccupied. I was in turmoil.

It was Thursday, 22 June 2006, the day I went from being the bloke who had a good chance of refereeing the World Cup Final to the clown who would always be remembered for a cock-up.

Billions of people around the world know that a football referee shows a player a yellow card when he cautions him. If he has to caution him a second time, and has to show him a second yellow card, then he must also show him a red card and send him off. Two yellows equal a red – simple. Most of those billions around the planet also know that I got it wrong. Mistakenly, unforgivably, I cautioned Croatia defender Josip Simunic three times, and showed him three yellow cards, before producing the red.

As I looked up, unseeingly, into the nearly deserted stands, and through the halo of the roof into the night sky of Germany, I thought about the magnitude of my mistake. Its implications kept going around in my head. I was too upset to think about the future but I did conclude that my twenty-six-year career was ending there and then. I worked out later that the game in Stuttgart was my 1,500th match, exactly. At that moment, I assumed it would be my last.

I became aware that there were other people out on the pitch area and saw that assistant referee Glenn Turner was standing, appropriately enough, by the touchline. I walked over and he gave me a hug. Neither of us said anything. Neither of us could. Finally, I left the pitch to make my way to the official car which would take me back to the hotel. But I took one last, lingering look back at the stands, the roof, the lights and the scoreboards. I was convinced I would never referee in a top stadium again.

There were even lower ebbs to come. In the days that immediately followed, I was in a dark, black cave. And for a long time afterwards there were bleak moments when the harrowing events of that night in Stuttgart came back to overwhelm me. I don't suppose I shall ever stop having nights when I lose sleep. I have a life sentence of asking myself, 'Why?'

But I did not let my career end there. I did not want to be defined by Stuttgart. It is only part of my story.

Yet I know that other people do define me by Stuttgart and the biggest mistake I made. It became clear, in the season that followed, that the wound my career suffered that night was, indeed, mortal. So we shall return to the Gottlieb-Daimler Stadion in this account, just as I return there in my mind all too often. And I shall explain what happened – even though I cannot explain why.

But first I want to tell you how, in the season that followed the 2006 World Cup, some very good folk, like David Beckham, tried to heal that wound. I also need to tell you how others, like John Terry, made the pain impossible to ignore.

CHAPTER TWO

Beckham Calling

The first telephone call I received when I arrived home from the World Cup was from David Beckham.

My wife, Julia, picked me up from Heathrow airport on her own, without our three children. Neither of us wanted pictures of the kids in the newspapers. She thought, as well, that I would need a bit of time alone with her, a bit of support, before being strong in front of our two daughters and our son.

Then, about an hour after I had arrived back, at last, to my home in Tring, my mobile rang. I did not want to talk to anyone but I answered it and a voice said, 'Graham? It's David. David Beckham. Becks.'

I thought it was a joker or a hoaxer. But he said, 'Remember I got that shirt for your daughter, Gemma?'

So I knew it was him. It was the England captain. He was in a hotel in Gelsenkirchen and the next day he was going to lead his country in a World Cup quarter-final. Yet he had taken time to telephone me. I had already received one message of support from him. The England squad had watched my own

World Cup implode and several had sent messages to me via another referee who visited their base camp. I was told that Beckham, the captain, had made a special point of saying, 'Tell him to keep his chin up.'

Now Beckham was on the telephone; a man and a father who could empathize with me and who wanted to reach out in friendship to me and my family. He knew all about making a mistake at a World Cup – and more than anyone about being vilified for it. People in England had hanged effigies of Beckham after he was sent off in 1998 against Argentina.

I had played a small part in helping him after 1998, by encouraging him during the Community Shield match which began the next season. He was only twenty-three then. Now, in 2006, Beckham was such a global mega-celebrity that when he phoned me, I was as excited as a star-struck kid.

I had been there, done that and got all the refereeing shirts. I was blasé about celebs. And at that moment, I didn't care about much at all, because I was so crushed by Stuttgart. Yet when Beckham phoned I fumbled with the buttons, trying to put the mobile on 'speaker' so that Julia could hear. I did not manage to find the right buttons. In any case, what the England captain said was a personal message for me.

He told me not to let it get me down. He told me it would pass. He asked if there was anything he could do.

What a man.

Friends and family had helped me when I was in the black cave of my abject despair in Germany. Thinking about the precious people in my life had provided the first pin-pricks of light. Now, back in England, Beckham's humanity gave me real inspiration.

A lot of good people also helped persuade me to keep going. The saying is that 'you learn who your friends are' and that is true. But you also learn that some people you barely know are decent as well. I remember collecting my son, Harry, from school one day in the season that followed the World Cup, when Burnley manager Steve Cotterill telephoned. He said, 'I hear you're thinking about packing it in, Pollie. Don't do it.' I had only refereed Cotterill's team once and yet he had made the effort to find my number and contact me. Gestures like that meant a lot, and so did the support of Keith Hackett, the man in charge of England's professional referees, who said to me, pointedly, 'Tell me why you should give up?'

So I kept going and the first match I refereed after the World Cup was a friendly between Tring Athletic and Bedmond Social. I had promised my local club that I would do it and I did not want to let them down. There were only about fifty spectators and I could not help thinking, as I warmed up, 'This is my 1501st match. If things had gone differently, match number 1501 might have been the World Cup Final.'

During the game, one of the players hacked somebody down but, because it was a friendly, I didn't book him. I said, 'I'll tell you what, mate – in the season that would have been a yellow.'

He replied, 'And two more and I would have been off.'

It was the first joke made to my face about Stuttgart. I managed a wan smile. I felt no antagonism at all towards a player but, in that moment, I saw a future of endless similar jokes.

The next day I refereed another friendly – between Chelsea and Celtic at Stamford Bridge. Uriah Rennie became unavailable and they asked me. It went well enough and on the Friday I went to Chelsea's training ground to talk to the players about new interpretations of the Laws. José Mourinho, the Chelsea manager, had asked for me. That too, went very well. Everything was sweet.

But then came the first competitive match: Saturday, 12 August 2006 – Football League, Colchester United versus Barnsley. I could not face it.

The plan was to ease me back in. The Football League season kicked off before the Premiership and so it seemed a good idea for me to start at Layer Road, Colchester. But I was not even ready for that. I pulled over and sat in the car in a lay-by on the A12, with the radio off, alone with my thoughts. They were all negative thoughts. For the first time, in a career that had taken me from Division Five of the North Herts League to two World Cups, I did not think I could fulfil an appointment.

But of course I had to and of course I did.

Colchester had been promoted to the top division of the Football League for the first time in their history. Their ground held only 6,000 and there were just 4,249 present for their second home game of the season, the Barnsley match. Yet I knew there would be a big media presence.

Peter Drury of ITV had already telephoned me to ask if I would do a pre-match interview with Robbie Earle. Peter is a good friend and I had admired Robbie when he was a player and had grown to like him as a man. But I declined the invitation to talk to the nation. I had made up my mind that an interview I had given in Germany would be my last public word for a year at least.

An ITV crew was lying in wait as I got to the ground and a camera was trained on me for every step of my walk from the car to the dressing room. Robbie Earle asked for 'just one comment on the record' but I said 'No' again. Later I ambled out into the middle for the pitch inspection, faking total confidence. The camera followed me again.

In the press box, at the modest occasion of a Football League game, were some big-name, big-hitting newspaper writers: the columnists and opinion-formers. Most of them had formed their own opinion about me years before. They thought I hogged the limelight. But I really did not want any publicity from them, particularly on that day.

When I went out to warm-up I braced myself. At best, I expected merciless mickey-taking from spectators. At worst, I feared scorn and derision. What I received was applause and some encouraging remarks from spectators. I have never been more delighted about the English trait of rallying round someone who has suffered. As the local football paper, *The Green Un*, remarked, 'Rarely has a referee been so popular.'

Of course there was banter. In one area of one stand, a group of supporters had pieces of yellow card with the number three written on them by the same pen and in the same handwriting. Someone had gone to a lot of trouble. Perhaps it was a coincidence that an ITV camera was stationed in that part of the ground. Perhaps.

The game kicked off. Eventually and inevitably I had to take a player's name. Out came my yellow card and I heard the chant that was to provide backing music for my season: '*Two more … he only needs two more*.'

That time the joke brought a genuine smile to my face and I thought, 'You can cope with this, Pollie.'

So I was up and running. Now what I hoped for was six months of … nothing. No headlines and no controversy. I wanted the only reference to me to be the one at the bottom of reports, under the teams, where it said, 'Referee: G. Poll (Herts)'.

A week after the Colchester game, the Premiership season kicked off and I took charge of Arsenal's first match at the stunning new Emirates Stadium, against Aston Villa. It passed without incident and I was less of a story for the media than I had been the week before.

Fulham's match against Sheffield United at Craven Cottage was my 300th Premier League fixture, and the next time the Select Group of referees gathered together, there was a little presentation to mark what was a significant milestone. However, in my frail state of mind, I took it as a sign that my race was almost run. I knew I would not reach 400. I wasn't even sure of reaching 350. So instead of celebrating passing the 300 mark, I just thought, 'That is your last milestone, Pollie.'

The matches kept coming and I was successfully avoiding headlines. I refereed the Merseyside derby at Goodison, which Everton won 3–0. I took charge when Arsenal won 1–0 at Old Trafford. I was back at Old Trafford when Manchester United beat Liverpool 2–0. They all went well; high-profile matches with a low-profile Pollie. Excellent.

I had a European Champions League match involving Real Madrid. Beckham made a point of coming to see me in my dressing room and, again, wishing me well. More encouragement. More positive thoughts.

I took charge of Chelsea's home game against Aston Villa and should have sent off Chelsea's Claude Makelele just before the end. But the referee's assessor did not dock me any points for it. All was going swimmingly.

I was scheduled to referee Tottenham versus Chelsea. It was a Sunday afternoon game, which would be televised live, on 5 November. Inevitably, Sky TV's pre-publicity asked, 'Will there be fireworks on Bonfire Day?' They obviously hoped the answer would be 'Yes'. I was desperate for a 'No'. Sky got their wish.

CHAPTER THREE

Chelsea on the Attack

At the start of every season, referees note the fixtures they consider 'golden games' – the top matches. In the Premier League they are the fixtures between the top four clubs and the derby games with the fiercest rivalries. Tottenham against Chelsea was not quite up there in that top rank, but it was certainly near the top of the next tier. For me, games at Tottenham's White Hart Lane were enjoyable for two reasons. Firstly, they were easy for me geographically – the hotel in which officials gather before the match is a shortish drive from my home – and the second reason I enjoyed games at White Hart Lane was that the club looked after officials and their guests particularly hospitably.

The problem is that referees' guests are seated two rows from the front, in a section next to some of the noisiest, most partisan away supporters. So, although nothing in the build-up led me to think that the game would be in any way out of the ordinary, on that 5 November my wife and children heard a few choice adjectives about me.

Chelsea scored first, after fifteen minutes. Spurs failed to clear a corner and Claude Makelele spanked in a twenty-five-yard, swerving volley. A few moments later, I spotted John Terry pushing and shoving as the ball came over for a corner and so I awarded a free-kick to Spurs. It was a perfectly straightforward decision but, after I had whistled, Didier Drogba headed the ball into the Spurs net. Spurs goal-keeper Paul Robinson had heard my whistle, and made no real attempt to stop the header, but Chelsea supporters thought, briefly, that their team had doubled their lead.

Instead, Tottenham equalized after twenty-four minutes. Jermaine Jenas took a free-kick and Michael Dawson, Tottenham's six foot two inch defender, scored with a glancing header.

The first refereeing flashpoint was at what should have been a routine free-kick, moments before half-time. It was away on Tottenham's right wing and should not have perturbed Chelsea at all, yet Makelele and Ashley Cole would not go back ten yards. When Makelele retreated, Cole edged forward, and vice versa. They both knew I was not going to let them get away with that, so perhaps their pantomime was designed to take the mickey and undermine my authority.

I paced out the distance and called out, 'Claude, Coley ... back you come ... just here ... please.'

They stayed put. Cole told me to 'F*** off'.

I did not send him off for that. I know that those who disapprove of all swearing during a match will contend that I should have done; but I did caution both Makelele and Cole. I had done all I could to get them to retreat sensibly.

Aaron Lennon put Spurs ahead seven minutes into the second half. He controlled Robbie Keane's deflected centre and then placed his careful shot out of the reach of Hilario. After sixty-three minutes, I cautioned Terry when he felled Dimitar Berbatov in full flow. Terry's was the sixth name in my book and had no particular significance to either of us at that moment.

But as my watch ticked off the minutes, Chelsea, whose discipline had been poor all game, began to look spooked by the possibility of defeat. The Press Association reporter at the game wrote, 'Chelsea had been clearly rattled by Tottenham's fightback.'

Michael Ballack gave me some verbals, and when I cautioned him for dissent, a group of Chelsea players surrounded me. I restored order and dispersed the posse of players but felt it had been a concerted attempt to intimidate me. It was probably instinctive and not deliberate, but I made a mental note that I would have to report it.

Then, at a corner, Terry grappled with Tottenham defender Ledley King. He grabbed King's arm and dragged him to the ground. I realized that I would have to send Terry off if I cautioned him again, but my honest, instinctive opinion was that the incident deserved a booking. If it had been a player who had not been cautioned already, it would not have been an issue, and so fairness required that I took his name, again.

A group of Spurs players, including Pascal Chimbonda, were confronting Terry and, as they did so, the Chelsea player began moving away from the penalty area. But he collided with Hossam Ghaly and I knew that, if I didn't act quickly, there would be a really ugly scene. I called Terry over, showed him the yellow and then the red cards, and he left the field without a mutter of complaint. No other Chelsea players protested about their captain's dismissal either – although they had complained about nearly every other decision throughout the game.

They found enough to moan about again when I ended the game a little later. As we walked off, Cole swore at me and had a go at my decision making.

I could have sent Cole off for that. I could have red-carded him for using insulting language, or shown him his second yellow for dissent, but I let it go. José Mourinho made a snide remark in the tunnel. Again, I did nothing about it. I was focused on reaching the changing-room.

Perhaps I should have done something about Cole or his manager, but I knew the punishments would be inconsequential. I knew too that referees cannot report every player and every manager who says something out of order – we'd get writer's cramp.

So, if you had asked me at that moment whether I had handled the game well, my honest assessment would have been that I had been a bit lenient afterwards towards Chelsea. But I would also have said that it had been probably the best game of the season so far and that, yes, I had helped facilitate it. I had done my job.

Five minutes after I had reached the officials' changing room, there was a knock on the door. It was John Terry and Gary Staker, Chelsea's player liaison officer and administrative manager. Terry said, 'I need to know why you sent me off.' In theory, he was not meant to be in my room. Only managers were permitted to go to the referee's room, and then only thirty minutes after the game. The idea is to give people a chance to calm down and to prevent the referee's room being besieged. But I like to sort things out face-to-face and I had got on well enough with Terry for several years. So I said, 'You had already been cautioned and then, in my view, you grabbed Ledley King and pulled him to the floor in an aggressive fashion. It wasn't as if you just lent on him – you pulled him down.'

He said, 'Oh. It wasn't a straight red then.'

'No, John,' I confirmed. 'It was a second yellow card.'

The fourth official, Peter Walton, who was also in the room, chipped in, 'So it means you will only miss one game.'

'Does it?' said Terry.

'Yes,' said Walton. 'It'll be the Carling Cup tie against Aston Villa.'

'Fine … that's fine then,' said Terry. He left, looking relieved.

I was not sure what that was all about. His initial inquiry – 'I *need* to know why you sent me off' – was a bit odd. The referee's assessor, Gary Willard, and the match delegate, former West Ham midfielder Geoff Pike, were happy as well. Willard gave me a strong hint that he wanted me to report Chelsea for the incident when I had been surrounded by an angry group of players and both Willard and Pike made comments about Terry looking guilty, rather than surprised, when he was sent off.

I did not have an inkling that a firestorm of controversy was about to erupt. Out of the blue, Chelsea attacked me from three directions. First – and I probably should have seen this one coming – manager José Mourinho purported to be mystified by the disallowed Drogba 'goal' and by Terry's sending-off. He told reporters, 'I don't understand why John Terry was sent off. I cannot find a reason for that. The team gave everything and played high-pressure football. We had chances with one player less. But Mr Poll goes home, and nobody can ask him about the reasons behind his decisions. I never ask referees about their decisions because they always have an excuse. So why should I ask him? He would say something like "Didier Drogba was free and had a clean header but somebody thirty metres away made a foul." They always have an excuse for their decisions.'

There was some seriously flawed logic there. He seemed to think that I should have allowed Drogba's 'goal' to stand because Terry's foul was some distance away. That is self-evidently nonsense. On that basis, if someone thumps one of Mourinho's men a long way from the ball, the referee should take no action.

But Ashley Cole, who provided the second prong of the attack on me, made the same daft mistake in his reasoning. He said, 'Sure, JT got involved with someone on the edge of the box but it was nowhere near the ball.' So what, Ashley? It was a foul. It occurred before Drogba headed the ball. It was not a goal – and it should not have been a controversy.

Cole made a much more damaging allegation about me, however. He said I had told Chelsea, 'You need to be taught a lesson.' He said that Frank Lampard had told him I had said that. Most newspapers took Cole's word at face value. The implication was that I was deliberately harsh on Chelsea. Some reporters jumped to the conclusion that I was trying to inflict my own punishment on Chelsea for the way they had harangued Italian referee Stefano Farina in the midweek game against Barcelona.

There was only one problem with that theory. I had not said anything about teaching Chelsea a lesson.

I merely said the sort of thing I had said to players for twenty-six years. During the time when Chelsea were haranguing me about the Ballack booking, I said to Lampard, 'Your team are losing their discipline. You need to get it sorted out or I will have to.' There is a profound difference between what I said and how Cole reported Lampard's version of what I said. I had urged Lampard to calm down his team-mates. I had not implied some sort of vendetta on my part.

But the newspapers had their headlines. Some went with the angle that I had told the England captain to 'F*** off'. Some were more excited about my determination to teach Chelsea a lesson. Neither was true.

The third attack on me had not happened yet, but another blow did land and hurt. During the following week the FA told me they were not taking any action against Chelsea for surrounding me and haranguing me because I had not been intimidated. In other words, because I had been strong enough to deal with the incident without looking terrified, Chelsea were going to get away with it.

With that decision, the FA let down every referee in the country – especially the teenagers taking charge of parks matches. The FA signalled to every team in the land that it was perfectly acceptable for an angry mob to surround refs and scream in their faces.

The FA had let me down as well. That season, like never before, I needed their backing. I had made a big mistake at the World Cup and, if I was going to get back my credibility, the FA needed to stop players disputing every decision I made and undermining me by crowding around in a querulous gang.

I asked, in passing, whether Ashley Cole was going to be charged over what he had accused me of saying. The response from the FA astounded me. I was told, 'We need to investigate the matter thoroughly before making a decision.' So, instead of supporting me, the FA were investigating me. They thought I might actually have said that I wanted to teach Chelsea a lesson. I felt hugely let down.

Then came attack number three from Chelsea. It was launched by Terry himself in an interview with Chelsea's own television channel that was gleefully picked up by all the newspapers. He said, 'On the pitch Graham Poll said to me that it [the second yellow card] was for the barge on Hossam Ghaly where I just kept running. Then, after the game, he then said to me it was for the fall when me and Ledley King fell. So, you know, he's obviously had a look at it or got people to look at it and decided that's probably the best option for him as it covers every angle for him.'

This time the clear and utterly unfounded allegation was that I had changed my story and had produced a deliberately falsified account. The impression the England captain was trying to create was that he should not have been sent off. There had only been a minor collision and, on thinking about it later, the referee had changed his story to blame a different incident.

If Terry genuinely believed that is what happened he was completely mistaken. I had not changed my story at all. On the field I had not given Terry any explanation about why I was sending him off. That was why he came to ask me about it afterwards in my changing room. The account I gave him in the changing room was the only version of events I described for him. It was the only version there was, because it was the truth.

Perhaps Cole and Terry had simply forgotten that all the match officials were wearing microphones and earpieces throughout the game. Doh! Mine was an 'open mike'. The two assistants and the fourth official had heard everything I had said. They had not heard me say that Chelsea needed to be taught a lesson. They had not heard me tell Terry to 'F*** off'. They had not heard me say to Terry on the field why I was sending him off. They did not hear any of those things because I had not said them.

There were TV cameras as well as the microphone, and so I was able to say, in an email to the FA about Terry's accusation, 'There were no words exchanged at the time of his dismissal or indeed anything from the moment he fouled his opponent, Mr King, until after the final whistle. The video of the match shows this clearly.'

I sent off my email and waited for the FA to deal with the matter. It was to prove a long and frustrating wait.

CHAPTER FOUR

Big Time Charlie

I was outraged by the accusations by Cole and Terry, appalled that newspapers took them at face value and devastated that the Football Association investigated me. The biggest hurt was caused by the FA.

In fact, I don't blame Chelsea, their manager or their players for haranguing me on the pitch or the verbal assaults off it. They were encouraged to do and say what they did because, time and time again, they had seen the FA do sweet f.a.

As far as the accusations were concerned, I knew the evidence would exonerate me. I also suspected that the Chelsea players would back down. To persevere with the allegation that I had said they needed to be taught a lesson would have alleged also that both assistant referees and the fourth official were involved in a conspiracy of lies with me.

Yet there was no word from the FA of any charges against Chelsea. The affair was still being investigated. I was still being investigated. They had the reports from four match officials they were supposed to trust. What more did their investigation need? I am not sure I can convey how vulnerable that made me feel; vulnerable and betrayed. How was I supposed to command the respect of players in other matches if allegations about my integrity were not rebutted? If the FA doubted me, how was I supposed to repair my fractured credibility?

I asked to be taken off the Carling Cup tie between Everton and Arsenal on the Wednesday because I felt so downcast and devalued. Looking back, missing that game would have sent out the wrong message. It would have created the impression that I had been suspended because of the Chelsea accusations. So it was perhaps fortunate that I was told that I had to go ahead and referee the fixture at Everton. I would have to tough it out. Perhaps it would be a nice, incident-free match. Not a chance.

In the twentieth minute Everton appealed for a penalty when Andy Johnson was tackled. It looked like a fair challenge to me, so I span away from the incident to follow play. I was aware that James McFadden was chasing after me but I was concentrating on the game. Then, as clear as anything, I heard McFadden shout, 'You f***ing cheat!'

His team-mate, Tim Cahill, was near me and grabbed my arm. He said, 'Don't do it, Pollie.' Cahill knew, McFadden knew and I knew what the Scot had said.

Whatever nonsense people say about me seeking controversy, I ask you to believe that the last thing I needed that night was more back page headlines. But McFadden had run thirty or forty yards to call me a cheat. It was not a spontaneous, heat-of-the-moment remark. Other players had heard it.

Referees hate being called a cheat. The whole foundation of refereeing is that you make honest decisions. You want to get those decisions right – you strive to get them right – but if there are mistakes, they are honest mistakes. I would have betrayed my profession if I had not sent off McFadden. So I did.

The ground erupted. It had to be a home player, didn't it? And Everton manager David Moyes proved a major disappointment. Before the match, during my warm-up, he came over and said, 'Don't let them get to you, Graham. We all know you are the best referee.' Yet after the match he staged a theatrical stunt at the media conference. He produced McFadden, who denied that he had called me a cheat. Everton's case was that the player had said 'f***ing shite' rather than 'f***ing cheat'. So that was all right then! But I know what he said.

Moyes told the assembled media, 'Once again we have a situation where Graham Poll says a player says one thing and the player says he said something different. Who do you believe?' That 'once again' comment was a reference to the Chelsea accusations.

After reviewing the match report – which included the explanation that McFadden had been dismissed for calling me a cheat – Everton decided not to appeal against the decision. So I was once again exonerated.

The assessor, Mike Reed, thought I'd had a 'brilliant' game. But, when I got back to my hotel, a group of Everton fans did not share that view. By then they had probably heard the Everton version of McFadden's abuse, so they spat out some expletives of their own at me.

Next morning, when I turned on my mobile, there was a text message and a voicemail from Keith Hackett, manager of the referees' Select Group. He was in Switzerland at a UEFA meeting. He had instructed me to call him urgently 'about a financial irregularity regarding car sponsorship'.

A what? I could not believe it. I phoned UEFA and demanded that they dragged Keith out of his meeting. With mounting paranoia, I shouted at my boss. I yelled, 'What the hell is going on, Keith? Is this being pushed out by a club? Where is all this coming from?' He asked me if I had a sponsored car. I said, 'Why do you need to ask that? I have my own car and my bank statement can show that I pay for that car every month.'

He said, 'The Premier League press office have been phoned by a paper. The paper say they have a copy of an agreement showing that you have a sponsored car ...'

I replied, 'Point one: I don't have a sponsored car. Point two: is it wrong if I did? Dermot Gallagher has one with the sponsor's name across the side. Keith, somebody is trying to do me, turn me over.'

My boss went back to his meeting and I made a mental tally of recent events. I had been maligned by two Chelsea players, one of whom was the England captain. I had sent off an Everton player for questioning my integrity. His manager had questioned my veracity. I had been abused by supporters. I had been accused of some sort of financial impropriety. Oh, and I had been betrayed by the Football Association. All in just under four days.

At breakfast I read a report of the Everton game in *The Guardian*. The writer said that if I was offended by being called a cheat, I needed to get out more. I did not read any other reports but I now know they were scathing. The *Mirror's* headline was 'POLL POTTY' and, in a later edition of *The Guardian,* Dominic Fifield came to this considered appraisal of me:

> Already under investigation by the Football Association after allegations made against him by Chelsea's disgruntled players in defeat on Sunday, his penchant for the theatrical

> is stripping him of credibility, his apparent desire to be the centre of attention – he was signing autographs prior to kick-off – unhelpful when he attempts to officiate. He would argue, with some justification, that it was McFadden's folly which prompted the red card, but it appears that he revels in the notoriety such controversy affords him.

Other reports pointed out that I was already in the spotlight over my 'much-criticized decision' to dismiss John Terry. Some reminded readers that Terry said he had been given two different versions of why he was shown a second yellow card and that team-mate Ashley Cole accused me of bias against his club. Very few reports bothered to add that I had denied the claims of Terry and Cole.

In the car on the way home, I turned on the radio – to hear a phone-in caller repeat the comment that I had indulged in an autograph-signing session before the previous night's game. The caller said, 'He's Mr Big Time Charlie, Mr Superstar who loves the attention.'

The truth, if anyone is bothered about the truth, is that before the game and before the ground was open to the public, there were three or four lads by one of the dug-outs who were with one of the club officials. They asked for my autograph. I obliged. If I had not, then presumably I would have been a Big Time Charlie who thinks he is too important to bother with kids who want his autograph.

On the way home, as I drove off the M6 toll road and pulled onto the M42, I looked at my eyes in the rear-view mirror because I knew they were brimming up with tears. Alone with my feelings, my emotions had spilled over.

In any other period of my refereeing career, I would have been angered by the accusations and understandably upset by the crescendo of criticism, but I cannot imagine they would have made me tearful. Now, however, five rough days had brought confirmation of a truth I had been avoiding: I had fallen out of love with refereeing. Not football – I still loved football – but I no longer loved refereeing. That realization brought a dead weight of sadness.

Refereeing had been so important to me for half my life, but I had refereed the Everton game really well and yet still had my competence and integrity doubted. It was clear to me that my credibility was gone forever. The disillusionment and deep, deep disappointment I felt as I drove home from the city of Liverpool was intense and oppressive.

Earlier that week, on the morning of the Spurs–Chelsea game, Patrick Barclay had written a short little tribute to me as a 'PS' at the bottom of his column in the *Sunday Telegraph*. The brief article finished with two points which meant the world to me. I am not sure journalists realize how their words can hurt or heal. But, after referring to my three-card trick at the World Cup, Paddy wrote:

> Two thoughts arise. The first is that I'd rather have a referee who makes an isolated technical mistake than one as weak as Stefano Farina proved in Barcelona last Tuesday. The other is that if England's players, many of whom did far worse than Poll in Germany, were ever to show half the character he has displayed since the resumption of hostilities, they might yet win something.

I have chosen to reprint the piece of flattery from the *Sunday Telegraph* because of the contrast between the kind picture it paints of me and the state I was in a few days later, on that journey home from Liverpool. If Patrick Barclay had seen me close to tears in my car, he might have had less praise for my strength of character; or, I suppose, he might have understood how difficult season 2006/07 really was.

Soon after I reached my home, a woman reporter from *The Times* arrived at my door to ask some questions. I had given one interview, to Sky TV, in Germany after my Stuttgart misadventure and had taken a vow of silence since. So I asked *The Times* woman to leave. Unable to write anything much about me, she wrote some spiteful things about Tring. I was upset about that, because the people of the town had been very supportive.

It had not been a very good week so far. The next morning, Friday, a letter arrived, addressed on the envelope to 'G Poll, Tring'. That was all. My instinct told me it would be abuse from a Chelsea supporter or a very quick Everton fan. I told myself not to open it, but I did. It was from a lad named Thomas from an address in Bishop's Stortford, Hertfordshire. It said:

> Dear Mr Poll
> I am typing this on my dad's computer. I am training to be a ref and am 14-years-old. I watched the game on Sunday and thought you had a good game. I think it is wrong for players to question referees decisions and I think it was god *[sic]* for you to tell the Chelsea players they needed to learn a lesson on discipline. It is not just them it is players from all teams. Some-times I think refs need to be stronger and tell these players these sort of things. Anyway got to go because my dad wants the internet. I haven't got your address but I know you live in Tring so I hope you get this. I am reffing game on Sunday and will try and be like you.

Interestingly, even this young man assumed I had told Chelsea they needed to be taught a lesson. But his letter reminded me that I owed a responsibility to all the referees in the entire football pyramid. My responsibility to them was not to be broken or cowed by false allegations. Thomas cannot have known the positive effect his letter had on me. I wrote back to him, enclosing some refereeing 'goodies'.

A little later that day, I headed back to the North-West to stay overnight ahead of my Saturday fixture: Manchester City versus Newcastle. The match was going to be live on Sky at lunchtime and they were billing it as, 'Graham Poll's next game'.

Somewhere between Stoke and Manchester, as I sat in the stationary queue of traffic which seems mandatory on the M6, I was telephoned by Brian Barwick, the chief executive of the Football Association. He wanted to draw my attention to some mildly supportive comment pieces in some newspapers. He said, 'I hear you have been thinking about possibly giving up. Well, I hope you have been reading the more positive press coverage today.'

All my anger and frustration at his organization exploded. I told him how disappointed I was that Chelsea had not been charged with intimidation – a signal that it was all right to mob referees. I was doubly disappointed that nobody at Chelsea had been charged with anything for making allegations about my integrity. And I told him it was an absolute disgrace that the FA themselves had decided to investigate me and then had let that investigation drag on.

I said, 'It is because the FA is not strong with people who say things about referees, and do these things to referees, that James McFadden believes it is OK to call me a cheat.

'You, the FA, should have backed me straight away after the Tottenham v Chelsea game, or conducted a very quick inquiry. Then you, as chief executive of the Football Association, should have held a press conference saying it is wrong to question the integrity of referees.

'You should have done that – not for me, but for every referee in the country. But you didn't and so there will be 27,000 referees going out this weekend knowing that they cannot rely on the support of the Football Association. When a referee takes firm and correct action you don't support him.'

Barwick huffed and puffed but didn't know what to say. My final comment to him was a question. I asked, 'How on earth do you expect me to go out and referee a football match tomorrow?'

Richard Scudamore, chief executive of the Premier League, also telephoned me and I asked him the same question. Scudamore said, 'You will go out tomorrow and referee brilliantly as you always do.'

I responded, 'And you take that for granted. You think that just happens. You have no idea how difficult that is – not just for me but all referees, given the scrutiny we are under. This is the hardest it has ever been to referee well in the Premiership. It won't get easier and it is not pleasant any more.'

As soon as I reached the City of Manchester Stadium, I was dogged by a Sky TV crew. The cameraman followed my every step as I went inside and again later as I checked the pitch. But the game between City and Newcastle went off without a goal or controversy. The assembled media pack was greatly disappointed. I was delighted.

CHAPTER FIVE

No Defence from John Terry

The Chelsea affair was dragging on. I telephoned FA headquarters at Soho Square every day to check if there was any progress. I wanted the cloud of suspicion over me dispersed. I talked to Graham Noakes, the FA's Director of Football Administration and Refereeing, or to Tarik Shanel in the FA's Compliance Department. Every day the answer was the same: the investigation was 'ongoing'.

Why? My report, and those of the other match officials, had been submitted within twenty-four hours of the game. Why, after all this time, had they not supported their four officials? I knew that the Compliance Department had compiled a full video sequence of Terry leaving the pitch. It confirmed that he had said nothing to me and that I had said nothing to him. The Chelsea and England captain's version was clearly wrong. Yet the FA seemed reluctant to conclude their inquiry. Did they not want to charge the England captain?

By the evening of Friday, 17 November – twelve days after the match at Tottenham – I'd had enough waiting. I telephoned Graham Noakes at the FA and threatened to pull out of the following day's game (Reading versus Charlton) and said that unless there was some action on the inquiry I would give a story to a newspaper telling them of my disgust with the football authorities. I would say that the FA had failed every referee in the country. After all, that is exactly what they had done.

Just making my double warning endangered my career. If I had actually carried out either threat, then who knows what would happened. The authorities find it a lot easier to sack a referee than to back him.

I did referee Reading's game against Charlton, but I should not have – I was terrible. My confidence was shot to pieces. The FA knew I would go through with the other threat if necessary. I would definitely take my story to a newspaper because I'd had enough.

Finally, on 30 November, twenty-five days after the Spurs–Chelsea game, the FA published a statement on their website. It said that John Terry had been charged with improper conduct for making his allegation that I had changed my story about his sending-off. The rest of the FA statement is worth reporting because it tells you all you need to know about that organization. It read:

> Graham Poll has also been cleared by The FA of saying anything inappropriate towards Chelsea players during the same match regarding their discipline. Responses sought from Ashley Cole, Frank Lampard, Chelsea FC and the match officials confirm that Poll did not say that Chelsea needed "to be taught a lesson". There will be no action against any parties on this matter. Chelsea manager José Mourinho has been reminded of his responsibilities for media comments related to Poll's performance in the same match and asked to use the relevant official channels

to give feedback on the performance of referees. He will not face any formal disciplinary action.

Once again, I was vindicated. I had not said that Chelsea needed to be taught a lesson. I had been cleared. Cole, however, was not punished at all for glibly making the accusation, nor was Mourinho punished for suggesting that I was incompetent and that I did not care. The Chelsea manager had been 'reminded of his responsibilities'. That was telling him.

Terry had fourteen days to respond to the charge. Initially Chelsea indicated that he would request a personal hearing. Chelsea normally hire top barristers for disciplinary hearings and it seemed they were gearing themselves up for another fight with authority, but then on Monday, 8 January, more than two months after the match, Terry – or someone on his behalf – contacted the FA to withdraw the request for a personal hearing and to admit the charge. The England captain's admission was an acceptance that his version of events was inaccurate.

The next day the FA held their hearing, using only written submissions. Terry was fined £10,000 – about a morning's wages. That was telling him as well. However, the FA issued an unprecedented statement. It said: 'We were extremely disappointed the integrity of Poll was questioned. We note the late admission to the charge and the excellent previous disciplinary record of John Terry. But we are also disappointed that no public apology had been forthcoming for his admitted improper conduct.'

It was a limp, puny condemnation. But it was still a condemnation of the England captain by the Football Association and so it was, in its own way, remarkable.

Ashley Cole had blithely sworn at me and then made shocking accusations about me, but at least his remarks had been straight after the game when he was steamed up about losing to Spurs. By contrast, Terry had produced his inaccurate allegations two days after the match, when he had had time to think about what he wanted to say about his sending-off.

His account had made damaging allegations about what I had said. Video recordings disproved his account – and yet he simply kept quiet. He simply let the FA case against him proceed and paid the paltry fine. He did not apologize for his account, even though it questioned the integrity of a referee and added to the corrosive criticism of officials which erodes the entire game.

David Beckham, Terry's predecessor as England captain, demonstrated privately to me that he is a decent, caring human being. By sending me a message of support in Germany and then telephoning as soon as I got home, he behaved as I think an England captain should.

John Terry had his version of events proven false and then was not big enough to apologize or even acknowledge publicly what he had done.

You will make your own judgement about whether that behaviour befits an England captain. I know what I think.

CHAPTER SIX

Stop the Ride

By the time the Football Association's disciplinary wheels started to move to exonerate me, Julia and I were on our way to Lavenham, in Suffolk, for a break. But there was no break from recognition.

We were pulled over by a police car after a slightly dodgy overtaking manoeuvre but the officers really stopped me because they realized it was me. They let us continue on our journey after they told me they were Ipswich fans – and after I pointed out that I had refereed their club's 9–0 home defeat by Manchester United in 1995.

After checking in at the hotel, we went for a walk but a white van stopped and the driver wanted to ask us for directions to somewhere or other. He climbed out of his van and the first thing he said was, 'It's Graham Poll.'

Then, that night, we ordered drinks in a pub and a guy in his mid-thirties said, 'I'll get those ... it is Graham isn't it? I feel for you. You've had a rough time. I've started refereeing this season and I base my game on yours. So I'm shit as well.'

Next, at dinner in our hotel, a couple at a nearby table started talking about me loudly enough for me to hear. And finally, after signing the bill but then deciding I wanted to add to it by buying a bottle of wine, I was told that two waiters had taken the bill because they wanted to copy my signature.

I was not quite sure what that was about. But I was sure that Julia and I would never 'get away from it all' while I remained controversial Graham Poll, the referee who made the huge mistake in the World Cup. I started to understand that the 2006/07 season should be my last as a referee.

There is no upper age limit for referees in England now, thanks to anti-age discrimination laws. But FIFA referees must retire from the international list at the end of the calendar year in which they reach 45. So I would come off the international list in 2008, and I had always intended to stop refereeing altogether that year. The plan was that I could either quit after the 2008 European Championships or at the end of that year. I would not continue refereeing in England without the international badge. I had worked so hard to earn it.

After the 2006 World Cup, I knew I would not be going to Euro 2008. But once I had decided not to quit there and then, I still had 2008 in my mind as my retirement year. That meant at least two more seasons and possibly two and a bit. But as the first of those two seasons unfolded, and I became dispirited and disillusioned, I began to think that I would hang up my whistle – as the cliché goes – in the summer of 2007.

In November 2006 I went to see Graham Barber – the ex-referee and a good, good friend – at his place in Spain and he said, 'Get through this season and then see how you feel.' He told me I should not let 'them' beat me. By them, he meant the unsupportive football authorities. But, increasingly in the next few months, I began to suspect that I was already beaten.

I had come home from the World Cup with a terrible, mortal wound. To keep going for two more seasons, as I wanted, I needed support from the FA. Yet they allowed my integrity to be questioned. Instead of supporting me, the FA just looked on as my wound was ripped open and made worse.

In December 2006, I refereed AC Milan against Lille in the Champions League. As the teams were waiting in the tunnel before the tie, Dario Simic, Milan's Croatian midfielder, came over to me. I had sent him off on that fateful night in Stuttgart. In Milan, Simic looked me straight in the eyes and said, 'I am so sorry for what happened. We knew Simunic had already been booked. We should have told you. I am so sorry.'

Lille won 2–0. After the game, Simic came over to me again. He repeated. 'I am sorry. Please accept my shirt.' I did not know whether to laugh or cry, hug him or hit him. In the end, I just accepted the shirt – in the spirit in which it had been offered.

Later, Simunic promised to send me a shirt as a memento of the night we made history. I accepted that gesture as well with as much good grace as I could muster. But there could be no closure about Stuttgart. Every time I was involved in a refereeing controversy, it coloured people's perception of what had happened and was usually mentioned in the media reports.

Yet one game gave me a glimpse of how things might be different for me, and for all referees – if all managers were as honest as Stuart Pearce. In the very next match I reffed after going to Milan, I red-carded Manchester City's Bernardo Corradi in the final minutes of a defeat at Old Trafford. I had already cautioned him and then, in my opinion, he 'dived' to try to win a penalty. I cautioned him again and so sent him off.

My decision was widely praised, but only because Pearce, the City manager, backed me and not his player. Pearce said, 'I have no complaints about the sending-off. Bernardo went down a little bit too easily and I am not like the other nineteen managers, who would sit here and give you a load of cock and bull about it.'

Great. That is what you want to hear when you have sent someone off. How could the fans or the press have a go at me when Pearce had not? That lifted my spirits, and that game at Old Trafford was followed by a run of matches which went well. But then my last two assignments of 2006 brought two more rows.

Late in the Charlton versus Fulham match, on 27 December, assistant referee Steve Artis flagged for handball by Charlton's Djimi Traore. I was in no position to see, so I backed my assistant. Fulham equalized from the free-kick. TV replays showed it was not handball and so Charlton, who were battling to avoid relegation, felt robbed. After the game, Charlton manager Alan Pardew complained, 'In the last few minutes of the match, when my players have forgotten what it's like to win a game of football, I expect them to be nervous and make silly mistakes. I don't expect match officials to make similar mistakes.'

The point, surely, is that officials do make mistakes, exactly like players. It was Artis's first season but I wrote in my official report that I would be happy for him to run the line in any game I refereed. He had been outstanding until that one, human, error.

Then, with four days of 2006 remaining, I was fourth official at Vicarage Road for Watford against Wigan. In the second half, with the score at 1–1, torrential rain turned the pitch into a paddy field. Steve Tanner, who was in charge of his second Premier League game, asked my advice but it was still his decision to abandon the game. It was the correct decision, as well. But it was not the weather or even the ref who got the blame. According to the many media reports that highlighted and criticized my involvement, it was me. When I raised a glass on New Year's Eve, the toast was, 'Good riddance to 2006.'

January was like December, with ups and downs. I believe the expression is 'a rollercoaster of emotions', but the truth is that, by then, I knew I wanted to get off the ride. That thought became sharper and more definite in January and soon it was an irrevocable decision. There were still plenty of 'ups' but they were never sufficient to make me change my mind. The 2006/07 season would be my last.

On the last day of January, I was appointed to a Chelsea match for the first time since John Terry had made up that story about me. The Premier League had waited and waited, but we all knew that I had to officiate with Chelsea again.

Terry was injured and not playing. But as I was warming up, he walked past me and made a small gesture of acknowledgement – a slight nod and a partial raising of his open palm. Was it to say, 'Hello'? Was it to say, 'Sorry'? Who knows?

The other Chelsea players started the game by ignoring me completely – not rudely, but just not indulging in any of the usual banter or comments. Then, slowly, things began to get back to normal. At one point, when Ashley Cole was being put on a stretcher, Didier Drogba said to me, 'Ignore all of them. We know you are a good referee.'

By 'all of them' he could have meant the crowd, who were abusing me, or the media or even the other Chelsea players. I didn't know what he meant, and it didn't matter. He was just trying to encourage me. With that, he went to give me a 'high five'. I responded instinctively and we slapped palms. I dare say I got more criticism for that – for being over-familiar with players and a bit too 'show biz', but, for me, it was a lovely moment. There were other good moments too, but by then I knew I was going to finish.

When I had decided, after Germany, to keep going, it was the right decision but for the wrong reason. I had thought, 'You could get a Champions League Final, Pollie,' but that was the wrong type of motivation. You can't referee just because of the possibility of one match – not least because, as happened in 2005, 2006 and 2007, English teams might reach the Champions League Final which would mean I could not referee it. Carrying on purely for the chance of a Champions League Final was the wrong motivation for another reason as well. It was wrong because the only inducement that really works is that you love it – and I no longer did.

I was still refereeing well, I believe. Certainly I was still making big calls without worrying about anything other than whether I thought they were right. In February, Tottenham's Robbie Keane scored twice against Bolton, but then he stopped a shot going into the Spurs goal with his arm. To me, it was a deliberate act. So it was handball. So it was denying the opposing team a goal. So it was a sending-off. Robbie said, 'On my life, it was an accident,' but I went with what I believed I had seen. That was the only way I could referee. So when Robbie said, 'I've never been sent off,' I replied, 'You have now.'

An injury prevented my refereeing Liverpool–Manchester United and I was really disappointed – because it would have been my last time in charge of one of English football's big, set-piece fixtures. Why did I care if I no longer loved refereeing? Well, I suppose that I was noting the milestones as I neared my finish.

If I had any lingering doubts about finishing – if there were any tiny doubts loitering anywhere in my mind – they were eradicated by another game, another fresh set of accusations and a reporter and a photographer appearing on my doorstep.

The match, on 9 April, Easter Monday, was Charlton against Reading at The Valley – or relegation-threatened Charlton, as the media felt obliged to call them, at home to the season's surprise success story.

In the first half, Charlton's Alexandre Song Billong committed a bad foul, and so I booked him. At half-time, Alan Pardew, who had been so upset with an assistant referee's decision the last time I had been to The Valley, came to my changing room. In theory, managers are only allowed in the referee's room thirty minutes after the finish of the match and, normally, I would have kept him out. But he was in before I realized it was him and, besides, lots of managers make comments at half-time, usually in the tunnel on the way off. Arsène Wenger does it, for instance, and so does José Mourinho. Most of them do. Whether they are just getting something off their chests, or hoping to influence you in the second half, it doesn't matter. You are not going to be influenced any way.

Pardew said, 'All I want to say is be careful with Song. Don't send him off.'

I said, 'Alan, give me some credit,' by which I meant that I would referee properly. I was not seeking to send off Song, or anyone else.

He said, 'Thanks' and headed off.

In any game of football, if a player has one yellow card and then commits a foul which is not worth a second caution, you call him to you and make it clear to him – and to everyone in the ground – that it's 'one more and you are off'. You pointedly indicate the tunnel, to make it clear, 'That is where you will be going if you are not careful.' The reason you do that is to sell your next decision. You are telling him, and telling the crowd, what might happen. Then, if it does happen, everybody accepts it.

So, in the second half, when Song committed a foul which was not worth a second yellow, I went through that whole warning routine with him. Soon after that, Pardew took Song off and replaced him with a substitute.

I went home after the game, content with another job well done. But, unbeknown to me, at his press conference, Pardew said, 'At half-time I went to see Graham Poll and I said "I need to have some signal if he is getting close to being sent off." He sent me that signal so Alex had to come off. It was full credit to Graham. That's the sort of refereeing you need.'

Pardew was trying to praise me. His recollection of our conversation was a little different to mine, but not significantly so. But the media took his comments to mean that he and I had concocted some secret deal. The implication was that I had favoured Charlton.

The next day, when I was sitting in my study, I saw two men pitch up at my front door: a little chap with a notebook and another bloke with a camera. Julia went to the door.

They told her they were from the *Mirror.* She told them I was busy. So they went to wait in their two separate cars.

Next, two football reporters from another newspaper telephoned me separately. One admitted, when I asked him, that it was only a story because it was me and because of Stuttgart. The other writer from that newspaper, a friend, said he needed a bit of information so that he could 'kill' the story.

I thought it was all unbelievable. I had refereed the game really, really well and yet I had headlines in the papers and people on my doorstep. There had been no clandestine deal, no special signal for Alan Pardew. Yet newspapers and their readers were quite ready to believe that I would do something partisan. That assumption – that I would favour one side – was what hurt.

One reason for that assumption was that people are always ready to assume the worst about any referee, but another reason for the assumption in this particular case was because it was me – the bloke who had messed up in Stuttgart. I'd made a big mistake in Germany. I was fallible. I could easily get something badly wrong at Charlton. That was the reasoning, and that was why I had to pack up that season.

CHAPTER SEVEN

Despicable Outburst

I kept my decision to retire a secret for as long as possible. If I had announced it straightaway then pundits would have speculated that it was because of Stuttgart. They would have been right, but I did not need Stuttgart discussed again.

I told my family, of course, and the youngest member of the clan almost gave the game away. Harry, my little son, had a 'secrets book' at school. It was part of his school's anti-bullying policies. If a child was bullied, he or she could write about it in the secrets book. Harry wrote in his book, 'I can't tell anyone but my dad is going to stop being a referee.'

I did a rather better job of keeping my secret, although it caused a few problems. For instance, I knew that I would not be refereeing any more international matches after that last season, 2006/07, and I knew that my final total would be close to one hundred. As someone who always set himself targets, I thought it would be excellent to reach that landmark, but, of course, UEFA did not know that my career was ending and were in no hurry to give me match number 100.

I reached ninety-eight before Christmas, but then there was a long, unexpected gap between appointments. When match ninety-nine arrived, it was a UEFA Cup clash between Paris Saint-Germain and Benfica in Paris – the only major European city in which I had not refereed. That was great, but I began to wonder if I would actually reach three figures.

I was not appointed for any of the March internationals and so I spoke to the FA and asked if there was a problem. They said, 'No' and that I was going to get an international in June. They thought that was good news for me. I could not tell them that it meant I would either have to delay my retirement or accept that it would be ninety-nine and out.

Then my friend Yvan Cornu, UEFA's referees' manager, hinted that I might not have to wait until June for game 100, and I started trying to work out what he meant. Three English clubs reached the semi-finals of the Champions League, which ruled out an English referee. The first legs of the UEFA Cup semi-finals were also out because I was speaking at a dinner with Pierluigi Collina – he was on the UEFA referees' committee by then, and I assumed that he would not want to mess up the plans for the dinner. That left only the second legs of the UEFA Cup semi-finals.

I wanted family and friends with me at my 100th and last international game, and so, forewarned by Yvan Cornu's card-marking, I investigated flights and hotels for the two UEFA Cup second legs – in Seville and Bremen.

I have told you all these arcane details to try to capture both the anticipation and frustration of waiting and hoping for an international appointment. It is all a bit cloak-and-dagger and if you make any assumptions about your own appointment, UEFA are likely to take the game away from you.

I waited impatiently for notification of game number 100. When it was announced, it was Seville – the match between two Spanish clubs, Sevilla and Osasuna. I am sure Bremen can be a lovely place, but I was very pleased by the news. Even if I had scripted it myself – setting out exactly how I wanted my one hundredth, and final, international match to unfold – I could not have improved on the actual events. Throughout this book I am trying to answer the question, 'Why would anyone want to be a referee?' The semi-final, second leg of the UEFA Cup provides one answer.

For Dutch referee Eric Braamhaar, the first leg did not go so well. He tore a calf muscle and there was a seven-minute delay before he was replaced by the fourth official. The only goal of the game was scored by Roberto Soldado of Osasuna, ten minutes into the second half.

I was at that dinner with Collina when the first leg was played, but I recorded the match and watched it when I arrived home in Tring, to pick up some pointers for the second leg. It was not difficult to glean what my game would be like because the theme of the first match was the mutual lack of respect between the two teams. The sub-plot was the frequency with which players went down unnecessarily, and stayed down, pretending to be hurt. I also saw Osasuna striker Savo Milosevic, the former Aston Villa player, appear to shove an opponent in the face out of sight of the referee. And at the finish there was a nasty mêlée. The second leg was going to be interesting then.

Peter Drury, the ITV commentator who was working at the first leg, lives in Berkhamsted, near Tring, and talked to me about some of the refereeing issues. He said, 'I pity the poor so-and-so who has to referee the second leg.'

'Thanks.'

He said, 'It's not you, is it?'

Knowing he could be trusted, I said, 'Yup.'

My team for the second leg was Darren Cann and Roger East as assistants, with Mike Dean as fourth official. My other team was the family and friends who came to share my secret big occasion – Julia, my sister Susan, brother-in-law Tony, Rob Styles and Rob's wife Liz. I told the assistants and fourth official that the reason for the suspiciously large contingent of family and friends was that it was game number 100.

In order for it to be a celebration, and not a wake, I had to have a decent match. The UEFA liaison officer warned us, 'This is going to be a difficult game. These teams really don't like each other.' But I was up for it – I had ninety-nine international fixtures behind me and I had learned how to referee as a European instead of an Englishman. For example, on the Continent, when a player goes into a challenge with his studs showing, it is always a foul. In England, unless contact is made it is commonplace to play on.

Mind you, I had learned how to referee on the Continent the hard way – by being rubbish at one European game. That was another all-Spanish fixture, in November 1998: Real Sociedad versus Atletico Madrid in San Sebastián. I had a complete disaster, yet thought I had done well. I refereed as I would have done in England and ended up showing eleven yellows and two reds. But I was not in tune with Spanish football: the attitudes were different; the fouls were different. Consequently, the refereeing should have been different. I misread the game completely.

Spanish fans show their displeasure about refereeing decisions by waving white hankies. That night in San Sebastián there were 27,000 people in the stadium and probably

26,900 or so waved white hankies. The others must have forgotten theirs. It looked like a huge parachute had enveloped the stadium. We had to be smuggled out of the ground under a blanket that night.

That was in 1998. By May 2007 I was a better referee. But, because of the first leg, I was still anticipating that the second game would bring eight yellow cards at least and perhaps a couple of reds. On the morning of the match the representative of Sevilla came to me at the ground with a letter which did nothing to make me revise my forecast. The letter was written in English and couched in a very aggressive tone. It said, among other things, that Osasuna had disrupted the first leg by feigning injury and so Sevilla intended to ignore any apparent Osasuna injuries in the second leg. Sevilla would not kick the ball out and would not stop play if an Osasuna player was on the floor, looking injured. The letter asked me to tell Osasuna about Sevilla's intention to play on. I was sure that if I read that letter out to Osasuna, it would only increase the enmity. Indeed, there might be some genuine injuries sustained before we even kicked off.

When the meeting with club representatives took place, without planning it in advance, I hit on the perfect thing to say. The Laws of the Game, I explained, made the safety of players the responsibility of the referee, not of the other players. I told the club representatives, truthfully, that in England we had adopted a new policy when players appeared injured. Neither side was expected to kick the ball out. Instead, the referee, and only the referee, decided when to stop play for an injury. I told the meeting that I intended to use that English policy.

Once the game kicked off, the first time someone went down and stayed down, I gave the free-kick but I stood over the player on the floor, smiled, offered him my hand for a handshake and pulled him up, still smiling. Players continued to hit the turf as if felled by snipers, but I repeated my performance three or four times: nice smile, handshake, pull him up.

I also completely discarded the diagonal system of refereeing – which I probably need to explain briefly here. The referee patrols the pitch in roughly a diagonal line. The two assistants patrol opposite halves of their touchline – from the goal-line to the halfway line. The idea is for the referee to keep the ball between him and one of the assistants.

The method of diagonal patrolling is used throughout football and I used it in most of my 1554 games – but not all of them. I discarded it if I thought I needed to keep closer to incidents and so I abandoned it that night because I was determined to keep on top of every incident. When I blew my whistle and the players looked around, I wanted to be only a few metres away.

My tactics meant a lot of running as well as a lot of smiling and a lot of shaking hands. I must have looked manic – but the approach worked. Players knew I was right behind them and they knew as well that I was giving fouls when appropriate. They realized I was not letting anyone stay down if he was not hurt, and so they soon stopped writhing about on the floor as if they had been the victims of heinous assaults.

I was totally on top of that game from start to finish. I let it flow, but I was utterly focused and completely 'in the zone' – as sportsmen and women from all sorts of disciplines say. In the entire ninety minutes, neither trainer came on once – not once.

Luis Fabiano scored for Sevilla from six yards after thirty-seven minutes to make the aggregate score 1–1 and we reached half-time without a single caution. The liaison officer was shocked but delighted. He called it an exceptional first half.

Dirnei Renato put Sevilla ahead with a clever, cushioned volley after fifty-three minutes, and although there was a tough period in the second half, when I had to take the names of five players in eleven minutes, the game needed those cautions. After I had administered them, it calmed down and flowed again.

Near the end, I was in one penalty area and the ball was heading for the other. I needed to get up the pitch. I had very little left physically, but I went for it. As I forced my tired limbs into a sprint, I pretended to whip myself, like a jockey urging on an old nag. In my earpiece I could hear both assistants and Mike Dean, the fourth official, laughing. Deano obviously thought I looked more like a train than a horse and I heard him telling me, 'Put some more coal on, Pollie!'

I made it to the other end of the pitch, stood in the six-yard box to indicate a goal-kick and then immediately span and raced back to the halfway line. I glanced at the heart monitor on my wristwatch. It showed more than 100 per cent, which theoretically was not possible. It meant that I had got something extra out of my old system.

In the few moments remaining, I took several long looks around and stored the scene in my memory bank. It was a typical Spanish stadium, with big stands but no roofs. It was full. It was a tremendous occasion. I even managed to spot Julia in the packed stand. Magical. Memorable. When I whistled for full-time, I felt a rush of emotion. I could have ended my entire career at that moment and have been completely fulfilled.

The floodlights went off momentarily, which was interesting, but they came back on and we made our way off the pitch. The assistants and Deano hung back a bit, because they sensed this was a special moment for me and that I was emotional. But Christian Poulsen, Sevilla's Danish international, gave me a hug and his shirt.

In domestic matches I just used an ordinary coin of the realm for the toss-up but in international matches I always used a special FIFA coin. My routine was that, after using it, I gave the FIFA coin to an assistant and he gave it to the fourth official for safe keeping. Then, at the end of the match, the fourth official always returned it to me – but not that night. In the dressing room after the game, Deano hugged me and started to return the coin. I said, 'You keep it. It is yours. I won't need it.'

That was how I told the officials that I was finishing at the end of that season. Deano said he had guessed, because of the intensity of my performance. He said, kindly, that nobody in Europe could referee better. I thanked the three guys for their help and support and stressed that it was not a moment of sadness for me: it was an occasion of celebration and achievement. I knew I had dredged up a performance which, in terms of fitness, decision-making, man management and concentration, belonged to the time, three or four years earlier, when I had been at my absolute peak. I knew that I would not be able to scale that peak again.

So the two teams – the team of officials and the team of family and friends – went for a meal and on to a tapas bar, which we left when they kicked us out at 4 am. UEFA rules prohibit family and friends from staying in the same hotel as the officials, but we had managed to find another (cheaper!) hotel very close by. So at 4.10 am I kissed Julia goodnight on the street. She went to her hotel and I went to mine.

I still did not want the night to end. Deano and the others came to my room and we talked about the game and about life until they gave up at 5 am. They left me with my thoughts and with the thirty or so cards from other English FIFA officials, past and present, which Deano had organized. The cards congratulated me on reaching 100 international matches. Those who sent them did not know that I was 'declaring' after reaching three figures, but their messages made a significant night even more unforgettable.

My next match, three days later, was a charity friendly: Tring Tornadoes Managers against Tring Tornadoes Under-16s. Attendance? About 350, or 44,650 fewer than in Seville.

Then, on Wednesday, 9 May 2007, I took charge of Chelsea against Manchester United. When I had been appointed for that fixture, it was expected that it would be the title decider. Chelsea, who had won the Premiership on each of the previous two seasons, trailed United for most of the 2006/07 campaign but hoped to leapfrog them to the top of the table in that crucial game at Stamford Bridge in May. It was expected to be an epic encounter, with the winner almost certainly taking the title.

Chelsea and Manchester United had also both won their FA Cup semi-finals, and had booked their places in the first Final at the rebuilt Wembley. That gave added significance to their League fixture, and for me to be awarded the appointment was confirmation that I was back at the top. I was number one again, which was important to me. The temptation to quit after Stuttgart had been very, very strong, but I did not want my career to end like that. I wanted to prove, to myself and to others, that I could recover, re-focus and referee consistently well. The Stamford Bridge showdown between the top two teams in the Premiership was an affirmation that I had succeeded.

It would be a big match for two of my children as well. Gemma wanders around the house in a Manchester United shirt and Harry is always wearing his Chelsea shirt with 'Lampard 8' on the back. Gemma has her drinks in a Man U mug; Harry drinks out of a Chelsea cup. Fortunately, there is nothing in the rules about children not supporting teams that their dad referees!

The match, however, was not the titanic encounter that had been expected. The weekend before the game at Stamford Bridge, Manchester United won at Manchester City and Chelsea drew at Arsenal. United were the champions. Gemma was delighted, but my match at Stamford Bridge was rendered meaningless. That did not mean it would be easy to referee – in fact, with both teams picking fringe players who were out to prove themselves, I sensed it could be quite challenging. And sadly, José Mourinho decided it would be me a night for me to remember, although not with fondness.

FIFA referee Peter Prendergast, my mate from Jamaica, flew over with his wife to spend a couple of days with us in Tring and come with us to Stamford Bridge, because he was in on my secret and knew it was going to be one of my last games. In the referee's lounge before the game – a cramped little room, with a couple of sofas, in the dressing rooms area at Chelsea – we were having a cup of tea when John Terry walked past. He saw the door open, glanced in and smiled. I smiled back and so, after doing whatever he had to do, he came back and entered the room.

It was the John Terry I knew from a few years back: friendly, polite, jokey. It was nice for Prendy to meet the

England captain, and I appreciated JT making the effort to shake everyone's hand and have a little chat. Yet once the game kicked off, he was snarling and swearing at me at every opportunity. Once, when I started to have a bit of banter with Joe Cole, JT said to his team-mate, 'F*** him off, Coley. Don't talk to him.'

The first twenty minutes of the game were turgid. Nothing happened. But I kept my concentration because I knew one incident could change the nature of the match – and that one incident proved to be Alan Smith's foul tackle on Chelsea's John Obi Mikel. I should have given Smithy a talking to, so that the Chelsea player's sense of grievance was salved and he had a moment or two to calm down. Instead, and wrongly, I let Chelsea take a quick free-kick and did not talk to Smith. So John Obi Mikel was still wound up and, within moments, he clattered into Chris Eagles with a bad foul.

Sir Alex Ferguson jumped up out of his seat, stomped up the line and started demanding that the Chelsea player should be sent off. What Sir Alex didn't shout was that if I red-carded the young Nigerian, he would miss the Cup Final – but I knew. The challenge by John Obi Mikel was rash, but he kept low and did not really 'endanger the safety' of Fergie's player. So I showed the Chelsea player a yellow card and not a red.

Then I imposed a segment of tight refereeing. I whistled for every infringement, to close the game down, and let tempers cool. Sky television 'expert' Andy Gray told viewers, 'Referees have been successful this season because they have played "advantage", except for Graham Poll.' That just shows you that you can know a lot about football without understanding anything at all about the job of referees.

Fergie must have stirred up his men at half-time because they started the second period with extra commitment and I had to caution two of them within about five minutes. Now, I did not want to make anyone miss the Cup Final. If someone punched an opponent, or did something really awful, then I would have sent him off, of course, and he would have been suspended for the Cup Final. But for situations which I could manage with cautions, I just gave cautions. To be scrupulously fair, I applied the same principle to fringe players who were unlikely to be involved in the Cup Final. In other words, I refereed both teams in exactly the same way, within the spirit of the game but with one eye on the Cup Final.

Was that the right thing to do? You can discuss it among yourselves. I believe it was exactly the right thing to do, although those 'experts' who always claimed that I deliberately sought out controversy might like to ponder my approach. If I had wanted controversy, I would have sent a couple of players off, preventing them playing at Wembley and made sure I was the centre of attention again. Yet the truth is that, throughout my career, I never made a decision because it was controversial. I frequently had to make decisions despite them being controversial. On that night in May 2007 at Stamford Bridge, I most definitely did not seek the confrontation with José Mourinho which erupted in the second half.

Chris Eagles had put in a bad tackle on Shaun Wright-Phillips but the Chelsea player got straight up, made no fuss and was not badly hurt. Working to the same principle that I had with the Chelsea players, I showed Eagles a yellow card instead of the red which his foul might have earned in another match. Mourinho was up and looking apoplectic in his technical area, as Sir Alex had been in the first half. That was OK. That was understandable. But what happened next was not acceptable.

The Chelsea manager made deliberate eye contact with me from twenty yards away and hurled abuse at me. I went towards him, not to 'get on the camera', as some claimed, ludicrously – the cameras were on me all the time – but to calm him down. I accepted that he was overwrought. After all, as pundits are wont to say, football is a passionate game, and most managers swear at the referee from time to time. Some of them – Sam Allardyce and David Moyes come to mind – can have a right go at a ref in the heat of the moment. Some, like Sir Alex Ferguson, have mellowed with age and consistent success. Arsène Wenger was very calm during successful seasons but entirely different during less successful seasons. So it is often all about stress.

Perhaps, throughout my career, I should have adopted a more stern approach. Perhaps, if referees had more backing from the FA, we would send managers off as soon as they tell us to f*** off. Then, perhaps, the routine abuse would stop.

Anyway, back in the real world, I approached José, assuming that he was just reacting to the pressure of his situation. I wanted to say, 'José, you are under pressure, which I respect. But I would like you to respect me. Please be careful what you say to me.' That is what I wanted to say and it is what I would have said to any other manager in that situation. Nineteen other Premiership managers would have responded to the calm man-management by apologizing, or at least by stopping swearing for a while.

But before I could say anything at all to Senhor Mourinho, he leant his head into me and produced a foul tirade which included a disgraceful personal comment about me and Sir

Alex Ferguson. I was stunned. I was appalled. The inference was bad enough – that I was favouring Manchester United – but the way he expressed himself was just awful.

A test I often apply to myself is this: would I be happy explaining this behaviour to my family? Do you think José Mourinho would have been proud that night to have gone home and said to his wife and children, 'Guess what I said to Graham Poll'?

Immediately after his despicable outburst, and before I could respond, he retreated to the back of the technical area and climbed into the seating behind the dugout, as if he had been sent off. Why did he do that? Perhaps José Mourinho thought he deserved to be 'sent off' that night and perhaps he wanted another dispute between Graham Poll and Chelsea.

I understand the pressure he was under and, as I say, other managers tried to apply psychological pressure and other managers swore at me without much restraint. I expected Mourinho, who is a fighter and wants to win everything, to go further than most – but not that far. Nobody in my twenty-seven seasons had used such deeply offensive language to insult and abuse me.

Yet, as I stood there, still in shock at the verbal assault I had suffered and looking on as Mourinho clambered into the seats behind the dugout, I thought to myself, 'I do not need this hassle … I have got three games left after this. I do not want to spend weeks and possibly months after that waiting for a disciplinary hearing for José Mourinho, at which he will get the equivalent of a slap on the wrist.' So I did not send him off. If that was a dereliction of my responsibility, then I apologize. But before you ask yourself whether I was wrong, ask two other questions. Firstly, was it right that José Mourinho should behave like that? Secondly, was it right that he was confident that he would get away with it – that any sanction imposed by the FA would not seriously inconvenience him or his club? I think it is a terrible indictment of the Football Association that a referee suffered that filthy defilement and yet concluded that there was no point in responding.

Because of events in my last season – John Terry's inaccurate account of his sending off and José Mourinho's grotesque verbal attack on me – there is a danger of this book turning into me versus Chelsea. But other referees will tell you similar stories about other clubs and, while I certainly think that the actions of JT and JM were unforgivable, I have no doubt that they were encouraged to behave as they did by the contemptibly timid Football Association.

So, as I stood there nonplussed by Mourinho's outburst I felt it was simply not worth the grief to respond. It was not worth getting fifty foul letters to my home from Chelsea supporters saying that I was this and I was that – which I knew from past experience is what would have happened. Yes, I was a referee, but I was also a man with a young family. I did not want threatening letters arriving at my family home.

Steve Clarke, Chelsea's assistant manager, thought I had sent off his boss, and accused me of doing it for the cameras and loving the attention.

John Terry made it his business to come over to the side of the field and give me an earful. His theme was identical to Steve Clarke's – so much so that it made me wonder whether it was a key message that Chelsea had decided in advance. Was it a premeditated campaign? And did John Terry want a yellow card from me, to provoke more controversy and to suggest that our dispute earlier in the season was because of bias or animosity?

I used my lip-microphone to say to the fourth official, Mark Clattenburg, 'Make it clear to Mr Mourinho that he has not been sent away from the technical area.' I also told John Terry that I had not sent off his manager, but at this stage he wasn't prepared to listen to anything I had to say.

I walked away and we finished the game. It was a draw. In his after-match media conference, José Mourinho was asked about what had happened with me. He said, 'I was telling Mr Poll a couple of things I have had in my heart since the Tottenham game at White Hart Lane. But it was nothing special. I was cleansing my soul. I think he [Poll] was what he is always. He had a normal performance when he is refereeing a Chelsea match. Do we jump with happiness when Mr Poll comes? No, I don't. I just say he is a referee Chelsea has no luck with. If we can have another referee we are happy. We do not like to have Mr Poll.'

There we are then. His noxious outburst was nothing special. It was just Mourinho cleansing his soul.

When I read what Mourinho had said, and considered how Clarke, Terry and the Chelsea manager had delivered the same 'key message', I did wonder whether it was all premeditated. Of course, Chelsea's comments to me and about me that night might have all been just hot-headed reactions, but there were three potential benefits from their outbursts.

Firstly, a big row with me would dominate the headlines the next day and distract everyone's attention from the real story of the night, which was that Chelsea were no longer champions. They had been forced by protocol to form a guard of honour for Manchester United at the start of the match. That hurt the Chelsea players and supporters and signalled José Mourinho's failure.

Secondly, a confrontation with me, following the storm earlier in the season about John Terry's sending off, would also ensure that I would not referee Chelsea again for a long time. Unaware that I was retiring, Mourinho did not like the fact that I stood up to Chelsea Football Club and that I refused to be intimidated. It was not difficult to calculate that, if there was another huge row, the Premier League would not give me Chelsea fixtures for a while, or I would impose my own ban on taking charge of Mourinho's team, because to referee them would be asking for trouble.

Thirdly, Mourinho knew any incident involving me would not be dealt with before the Cup Final and that, when he was eventually 'punished', the FA would impose a paltry fine or some puny sanction. So I wonder whether he was trying to send out a message to other referees. Did he want to say, 'Look, I have seen off Graham Poll, your top official. All of you need to tread carefully with me.'?

Here is another question, this time for the media. Is it right that the totally one-sided reporting of refereeing incidents – based, usually, on the assumption that the referee is wrong and, in my case, based on the view that I loved controversy – makes the situation a thousand times worse? Because it certainly does.

As an example of that, let me tell you about one report of Mourinho's torrent of outrageous vilification. Rob Beasley, a football reporter with the *News of the World*, is a Chelsea fan and has good contacts at the club. The rumour that I was about to retire had surfaced and here is what appeared in Rob Beasley's newspaper under his name on the Sunday after that match at Stamford Bridge:

> Chelsea have rubbished retiring referee Graham Poll with a savage send-off.
>
> Poll, 43, is hanging up his whistle this summer and that's brought nothing but glee at Stamford Bridge.
>
> One top Blues star said: 'No one here is sad to see the back of him. He always had to be the centre of attention.
>
> 'He was at it again when we played Manchester United. He confronted José Mourinho on the touchline and was obviously playing up to the cameras, it was embarrassing.
>
> 'What's sad is that he fancied himself as one of the top referees around, but he'll be remembered as the ref who gave three yellow cards to the same player at the World Cup. What a joke!'

Well, Rob got my age right.

The day after the Stamford Bridge game, the referees gathered at Staverton for one of their fortnightly sessions of analysis and training. I told the others about Senhor Mourinho's rant. We had a discussion about the behaviour of managers in their technical areas, because Keith Hackett, our manager, wanted a crackdown on all the swearing and abuse for the following season. Several top referees told the meeting that none of them took action against inappropriate comments, language or behaviour in the technical area because the FA would not back them. I agreed completely. That tells you all you need to know about the state of the game and how referees felt abandoned by the Football Association.

As far as I was concerned personally, in the course of six days I had experienced the exhilaration of performing at the peak of my powers in Seville and the degradation of being foully derided at Chelsea. Both matches confirmed my view that it was time for me to finish refereeing.

The rumour that I was retiring had found its way into newspapers. Quite a few people knew my plans by then and I suppose it was inevitable that the news would get out, but it caused a few anxious days. I had been told that I would referee the Football League's Championship promotion Play-off Final at the rebuilt Wembley. Would the fact that I was retiring make the authorities reconsider?

Richard Scudamore, chief executive of the Premier League and effectively the man who made the decisions about the professional referees, telephoned. He asked, 'Is it true?' I told him it was indeed true that I was retiring. I made it clear that it was not because of Chelsea. It was a decision I had made because I no longer enjoyed refereeing. He said, 'Well, then it is the right decision. But I am sorry to hear it. The Play-off Final at Wembley is an appropriate end for you and a way for football to thank you for all you have done.'

My final Premiership match was Portsmouth versus Arsenal. There had been heavy rain, but the pitch was playable and I just conducted my normal, routine inspection. However, because of the accurate speculation that it was my last Premiership match, there were fifteen photographers following me as I walked out to look at the pitch and apparently someone commented on radio that, typically, I was milking the moment. Yet one of the reasons I had tried to keep my retirement secret was that I did not want the last games to become a circus.

I disallowed a 'goal' for the home team by Niko Kranjcar for offside. Television later proved it was the correct decision and the match finished scoreless. If Portsmouth had won, they would have qualified for the UEFA Cup for the first time in their history but, because the match was a draw, they finished ninth in the table and Bolton went into Europe instead.

Now, one way of reporting those events would have been to say, 'Graham Poll made a correct decision which ensured Bolton justly earned a place in the UEFA Cup.' But, back in the real world again, everyone took the line that I had cost Portsmouth their European adventure. Many reports said I had got the decision wrong and most added the implication that I enjoyed the notoriety the decision had caused in my final Premiership fixture. *The Guardian's* headline was, 'Fingers point at Poll as European dream dies'.

There were other important games on that final day of the Premiership season, especially those at the foot of the table which determined who was relegated. There were other big refereeing decisions that day. Yet the only referee whose name was in the headlines the next day was Graham Poll.

Again, it provided more confirmation that it was time to go. There was no possibility that I would ever again be treated evenhandedly by the media. I was Graham Poll, the man who had blundered at the World Cup and who was 'always seeking controversy'. The easy, lazy way of reporting my matches was to focus on one of my decisions, say that I had got it wrong and suggest I had done it to get the headlines. I was going to walk away from refereeing earnings of about £90,000 a year but, as I had told Richard Scudamore, I was no longer enjoying it.

Yet my penultimate match was a cracker. The League One play-off semi-final second leg between Nottingham Forest and Yeovil at Forest's City Ground saw the advantage swing one way and then the other. It went into extra-time and ended with Yeovil winning 5–2 on the night for a 5–4 aggregate victory. Yeovil had been playing in the Conference only four years before yet they had beaten Forest, who had been European champions twice. I had to send off Forest's David

Prutton for two cautions but nobody could quibble with the decision and it was a truly spellbinding match that I thoroughly enjoyed.

Then, as the days ticked away towards my final game, some of the top men in refereeing became nervous. By then, my imminent retirement was an open secret and they thought I might give an explosive interview before the last match, or make some grand gesture during the action (I am not sure what – perhaps they thought I would leap and head in a goal, although they wouldn't have thought that if they'd ever seen me play). I was upset that they even thought those things. In fact, the precise opposite was true. I fended off all approaches from the media before my final match because I wanted to ensure that the fixture – between West Brom and Derby – was about the clubs and their fans, not about the referee.

Six days before the West Brom–Derby game, I was a guest of Vodafone at the Champions League Final between Liverpool and AC Milan in Athens. My hosts paid me a fee to referee a little match between the media and some of their other guests and to host a pre-match Q & A with Teddy Sheringham. But when they suggested I might take part in a press conference, I had to say 'No'. All the questions would have been about my retirement and if I had answered honestly, then my last game would have become the circus I was trying to avoid.

And so, after twenty-seven seasons, I reached my final game, match 1554, at Wembley – and I make no apologies at all for being absolutely, utterly, overjoyed to bow out at the national stadium. There were three reasons for that feeling. Firstly, I was still the official the authorities wanted to referee a game worth at least £52 million to the winning club.

Richard Scudamore, Keith Hackett and the rest were confident in my ability to take charge of that match and that meant a lot to me. It gave me a sense of pride. I see no reason to apologize for that. Secondly, it was natural for me to want to referee at the 'new' Wembley. I had taken charge of the last FA Cup Final in 2000 before they pulled down the old stadium and of course, like every other football fan in the country, I wanted to experience the new place. Thirdly, it provided the perfect way of saying 'thank you' to some important people. I scrambled around getting tickets and managed to ensure that, as well as Julia and our children, my mum and dad, two of my sisters and some friends were there to share my last big occasion as a referee. It was profoundly important to me that my mum and dad, who were there when my refereeing career started, were there when it finished.

I am delighted to report that it finished well. The match officials were put up at the Hendon Hall Hotel, which was where I had been before 'my' FA Cup Final and which has a unique place in English football history because it was where the England team stayed before the 1966 World Cup Final. Staying there in 2007 gave the occasion a special feel for me, but I can honestly say that I was not at all emotional. The time had come to call time on my career, and it just felt right.

People who were in on the increasingly unsecret secret about my retirement noted that I sung the national anthem lustily that day at Wembley, but those who knew me well realized that I always did. Belting out 'God Save The Queen' was my way of forcing out any last-minute nerves. I will admit that I could not look across to where I knew my mum was sitting, however. She had said to me, 'Think of me when you sing the anthem.' So I knew she'd be looking and that if we had made eye contact, I would have lost it. I will also concede that when I stood there, on a red carpet at a full house at Wembley, singing the national anthem, I did think back to those games in the parks when I started. The truth is, I always did that during anthems before big games that I was about to referee. For some reason, my mind always went back to games in a particular park in Stevenage – Hampson Park, an exposed, windy plot up on a hilltop near a water tower.

At Wembley, on 28 May 2007, it was a great help to have two really good assistants, Darren Cann and Martin Yerby, plus Mike Dean as fourth official. They all knew it was my last game and I also told Jim Ashworth, the manager of the National Group refs, who was 'in charge' of the officials for the Play-off Finals. Jim was also retiring, so the Derby–West Brom match was his last as well, and I told him the truth about my finishing so that we were all relaxed about the situation. I was lifted by the little words and gestures by which Jim and the others let me know they wanted my last game to go well.

Twelve minutes into the match, West Brom's Jason Koumas danced past a couple of opponents and into the Derby area. Tyrone Mears slid in with a tackle and upended Koumas in the process. I was really close to play and signalled 'no penalty' by slicing the air with both hands like a giant pair of scissors. Martin Yerby, the assistant who was on the far side of the pitch but in line with the incident, said, 'Great decision, Pollie', but I heard Deano, my mate the fourth official, mutter, 'Oh no!' I am told that my mum and sisters, who were also in line with the incident, glanced at each other with a wide-eyed, raised eyebrows look. They didn't say anything to each other, but they thought it was a penalty. I would suggest that 80 per cent of the paying public inside the stadium probably agreed with them. The West Brom fans certainly did, and started to let me know. But we had a fifth official, Trevor Massey, to cover for injuries. Where he was sitting, he could see a TV monitor and he ran down and said to Deano, 'He got it right. The defender got the ball. Pollie got it right.'

It was enormously satisfying to get such a big call correct in such a big game. There was another penalty appeal by West Brom in the second half which I turned down – it was a much easier call, but it was right as well. Yet, if I am 100 per cent honest with myself, I know I should have sent off West Brom's Sam Sodje and Derby's Tyrone Mears in the second half. Both had already been cautioned and each committed a second cautionable offence, yet I didn't get the cards out. That was because I knew that the headlines would have been about me sending players off in my last game. People would have said, 'Typical Graham Poll. It's his last game and so he has to use his red card.' So, although much of the media praised me for getting the penalty decisions correct, the honest truth is that my refereeing that day was compromised. I did not feel I could referee as I should have done; I did not feel I could send someone off for two cautions. I'd have red-carded someone for punching an opponent, or for a handball on the line, but not for two cautions. To mangle a well-known saying, I erred on the side of not cautioning.

But I certainly enjoyed the day. On the major occasions of my career – the big, set-piece matches – I always aimed to referee as if it were a normal game of football. Because it always was. Inside the white touchlines, it was just twenty-two blokes and me, as it had been all those years ago in Hampson Park. Yet, if by sixty minutes or so of a big match, things had gone well, I did allow myself a moment to take in the surroundings and the circumstances. A referee knows by sixty minutes whether he has 'got' the game – whether his decision-making and management have been good enough. Decisions become more critical in the last thirty minutes, because that is when the results of games are determined. By then, however, if a referee has had a good first hour, the players will accept the decisions made in the last half an hour, more often then not. And so, at Wembley in my last professional appointment, after an hour or so, I did permit myself to have a look around, soak it all in and think where I was and how far I had come. I took in the magnitude of what my job had been – refereeing huge matches like the Play-off Final – and acknowledged that it was ending. I did not experience an iota of sadness; I felt only that the race was run.

Not long after that, Derby's Stephen Pearson scored the game's only goal and provoked a really tense finish as West Brom pressed for an equalizer and Derby defended the lead which would carry them into the Premiership. In the dying moments, the tension exploded, and players from both sides squared up in a mêlée, but I was able to defuse the situation by getting in among the players, staying calm, pulling the instigator out and using some of the body language and people-management I had learned over the years.

I had intended to be in the centre-circle when I blew the whistle for full time, and I wanted the ball to be near me, so that I could grab it for a souvenir. I had thought about doing a dramatic, European-style signal as I whistled at the finish – putting both hands into the air, then moving them parallel to the ground and then putting them down by my side. But, when the moment actually came I was too engrossed in the action and too tired to do all that stuff. I was in the Derby area and I just put my two arms in the air and gave a peep on my 'Tornado' whistle to end the game and finish my professional career.

I felt drained. I think the mental pressure of the previous few months had taken its toll – the strain of knowing for so long that my career was finishing and the anxiety of hoping it would end well. After all, my life as a professional ref could have concluded very differently and far less satisfyingly. I might not have reached 100 international games. I might not have refereed the Play-off Final. Or I might have had a major controversy at Wembley. But it had all gone as well as I could possibly have hoped – with a terrific European match in Seville, an epic Play-off semi-final at Nottingham Forest and a farewell at Wembley. As I relaxed, I was engulfed by the overwhelming fatigue which comes when stress ends.

In Play-off Finals, wrongly in my view, the losing team does not go up to the Royal Box for any sort of presentation. Neither do the match officials. So we stood about in the middle watching Derby players climb the steps to receive their trophy and medals. I shook hands with the assistants and with Jim Ashworth. Deano and I hugged each other and then, after a very short while, I said, 'Come on, let's go.' It was over.

CHAPTER EIGHT

Fat King Melon

That is how it ended for 'Referee G Poll (Herts)' but there were so many good days and good stories. I want to tell you about the altercation in the tunnel between Roy Keane and Patrick Vieira and some of the tales from fourteen years as a Premiership ref. And I want to take you behind the scenes of my life as a referee and explain how I learned to deal with being 'The Thing from Tring', the wanker in the black, that ref everyone thought was arrogant.

So I have to start, briefly, with my parents. I have to start with my dad. He was a ref, so it is him I have to thank (or blame). I also have to start with my mum, who drove me to all my early games and stood, huddled in the cold and rain, watching me referee before taking me home again.

Throughout my career in refereeing, people asked me why I did it. I answered, 'Why wouldn't I?' I am a football fan and I have been closer to the action in big games than anyone other than the players. I travelled the world to see truly superb players – Zinedine Zidane, David Beckham, Andriy Shevchenko, Cristiano Ronaldo – in superb stadiums. I rose to the daunting physical and intimidating mental challenges of refereeing. In fact, I relished those challenges.

But it didn't start like that. It didn't start like that for my dad, either. For him, like a lot of referees I suspect, it began as a way to earn a few more quid. He needed the money for us, his family, which I was the last to join.

I was born in 1963. It was the year Martin Luther King delivered his 'I have a dream' speech, Bobby Moore became England captain, the Beatles released their first album and London was swinging. But in Hertfordshire, my mum and dad had more mundane concerns when I arrived in the world. I was born in the Hitchin maternity hospital but lived throughout my childhood and adolescence in Stevenage, an old market town which became the first of the 'new towns' – developments which were deliberately and dramatically expanded to re-house people after the Second World War.

Mum and Dad did their bit to aid Britain's recovery from the ravages of war as well – by contributing to the baby boom. They married in 1957, moved to Stevenage that year and started their family fairly quickly. Susan arrived in 1958, Deborah in 1960, Mary in '61 and me in '63 – just after Dad had got rid of a train set which is famous in our family.

The story is that he bought a toy train set when Mum was pregnant with Susan, in case the baby was a boy. He kept this train set, unused in its box, for years while Deborah and Mary came along. Then, when Mum was pregnant with me, he assumed the baby would be another daughter, so he got rid of the train set – just before little Graham arrived. If you put that story alongside the fact that Mum and Dad were both football mad, and that I had a career in football which they have enjoyed sharing, you can understand why, sometimes, my sisters felt a little vexed about little Graham – well, not about me as such but about all the time Mum and Dad spent with me at football.

The Poll family moved when I was one year old. We moved a short distance, in the same Stevenage neighbourhood of Shephall, but the new home – a four-bedroomed, terraced house – had more space. There were five houses in the terrace and ours was the second from the right. As I grew older, I made friends with boys in the terrace and across the street, and a crowd of us used to spend all our spare time 'over Ridlins' – at Ridlins Wood Athletics Track and Playing Fields, just behind the houses opposite our house. As well as the athletics track, there were swings and slides and five football pitches. We played football there from dawn to dusk.

If that all sounds mundane, I make no apologies. I realize that some autobiographies start with terrible tales of depravation or horrific accounts of childhood abuse. My story began with loving, hard-working parents in a normal home, but I am sure a shrewd sociologist would spot, in the child I was, clues about the man (and referee) I became.

For instance, why was I picked for the leading role of Fat King Melon in my primary school play? No, it was not because I looked like a melon. In those days I was as thin as a stick and my hair was so fair it was white. I was reminded about being Fat King Melon by one of the supportive letters I received when I returned home from the 2006 World Cup. Peter Browning, who taught me at primary school, wrote it and recalled that I had been in that school play.

I loved amateur dramatics. I suppose that sociologist would nod knowingly at that statement. My critics in the media, who have accused me of enjoying the limelight of publicity, would smile at the admission that I enjoyed being in front of the stage lighting. But my own analysis is that I liked acting because it was a way of dealing with an inner insecurity.

If I was told, as a schoolboy, to go to such-and-such a room, I would want to loiter outside, dithering about whether it was the right room and what people would think about me when I went in. So, to deal with that feeling, I would confront it. I would burst into the room and be completely over-the-top. I used to overcompensate.

Decades later, when I first reached the Football League referees' list and started going for medical checks, my blood pressure was always very high. That was anxiety – not about passing the fitness assessment, but about meeting people and about what those people would think of me.

So, at my schools in Stevenage – Ashtree Infants and Primary and then Thomas Alleynes – I overcompensated. I was the class joker and took to the stage. My first role at senior school was as a little girl in *HMS Pinafore*. I don't want the sociologist to even think about that. We also did old-time musicals, which I loved, especially when the local girls' school joined us for productions when I reached the fourth form (now known as Year Ten). I was one of the chaps who used to enter from one side of the stage to do 'I say, I say, I say' jokes.

My good friend in those days was Alan Crompton, who was one of those people who are good at every single sport. He was great at rugby, an outstanding cricketer and a very decent footballer – really annoying. In one old-time musical he and I dressed up as soldiers and sang a duet about being comrades. I am pleased to say, all these years later, that Crompo is still a comrade.

My schooldays were happy days because of those extra-curricular activities. But I wasted my academic abilities.

Thomas Alleynes, a boys-only school, changed from being a selective grammar to a comprehensive the year I started, yet it maintained grammar school attitudes. There were six academic 'streams' in each year. I was near the bottom of the top stream, but the boys I most aspired to befriend and imitate – the Jack the Lads who were quite bright but also liked a laugh – were in the second stream. My desire at school was to make the other kids smile. I used to mimic the teachers and spent more time kicked out of classes than inside. On one occasion, the physics teacher sent me out before I'd gone in, to save time later.

When I decided to leave school just before my sixteenth birthday, my parents were very disappointed, especially my dad. He would have given anything for the opportunity to go into further or higher education, but none of his three daughters chose to do so and now his fourth and last child was spurning that chance as well. He told me I could only leave school if I had a job. So I bought a three-piece, brown, pin-striped suit. Crompo bought a similar outfit in charcoal grey. The comrades were suited. He had an interview with Pearl Assurance; I had one at Prudential Insurance. We both got the jobs. The comrades were sorted.

Just over a year later, I began refereeing and so my two careers, in commerce and in football, had begun. Mum and Dad, I know, became proud of my achievements in both. You only begin to understand your own parents fully – their hopes and fears, their love and their pride – when you have children of your own, and so it was when I had a heart-filling moment involving my daughter Gemma that I appreciated how my mum and dad felt about me.

At the first parent-teacher meeting at Gemma's school, the teacher said, 'This is the most difficult meeting of this type I have ever had.' I glanced at my wife, Julia, wondering what was to follow. The teacher continued, 'Gemma is wonderful; a lovely, lovely child who is a pleasure to have in the classroom.'

Nobody has ever called me a lovely, lovely referee but, as I walked home from Gemma's school, I had a warm feeling of satisfaction knowing that my career in football must have meant a lot to those close to me. My mum, bless her, says there have been so many proud moments that she cannot pick just one, but when pressed, she admits it was the FA Cup Final – the last one at the old Wembley before the bulldozers moved in, and the one where I had to sneak out of the back door of my house to avoid a photographer hiding in the bushes.

CHAPTER NINE

Cup Final Blues

Studying the TV listings for Cup Final day in the year 2000, I remarked to Julia that television coverage was starting at 1 pm. 'That's ridiculous,' I said.

She replied, 'Yeah, two whole hours before kick-off.'

I meant, of course, it was ridiculous that the build-up was so brief.

As a boy, FA Cup Final day was spent camped in front of the television – for the entire day. Mum prepared the bread rolls the night before so that, once the TV build-up began at about 9 am, we could settle down and not be disturbed. We scoffed the rolls as we devoured the unbroken hours of football programmes. In those days – I sound like an old fart, I know – the FA Cup Final was the only live football coverage and the television companies made the most of it. So did we. We sat there all day, transfixed by *Cup Final It's a Knockout*, then *The Road to Wembley*, then *Meet the Players' Families* and so on. Then came the match. And that evening we'd watch the highlights again on *Match of the Day*.

By the year 2000, there was live football on television almost every day and so a lot less fuss was made about the FA Cup Final. My many critics will probably construe my disappointment about that as a desire to be in the limelight longer, because 2000 was the year I refereed the FA Cup Final, between Chelsea and Aston Villa.

I have to admit that I played my part, not at all begrudgingly, in the pre-match publicity. I let Sky TV film me having my hair cut in Berkhamsted. The BBC filmed me playing Mousetrap with my daughters. The *Bucks Herald* came and took a picture of me standing in my back garden, brandishing a red card. It seemed a bit corny, but I can't pretend I minded too much. I had a different response for a reporter and photographer from the *News of the World*, however.

On the Saturday before the Final, I was watching a video with the kids. Harry, my son, was not quite three months old. My daughters, Gemma and Josie, were six and four. At 9 am precisely, the reporter rang the front door bell. Turning up unannounced like that is called 'doorstepping', apparently. But the photographer wasn't on my doorstep. He was hiding just a little way up the road in some bushes with a long lens trained on my front door.

The reporter said, 'We are publishing a story tomorrow regarding a former allegiance of yours.' I had no idea what he meant. I wondered if it was about a former relationship with someone, but I could not think of anything that would be a story. Then he said, 'We have it on good authority that you used to be a Chelsea supporter.'

Their intention was to print a story saying, 'Cup Final ref is Chelsea fan'. It would create such a furore that I would be taken off the game. I replied, 'You are trespassing on my land. If you don't leave, I'll call the police.'

As I closed the door, he shouted, 'I'll wait. It would pay you to speak to us.' Clive, our postman, did call the police. He spotted these two characters sitting in our street, knew they were not locals, and telephoned the police, who said they could not do anything.

Meanwhile, indoors, I was piecing events together in my mind. The first clue was that, Nick Whitehead, who had been a friend of Mum and Dad when we all worked at Kodak, had called me three times during the week, out of the blue. He left two messages for me and then, when he managed to talk to me, wished me luck and made a couple of references to my having been a Chelsea fan. I thought he was trying to make a joke. I certainly did not think he could be serious, because it did not have a grain of truth and I assumed that he knew it was not true.

The truth, incidentally, is that when I was young I used to support a local boys' team in Stevenage called Gonville Rovers, and I have always supported England. As far as professional clubs are concerned, I am an ex-Leeds fan and a lapsed Queens Park Rangers supporter.

The first match that captured my imagination as a boy was on one of those lovely days watching the Cup Final. It was in 1970, when Leeds played Chelsea at Wembley. And, as young boys do, I decided that day that I was a Leeds supporter. I held on to that idea for about three years, and even had a pair of Leeds United sock garters. They had special, numbered tags. Mine had the number seven on the tags, which I thought might help me whack the ball at 70 mph, like Leeds number 7 Peter Lorimer.

But when Leeds stopped winning, I stopped supporting them, as young boys do. My dad was a QPR fan, so I declared myself a QPR supporter as well, although I seldom went to games. I was too busy watching my dad referee or cheering on Gonville Rovers. The professional team I saw the most was Arsenal, because I had a friend who was a Gunners' fan and we could get to Highbury quite easily by public transport from Stevenage. I went there quite regularly for about three seasons. But I was never an Arsenal supporter, because they were shockingly bad in those days.

All referees have to fill in a form at the start of each season with details of where they live (to calculate distances for expenses) and any potential conflicts of interest. They are asked about any club allegiances. I always left that section blank. I am prepared to own up now that I never declared my affection for Gonville Rovers.

Anyway, I was told that Nick Whitehead and another acquaintance from Kodak, John Elliott, attended a sporting dinner, at which England's finest former referee, Jack Taylor, was the speaker and answered questions. Nick asked the great man whether a referee could take charge of an FA Cup Final if he supported one of the teams. He was told, 'Of course not.'

Whether Nick honestly but mistakenly thought I supported Chelsea, and whether that answer set the cash register bell ringing in his mind, I don't know. Perhaps an alarm bell should have rung in my mind when Nick telephoned me out of the blue to talk about the Blues. Anyway, I was told that Nick had given the 'story' to the *News of the World*.

I made a telephone call to Adrian Bevington, of the Football Association's press office. He rang the *News of the World* and stressed that the FA knew that I was a lapsed QPR follower, not a Chelsea supporter. He said that if the newspaper alleged I would not be impartial at the Cup Final, the FA would sue.

The bloke in the bushes had not managed to snatch a picture of me when I had answered the front door. And I had some more disappointment for him. I smuggled myself and my family out of the back of the house and into the garage. We drove away without the *News of the World* realizing.

I've had 'gentlemen of the press' camped outside more than once in my career. I hope they all filled up with petrol locally on their way back to their offices, and bought ciggies and sarnies locally as well. I'd like to think that, whatever else they did, they helped the local Tring economy.

Numbers of potential customers for local shopkeepers have varied. An entire media circus made their way to the Tring exit of the A41 bypass immediately after my mistake in the 2006 World Cup. But there was just a meagre pair – a reporter and a photographer – after the match at The Valley the following season, when the myth was created that I had done a special favour for Charlton manager Alan Pardew.

I have never really worked out what picture the photographer in the bushes before the 2000 FA Cup Final thought he might get. Did he expect me to come to the door in a full Chelsea kit, with rosettes, a scarf and a rattle?

The *News of the World* still believed they had a story, but they relegated it to page nine. They published the results of the QPR games I had reffed. I think Rangers had lost five out of six, so any perceived bias by me had not done them much good.

I made another telephone call a couple of days before the Final. This one was to Aston Villa manager John Gregory to explain what had happened. He said, 'If I could have chosen a referee for the Final, it would be you.' I like to think, knowing what I do now about him, that he meant it, but it did not stop Villa using psychology to try to undermine me at Wembley.

I was thirty-six, and nowhere near the end of my career, I hoped. Yet I knew that this would be my only FA Cup Final. Nobody gets the top domestic honour more than once. It was an appointment I treasured and cherished. It is every referee's ambition to take charge of the Final and yet some very good referees never get the opportunity. Every year, the guessing game about who will earn the appointment dominates referees' conversations. We work out who has a chance, calculate who might be unlucky, and wait for the big announcement.

Ever since I had started refereeing – or at least from the days when I started to do well and begin to think I could scale the refereeing ladder – I had aimed to reach the Final. In fact, in about 1985 I told my mum, 'I will referee the FA Cup Final in the year 2000.' I meant that I was striving for it. It was my career target. In the succeeding years, I kept that target in my sights as I worked my way up that ladder.

So when the daft prediction that I had made as a young man actually came true, I was as proud as could be. Joe Guest, the FA's head of refereeing, telephoned and said, 'I'm calling to see if you are available on May 22nd.' For once, I didn't make a wisecrack. I resisted the temptation to say, 'I'll have to check.' I understood the importance of the FA Cup, the significance of the Final and the place the day had in the heart of real football fans. Plus, the 2000 Final was the first of the new millennium and the last at Wembley before the old ground, with its traditions and memories, was demolished to be replaced (eventually!) by a new stadium.

So, despite the best efforts of Nick Whitehead and the *News of the World*, I enjoyed the build-up to the big day. I wallowed in it. Neither am I ashamed to say that I enjoyed all the media attention involved. It made me feel special, but then, to my mind, the FA Cup Final was special and I was going to have a role in it.

Tradition dictates that the Wembley match officials and their wives are honoured by the London Society of Referees at an 'Eve of the Final Rally' – a social gathering which referees of all levels attend. As a young referee, I had gone to the Rally to gawp at icons like Neil Midgley and George Courtney. I was far too much in awe of them to actually approach them, but lots of the other refs wanted their moment with the Wembley officials, and so the Rally always went into extra-time.

The fact that I had been so many times to the Rally as a callow kid was another reason for me to savour the fact that I was going to referee the 2000 Final. Now it was my turn to be the principal guest at the Rally, but I was concerned it would end too late.

Peter Jones – we shall meet him again during my story – had been the Cup Final ref in 1999 and told me that he did not get back to his hotel from the Rally until just before midnight. He had to deal with a queue of people wanting autographs. He admitted that it was not ideal preparation for his big day.

So I asked to change a couple of things. I said that I'd arrange for the four match officials to autograph all the 200 or so programmes for the event in advance. Nobody would have to queue up at the end for signatures. And I said that I wanted to speak at the beginning of the function, rather than at the conclusion, so that I could leave in time for a proper night's rest.

Some of the blazer brigade thought it was sacrilege to alter the schedule. They concluded – like many before and since –

that Graham Poll was arrogant. I could argue that my need to prepare properly was the opposite of arrogance. But most people have already made up their mind about me.

Something else made the chaps in blazers splutter with indignation. Darren Drysdale, one of the assistant referees, had recently become engaged. He and his fiancée, Wendy, couldn't keep their hands off each other. Eventually I had to say, 'Can you give it a rest please? Or get a room.'

He replied, 'We can't help it. We're in love.' Obviously, I did not tell the other match officials about that at the first opportunity or take the mickey out of him in any way at all. I returned to the Hendon Hall Hotel at a respectable hour and had a good sleep. I can't tell you whether I dreamed or not – but then I had been dreaming of refereeing the FA Cup Final for nearly twenty years.

On the big day, I was determined to follow the advice of previous Final refs and seep myself in the atmosphere. They said they had enjoyed standing on the balcony, between Wembley's old twin towers, watching both sets of supporters walking towards the stadium along Empire Way. But when I stood there in 2000, Villa supporters who spotted me started to sing vile songs about my alleged allegiance to Chelsea. Joe Guest advised us to leave the balcony. I was grievously disappointed. Thanks, *News of the World*.

Then, in the dressing rooms, I did something else to outrage the blazer blokes – another break with tradition. FA official Adrian Titcombe always led the two teams out. The referee, assistants and fourth official brought up the rear. Over the years, when I had watched this, I felt it was wrong. I thought that it undervalued the referee and his team. So I asked that the FA follow their own regulation, which stipulated that the referee should lead out the teams. For the sake of every ref who has taken charge of Finals since, I am glad that I won that little amendment to the protocol.

The last FA Cup Final at the old Wembley was the seventy-second, and was decided by a goal in the seventy-second minute. Neither the game nor the goal was memorable. Gianfranco Zola took a free-kick for Chelsea, Villa goalkeeper David James fumbled the ball, knocking it against the chest of defender Gareth Southgate, and Roberto Di Matteo thumped the lose ball into the roof of the net. Di Matteo had scored the quickest goal in an FA Cup Final (forty-two seconds) three years earlier when Chelsea beat Middlesbrough 2–0. This time, in 2000, his goal was suitably scrappy for a poor game, and the most prestigious appointment of my domestic career was not a great occasion for me either.

In fact, it was a horrid, bitter experience. It was soured utterly by that *News of the World* article and the way some Villa players used the story to try to put me under pressure. During the game, Villa players repeatedly made snide remarks inferring that I was biased. They said things like, 'There's two teams playing, Pollie. Not one.' They said, 'Come on, be fair.' They hoped that, subconsciously, I would want to prove that I was not favouring Chelsea. They were hoping that I would react by giving the next marginal decision to Villa. And I am pretty sure that they had been told to use that tactic, because the players who did it the most were the right-back, the central midfielder and the left-forward. Because referees run a diagonal path throughout a match, those were the players I most often found myself near. I believed they had been instructed to target me.

The indignation I felt – the outrage – was because the allegation behind their remarks attacked my basic integrity. I had worked for twenty years to referee the Cup Final. It was my big occasion. Yet they were saying I was dishonest. Every little comment they made was like a slap in the face.

Then, right at the finish, when the teams were waiting to go up to collect their medals, a member of the Villa backroom staff said to me, 'You f***ing Chelsea fan. You c***.' That was the last straw. The comment touched a raw nerve. I confronted him and although I have never been someone who hits people, I honestly think I might at least have grabbed him if Joe Guest had not intervened. That would have given the *News of the World* a real story.

Then, as I climbed the famous thirty-nine steps to collect my own medal, the Villa fans booed and repeated the *News of the World's* false allegation. Peter Jones said the finest moment of his life – of his life! – was at the end of the 1999 Cup Final. In the moment before he left the pitch, he looked back at the scene, with the winning team doing their lap of honour and the fans cheering. He opened the presentation box in his hand, looked down at his medal, and thought, 'It doesn't get any better than this.' On my big day, the Villa fans were at the tunnel end and so I left the arena to catcalls from people suggesting that I was biased.

I can't leave the subject of that Villa squad without detailing some other exchanges with John Gregory over the years, because one of the things he said has stayed with me.

The first time he spoke to me was during a game against Charlton Athletic when he was Leicester City's assistant manager. As I left the pitch at half-time, Gregory said, 'You must be from Slough' and shook his carefully coiffured head. I did not have a clue what he was on about. Then, three minutes from the end, I awarded Charlton a penalty. It was not one of my best decisions. Charlton scored from the spot to condemn Leicester to defeat.

Within two minutes of the final whistle, John Gregory came to my changing room. 'Do you mind if I sit down?' he asked, as he sat down. I never objected to any coach or manager coming to ask any questions in a calm and dignified manner. How they approached me was more important than whether they obeyed the 'wait thirty minutes' rule.

Gregory stayed there, sitting in the officials' room, while I showered. Eventually, he said, 'Pollie, I can't face them. I can't face the players. You robbed us.' He, too, did not think the penalty was one of the best decisions I had ever made. There was no point in us having a long discussion, so I wanted to get rid of him. But I was still intrigued. 'Before you go,' I said, 'I've got a question for you. What was all that "You must come from Slough" business?'

He explained, 'I was born in Windsor and I hate everyone from Slough.' That cleared that one up then. He continued, 'You're a really good referee but you want to be popular. You want to be liked as well as being a good referee. Good referees aren't liked. We respect you. Don't try to be popular.'

He was spot-on. I remembered that remark. It helped me to be brave in decision-making later in my career and I have used the sentiment when talking to other referees. As I said in an interview with the *Daily Telegraph* before that 2000 FA Cup Final, referees are the Aunt Sallies of football. We are not there to be liked. We are there to try to make the right decisions.

So John Gregory gave me food for thought that day when his team lost to Charlton. He probably did not need to add, as he left the officials' dressing room, 'It was never a f***ing penalty.' But then I probably did not help by replying, 'I think we all know that.'

Because I like John Gregory, I was saddened that his players made snide remarks to me during the 2000 FA Cup Final. When I refereed Villa again, on Boxing Day 2000 against Manchester United at Villa Park, they were at it again. United won 1–0 and a number of Villa players made references to me being a Chelsea fan. This time, so did Gregory himself. I put it down to the fact they were all still disappointed about losing the Cup Final.

Then, in April 2001, I was in charge when Gregory took his Villa team to play Charlton at The Valley. I sent off Charlton defender Richard Rufus but awarded the home side a penalty. It was an exciting game which ended 3–3. Gregory again ribbed me about being a Chelsea supporter. I did not think I should have to keep putting up with that, so I asked the FA whether Gregory's continued sniping amounted to some sort of offence. They told me to rise above it so I decided that I needed to tackle it myself.

Gregory moved on and became manager of Derby. I next took charge of one of his matches in February 2002. It was at Pride Park, and Sunderland won 1–0. After the game, I went into the manager's office and gave Gregory a Chelsea hat and scarf I had bought especially for the occasion. I stood in front of his desk and sang, '*Chelsea, Chelsea*'. It was my way of saying, 'Look, I am not really a Chelsea fan, and we both know it, so let's laugh about it.' He did laugh. One–nil to Pollie.

A few weeks later I refereed Charlton v Chelsea and Gregory sent a package to The Valley marked 'for the attention of match referee Graham Poll'. It was brought to me by the Charlton secretary and I opened it in front of him. Inside were the same Chelsea hat and scarf. One–all.

Then I refereed Derby v Leeds close to the end of the 2001/02 season. In my dressing room awaiting my arrival was a number 9 Chelsea shirt with 'POLL' printed on the back. Two–one to Gregory.

Finally, just before I left for the 2002 World Cup, an envelope bearing Derby County's badge arrived at my home. Inside were four photographs of that Chelsea shirt with my name on the back and each photo had a message scrawled on it – things like, 'you wish' and 'in your dreams'. On the last one in the pile was the message 'Really good luck in the World Cup, Pollie'. Final score: 3–1 to Gregory. Game over.

Gregory lost his job at Derby sixteen months later and had a long period out of the game. When he did return to football management, in September 2006, it was at Queens Park Rangers, funnily enough. In one of our discussions about the daft allegation that I had been a Chelsea supporter I told him that my dad and I had watched him in his days as an outstanding player for QPR. We both liked him then. We both still do.

CHAPTER TEN

Collina, Dad and Me

Pierluigi Collina, the bald Italian, was probably the best referee anywhere in the world in the last thirty or so years. At the start of the 2002 World Cup, when all the referees sat in a room and were told, 'Aim for the highest. One of you thirty-six here will referee the World Cup Final,' we all looked at Pierluigi. It was at that same World Cup that I learned how astonishingly meticulous his briefings were to his assistants.

I was his fourth official for the game between Japan and Turkey. In the hotel room in which he told the assistants what he wanted from them, there was a whiteboard and he drew a pitch on it. I expected him to explain something straightforward – such as which areas of the field he wanted the assistants to make decisions. But on that whiteboard he wrote the names of both teams in their correct formations. He used the names he was going to call them if he needed to speak to them, rather than their formal names. Then he went on to explain, in fastidious detail, what would happen if Japan went a goal up or if Turkey took the lead. He explained how the losing side would change their tactics, or formation, or whether they would make a substitution. He detailed how the other team would probably respond. Then he indicated players who might get involved in incidents behind his back. He told the assistants who and what to look for and in what circumstances.

On another occasion, at a UEFA training session for referees, we were shown a video which included an incident when two players jumped for the ball. One elbowed the other in the face. UEFA said it was a red card offence. Collina thought otherwise. I asked him why, and his answer resonated with me. He said, 'Look at the player's hands. They are open. His fingers are extended. To elbow someone deliberately, you want to exert the force behind you, and to do that you clench your fist.'

I thought, 'Brilliant! Thank you very much, Pierluigi.'

I think he was spot on with his analysis, and that shows how he used to scrutinize the minutiae of everything associated with football to gain the knowledge he felt would benefit his refereeing.

Then there was Anders Frisk, of Sweden, another friend of mine and a top, top referee. He was the man who was struck on the head by a lighter hurled at him as he left the field at Roma. He was left hurt and bloodied. He was also the man hounded into retirement by threats to his family, allegedly by Chelsea fans. So he certainly suffered for his art. Yet he was entirely natural as a referee. His briefings to his assistants were extremely succinct. He used to say, 'Expect the unexpected and enjoy yourself.' That was it.

There are two broad categories of referee, I believe: manufactured and natural. The manufactured referee makes himself a ref. He thinks about where he should be and what he should do during a game. Everything he does is carefully considered. A natural referee goes with the flow a lot more. Both types have their virtues and their flaws.

In England, the top referees of recent years certainly fall into the two categories. Philip Don, who was appointed to take charge of the Select Group when referees became professional, was a manufactured referee. Keith Hackett, by contrast, who replaced Don as the Select Group supremo, was a natural referee.

David Elleray was manufactured. Paul Durkin was natural. Steve Dunn? Natural. Steve Bennett? Manufactured. Graham Barber? Natural. Graham Poll? Natural.

My style was a lot closer to Anders Frisk than to Pierluigi Collina. My style was a bit like pulling the cord to start the outboard motor and just letting the engine take me. I did not ponder where I needed to run. I did not think where I needed to stand. But I did have twenty-six years' experience which provided a subconscious structure to what I was doing.

Now, this doesn't mean that I think 'natural' is better than 'manufactured', because, although I say Steve Bennett is manufactured, I don't think he would ever have made the mistake I did in Germany. He is too considered in what he does to have made that sort of mistake.

My dad was more like Collina than Frisk (and not just because Dad was bald). Dad was also a very different referee to me. My memories of Dad, when I was a kid in our four-bedroomed, terraced house in Stevenage, are of a big man who was always working really hard; not for success for its own sake, but to earn more money to support his family.

Dad had been an electrical engineer for the Post Office (the GPO, as it was then) but I only remember him working for Kodak, the cameras, photography and photocopying company. I recall that Mum used to take us children with her to pick Dad up from Kodak after 7.15 pm on some nights, when he had been working overtime. I can also remember us driving over to collect him from Hitchin College, where he studied in evening classes to improve himself – again, to have a chance to earn more money to support us.

When the children were little, Mum was at home with us, but then she too took jobs. First she started part-time in the local greengrocers, then she worked for a photo-processors, next she also had a spell at Kodak and finally she worked for the local council.

Dad had a great quest for knowledge and a good memory to retain that knowledge. He had all the answers and was very clear about right and wrong. The rule he gave us was, 'Whatever you have done, if you tell me the truth, I'll support you. There may be some punishment if you have done something bad, but the punishment will be worse if you don't tell me and I find out later.' That is not a bad rule in my opinion. My wife and I have said the same thing to our three children.

Dad refereed to get more money to support his family. He never got higher than Class II (the middle of the three grades that existed then) but, during every season, he went out refereeing each Saturday afternoon and then Sunday morning and Sunday afternoon as well. Mum was football mad and so she and I used to go and watch Dad referee. My sisters came sometimes, but as they got bigger, they used to stay at home and watch an old film on TV.

If it did not clash with Dad's refereeing, we'd go and support Gonville Rovers – the boys' team which had originally started with lads from our road, Gonville Crescent. They were 'our' team. So it was football, football, football,

all weekend. Meal times, and everything else, were dictated by the football.

Also, on a Wednesday night, from the age of eight, I would go to bed at a normal time (between half past seven and eight o'clock), but then my mum would come and get me up at five to ten to watch *Sportsnight with Coleman.* I was allowed to sit up and watch the highlights of big European football matches, and they were magical.

I was Dad's linesman once when I was eight or nine. He said, 'Just ball in and out of play, son. I'll do the rest.' He refereed as he aimed to live his life – with a very firm, clear view of right and wrong. For him, the Laws of the Game, like the rules of life, were absolutely black and white. There were no grey areas at all. He was six foot three and sixteen or seventeen stone, had a military bearing because he had done his national service, and so looked very impressive. There are referees who command respect and those who demand it. Dad did both. His physical presence commanded respect. His no-nonsense approach meant that it was demanded.

When I was watching my dad all those years ago, I had no notion of becoming a referee myself. But I certainly adored football. I played for my primary school (at left-back, since you ask) but my secondary school did not play football. It was a rugby, hockey and cricket school. By the time I got there I was hooked on football and, as far as I was concerned, other sports could not compete. I could not compete very well in them, either, if I am honest. I did play basketball for the school and I did take up golf later with some success, but I joined football teams outside school to pursue the sport about which I was passionate.

My first club was Bedwell Rangers in the Stevenage Minor League and, probably because of my height, I was selected in goal. We lost the first game 8–0, the second 12–3 and the third 9–0. The defence must have been rubbish.

I was moved out of goal, played centre-half for a while and eventually ended up at centre-forward. But while my positions were going forward, I was going backwards in terms of the teams for whom I was playing – they were getting worse and worse. Nonetheless, I did make one-and-a-bit representative appearances at the age of thirteen.

My mum was social secretary of the Stevenage Minor League. Dad was the referees' secretary and fixtures secretary. I went with them when the squad representing the League toured Lancashire. I would not have been selected on footballing ability, but I went as a kid whose parents were going and who could play a bit. Then, as often happens, different boys were ill or injured and I was substitute in one game without getting on, then sub in another and went on. Finally, I played an entire match and performed well. I played at full-back and thought to myself, 'When you play with better players, you are a better player yourself.'

I did not kid myself that I would be anything other than a parks player but I certainly wanted to keep playing, so when I left school and began work for Prudential Insurance, in High Holborn, London, I played for the company. They had a team called Ibis, who played in the Southern Amateur League, which is a very good standard. All right, I did not actually play for the first team. They ran seven sides and I started in the sixth team, but I did work my way up to the second team. They played in Hammersmith, by the Thames, which was a long journey from Stevenage, involving a train, an underground trip and a bus ride.

I stopped being a man from the Pru after just under a year. The Prudential were using me as a pensions clerk and I wanted to do something less dull for more money. I went for a couple of jobs and landed a position with Shell Oil, based near Waterloo. That was an even longer journey and I decided not to join their football club. I could not travel all that weary way to and from work all week and then make the same tedious and tiring journey on Saturdays.

I was not quite seventeen at the time. Many of my school-friends were still at school and none of those who had left had done anything about playing football. This meant that I couldn't find a team in Stevenage who had players that I knew. Then fate, or happenstance, took a hand. Steve Coffill, who was then my brother-in-law, was a referee. He had been on a course learning how to teach others to become refs. He wanted to get his course notes in order and so he asked if he could practise teaching me. I persuaded a friend, Dave Ridgeon, to come along with me, and we let Steve teach us refereeing.

There was still no intention on my part to actually become a referee. Steve worked at Stevenage leisure centre and that was where we did the course. We were just having a laugh and knew that Steve could get us cheap beer in the leisure centre bar and perhaps a free game on the snooker table.

I took the course and, because I had done so, I also took the refs' test, although the exam itself was odd. There were two old refs, Fred Reid and Jock Munro – sorry fellas, but you seemed old to me at the time – who started playing Subbuteo, the table football game. I had no idea what was going on. Then they stopped. Jock asked, 'What was wrong with that, lad?' Unusually for me, I was speechless. I was supposed to have spotted some foul, or an offside or something, and that there was a corner flag missing. Their point was that a referee always has to keep alert and observe everything. It was a good point, except that I didn't want to take charge of Subbuteo matches.

One of the other questions they fired at me was: how would I check the pressure of a football? With youthful enthusiasm, I replied, quoting part of Law Two, 'I'd use a pressure gauge to ensure a pressure of between 0.6 and 1.1 atmospheres.'

The two old referees – let's call them experienced – shook their heads. 'Have you got a pressure gauge?' one asked. It was my turn to shake my head. Jock, I think it was, supplied the correct and commonsense answer: 'You press the ball with your thumbs, lad.'

Back then, that was how referees were examined. These days referees sit a written exam and an oral test. But young Graham Poll managed to survive the old-style grilling by the experienced refs. They told me I had passed. As I left the exam room, all the secretaries of the various leagues were sitting outside desperate to sign up referees. As a teenager, whose façade of self-assurance was a fairly thin veneer, it was very appealing to be wanted like that. So I thought, 'Why not?'

It was the summer of 1980. My journey from parks to the Premiership, from Stevenage to Stuttgart, had begun, but, of course, I had no inkling that I was embarking on anything of any significance. I was just going to do a bit of refereeing for some beer money.

My very first match, as a Class III referee, in my new black kit with a Herts FA badge sewn on by Mum, was on 6 September 1980, in Division Five of the North Herts League. Woolmer Green Rangers Reserves, the home team, beat the Anchor pub 6–0.

I still have those details recorded, neatly, along with the bare facts from every game I refereed. That, I dare say, makes me seem like an anal retentive, train-spotting, anorak of the first order. But so many referees have said to me, over the years, 'I wish I'd done that.' And my record-keeping started, like my refereeing itself, because of my dad.

When Dad was notified of a fixture, he would write it down, with a row of boxes for him to tick when the game was confirmed with the fixture secretary, when the kick-off time was confirmed with the home team and so on. He told me it was a really useful way of making sure you'd made and received all the necessary telephone calls. So, from the very start, I began doing the same and then, when I had refereed the game concerned, I just made a note of the score and jotted down if I had booked anyone.

I kept the list of games on one sheet of paper and, once I'd done it for half a season, it seemed sensible to keep going for the rest of the season. Then, in the summer, I had a full record of all my matches. So I did it for the second season – and continued to do so for every game and every season until I blew my whistle for full-time for the last time. They are all there: every game from Woolmer Green Rangers Reserves to Wembley.

The really wonderful thing, from my point of view, is that I can look at any season and almost any match and remember something about it. I remember, for instance, that in that first game in Division Five of the North Herts League all those years ago, Martin Hellman was in goal for Woolmer Green. He had a reputation for being a headache for referees, but he knew my dad and instead of giving me a tough initiation he nursed me through the game.

My second game was the very next day, a 7–3 away win for Bedwell Rangers in a youths game. Next up was a County Cup game, and the sort of one-sided fixture you can get in early rounds – an 18–0 romp for Cam Gears. I remember inspecting the pitch before kick-off and insisting that the home team repaint one of the penalty spots in the correct place. I bet they loved the officious, teenaged referee. Yet I note that I only cautioned five players in that entire first season and did not take anyone's name until game thirteen – unlucky for him. Mostly, I managed to control those big blokes with a whistle and my wits.

Don't worry, I am not going to go through all 1,500 matches here. But game number four for seventeen-year-old G. Poll was important to me because it was the one in which I really started to enjoy refereeing. It was a Saturday game and it was in the fourth division of the North Herts League. Icklefield Reserves drew 3–3 with Wymondley United. It was a terrific match, I recall.

The first part of the appeal of refereeing was the challenge. Teenaged, beanpole Poll had to go out and facilitate a game of football by properly controlling twenty-two fully-grown blokes. Some wanted to kick the ball and some wanted to kick other players. You had linesmen who were usually players who couldn't get in the side, or team officials or helpers. They were never completely neutral and sometimes they cheated. You had the mental challenge of knowing the Laws and applying them correctly and quickly – and doing it in such a way that players knew why you were doing it.

The metaphor that I use, and which makes sense to me, is of owning a beautiful, thoroughbred horse. If you have a horse like that, you don't want to tether it tightly to a stake in the ground, so that it can scarcely move, because you would be restricting it too much to see its grace and athleticism. But neither do you want to just let it go so that it runs away. You want to put it in a paddock. If you do that, you can watch it run and canter and buck. It is confined by clearly defined parameters, but those parameters allow you to appreciate the horse. It might not do exactly what you want it to do, but it will enjoy itself and express itself. I believe that, in football, the parameters are the Laws of the Game. The referee is the person who makes sure they are in place and are not breached.

After that 3–3 draw, my fourth game as a referee, players and other folk came up and shook my hand and said, 'Well done.' People say refereeing is a thankless task, but often it is not at all thankless. For a lad who had only recently turned seventeen, who had left school early and had not really done anything in life, to get praise from men like that felt good. People were telling me I was good at something. That was the moment when I thought, 'Yeah, I am enjoying this.'

CHAPTER ELEVEN

Running Backwards and Moving Up

When I became a Football League referee in May 1991, a month before my twenty-eighth birthday, my dad painstakingly made a certificate for me. It is still on the wall of my study, in a frame.

On a piece of stiff white card, he drew two ladders, displaying the rungs of my refereeing career. And in careful calligraphy he wrote, 'This record of progress is presented to Graham Poll who has shown that hard work, commitment and loyalty can achieve the referees' list of the Football League.' At the bottom he wrote, 'Presented by his very proud parents'.

What son has ever received a better present? Football has given me no greater reward than that. The words my dad believed were significant – hard work, commitment and loyalty – tell you about the family I grew up in and the values I learned.

But somewhere along the way, probably when I was trying to make my mates laugh at school, I also learned to be a cheeky, lippy what's-it. As I climbed those rungs of the refereeing ladder, I set two records: I was the youngest ever Football League linesman and there were more complaints about my tomfoolery than had ever been received before.

I never meant any harm by my mucking about. There was never any malice. But I can understand how I must have made people in the refereeing world think of me as a cocky upstart. I was a youngster making rapid progress up the ladder. The key figures in refereeing were quite a lot older and placed a lot of importance on doing things properly and with propriety. So the tale about how I took a fitness test with some portly, older refs, and ran around the track in front of them, backwards – yes, I can see how that might have added to the legend of my being an arrogant so-and-so. I honestly maintain that the truth about that day demonstrates as well as anything in my entire life and career how things can be easily misconstrued.

It was at Hornchurch, in Essex. It was the Isthmian League fitness test. We had to complete a set number of laps around an athletics track in a prescribed time. It required the refs to average two minutes a lap, and, as they say these days, it was a 'big ask' for blokes with big, erm, reputations.

But because I was young, it was not difficult for me. I could quite comfortably do three laps in four and a half minutes. And so, when I put in a couple of quick circuits at the start to break the back of the task, I lapped some of the older refs. After passing them, I span around, slowed down and ran backwards in front of them. It seemed a natural thing to do. I was confident that I would pass the test but some of them were struggling, so I started saying, 'Come on. You can do it.' That sort of thing.

They were not impressed. Between gasps of breath, they told me to eff off. So I joked and took the mickey a bit. I thought I was helping; I was not doing it to show off. But to onlookers and to some of the refs involved, I must have seemed like a swaggering braggart. I must have appeared an arrogant sod – but at least I was a fit sod!

I always tried to keep in shape and that too has often led to misconceptions. I am told, for example, that some broadcasters considered my warm-up routine on the pitch before Premier League games risible and commented on it on radio and television. They thought that the way I and my two assistants performed synchronized arm waving and so on looked like dancing. They thought that I was trying to attract attention to myself (again!) and that the whole routine said something about me. It did: it said I placed considerable importance on preparing properly. Perhaps their reaction said something about them, or at least something about how so many people routinely assume the worst of referees. Anything referees do is viewed through a prism of ill-will.

My warm-up procedure was specifically and carefully devised to do just that: warm up my muscles, sinews, tendons and joints. Then, when the game began, my body was ready. The routine I used was developed for me by experts. It was rhythmic because that helped me remember how many movements of each type I had made. Without a proper warm-up, I would not have been able to keep up with play and then the broadcasters would have criticized me for not being fit.

During an average Premier League match, I ran about thirteen kilometres. All our Premier League matches were translated onto computer graphics by a system called ProZone, which showed all our runs, our speed, our positioning and so on. Keith Hackett once pointed out that I was seldom in the middle of the pitch. He said, 'Graham believes strongly that the vast majority of the action is to be found at the end thirds of the pitch. We can see, from ProZone, that Graham sprints through the centre third of the field of play. The result is that he is always close to the action when tough decisions need to be made.'

That was a lot of sprinting to be in the right place. So fitness was, and is, a real issue for match officials. Before top referees became professional, we all had to arrange our training around our jobs. Amateur refs still do, of course, and that is why parks referees don't train much, if at all. I don't blame them or criticize them for that. You get home from work and you think, 'I really don't want to go for a run now.'

But then, as you start to clamber up the refereeing ladder, your physical condition becomes more important and is assessed, and so you think, 'I've got to train because I've got a fitness test.' Doing regular, structured training when you are working at another, full-time career certainly requires discipline and commitment. For instance, when I was living in Reading for a while – and holding down a high-pressure job directing a sales force for Coty – I really had to force myself to go out running when I got home after work. I used to think, 'If I don't go now, I won't go. Once I sit down and have a cup of tea, I won't go.' Football League referees, the officials just below the full-time professionals of the Premiership, still have to stop themselves from putting the kettle on when they arrive home. They hold down full-time jobs and yet are required to attain a quite remarkable level of fitness.

When I was training after work – and ignoring that tempting cup of tea – the fitness work itself was very different: less scientific, less structured, less suited to the actual demands of refereeing a football match. They just used to tell us to put our hearts under strain for twenty minutes a couple of times a week. My routine used to be: get in from my sales work, chuck my shorts on, no warm-up, straight out onto the streets. I'd do an 'out–back' – which meant I'd run for twelve minutes out, and I'd try to get back home in ten. Then no warm-down, no stretching. Straight in, shower, dinner. I'd do that two times a week. If you think about it, that was not correct preparation at all. In a match, when do you run for twenty-two minutes without stopping? You don't. As a professional referee, I trained for my matches, rather than to pass a fitness test, and, because I had been training for a long time, the test was one of the easier sessions. It changed considerably with professionalism, however.

The main component of the old assessment was a twelve-minute run, like the one I did backwards in Hornchurch. The distance you had to cover in twelve minutes depended on the level of referee you were and ranged from 2,400 metres to 3,000 metres. It was on a 400 metre track, so at the lowest level you were doing two-minute laps, which should be comfortable – with or without a grinning kid jogging around backwards in front of you.

For me, because I had been training for a long time, that pace was like walking, virtually. However, to be sure to complete 3,000 metres comfortably in less than twelve minutes I went faster than necessary and aimed to do eight circuits of the track and to complete each of them in one minute and thirty seconds. I look at Paula Radcliffe doing sixty-second laps – and thirty of them! – and just think, 'How does she do that?' That is supreme. Now, put Paula Radcliffe on a football pitch and she couldn't referee a game. It would be interesting television, though, and she'd do better than some refs I know.

The fitness test for referees which was in place for the final years in which I was professional was devised so that it was more appropriate to the job. It involved a series of 'accelerated runs' – not full-out sprints, but more like the quickening dash we performed during matches. It was electronically timed and you ran a metre – a stride – before the timer started: that way, there was less chance of injury from a sudden, explosive start.

The accelerated sprint was over 40 metres and referees had to complete it in less than 6.2 seconds. But the assistants, interestingly, had to do it in less than six seconds. The reasoning for that was that their short, sharp bursts along the touchline had to be quicker. They were keeping up with Cristiano Ronaldo, or someone similar.

So you did one 40-metre accelerated sprint and then jogged back to the start line and went again within a minute of the original start time. You did six of those 40-metre dashes. If you were over the permitted time on one, you retook it. But if you failed again, that was it, you were out. In other words, you had a maximum of seven attempts and needed to succeed six times.

Then came another running test, on a track marked off in sections. You ran for 150 metres and then walked for 50 metres to recover. You kept doing that all the way around the track. Everyone had to complete each of the 150-metre runs in thirty seconds, but the time allocated for the recovery period depended on whom you were and what you were. International referees had thirty-five seconds for each 50 metres recovery walk. Premier League referees did the same. Conference-level refs had forty seconds' rest. To pass, you had to complete ten laps, which is twenty repetitions of the run and the recovery.

Running 150 metres in thirty seconds is a speed of eighteen kilometres per hour and so, to replicate the test on a running machine, I used to stand beside the treadmill and turn it up to eighteen. Then I jumped on, using the handles to stop me shooting off the back, and within a stride or two, I got myself up to the speed of the treadmill. I maintained that for thirty seconds and then jumped off for thirty seconds. I kept repeating that sequence. That is being fit – and that is what a top referee can do.

Don't try that at home. In fact, even in a gym with helpers, my advice would be just to turn the belt up to eighteen and have a good look. Do not try getting on – it's flying.

One fitness test was far from a doddle for me – and it was the most important one of my career. In 1995 I was nominated for the FIFA (international) list for the first time but I went ill-prepared for the fitness assessment. I had a game the night before at Crystal Palace and then got up early the next day and drove to Bradford for the fitness test. That was not proper preparation but I was sure I would sail through.

It was the old-style laps, but I started to struggle and I began to doubt that I would complete 3,000 metres in the required time. My legs were heavy and I thought, 'You are not going to do this, Pollie. You might as well stop.'

Peter Jones started to catch me up. I've mentioned Peter before. He was the referee whose experience on the eve of the 1999 FA Cup Final served as a warning to me. We'll meet him again, in 2006, when he provided another, unwitting warning. But in 1995 on that running track in Bradford, he thought I was clowning around when I slowed down markedly. As he caught up, he said, 'Don't mess about, Pollie.' Then, when he realized that I was genuinely struggling, he said, 'Just come round with me for a lap.' He more or less dragged me round by encouraging me and running at a nice, sensible pace, and I kept going and passed the test.

As well as the backwards fitness test in my Isthmian League days, there were other incidents which have passed into refereeing folklore about me.

In December 1989, for instance, I took charge of an Isthmian League representative team versus an FA XI and after the game the officials were presented with a commemorative medal by a dignitary from the Football Association. Within a couple of days it was all round the league that I said, 'Cheers mate' when I was given mine. I honestly don't know if I did say that. If I did, then it was without thinking and certainly without meaning any disrespect. If I did say it, and the chap to whom I said it is still alive, then I would like to use this moment in this book to apologize.

Then there was the time when I had a chip in my mouth when I should have been blowing my whistle for a penalty. I suppose I should confess about that now. It was an Isthmian League game between Wokingham Town and Wivenhoe Town. The visiting chairman was standing behind a goal eating a bag of chips. So when Wivenhoe were awarded a corner, as I took up my position on the touchline near the goal, I leaned over and pinched one of his chips – a big one, covered in ketchup. As the corner came over, the Wivenhoe centre-forward was pulled down but I had a mouthful of chip and ketchup and couldn't blow up. I am pleased to say that the chairman did not blow up either, because his team won.

Perhaps my messing about like that was bluster; perhaps I was overcompensating again. Who knows? I do know that, right from the start, I got a lot of help and support from other referees and some of the senior people in football, so I certainly never meant them any disrespect or discourtesy.

In the very beginning I joined the North Herts Referees' Society. It was an active society full of really good people. We used to get together on Saturday evenings after matches and one of the older, experienced guys would ask me, 'Where did you ref today? Anything happen?' When I told him about how I had dealt with some incident or other, he would say, 'Did that work? Would you do that again?' It was an unofficial, informal but outstandingly helpful mentoring system – a form of on-the-job training.

Of course, I did not start in leagues with club chairmen or even crowds. I started in the parks. Invariably I was the youngest person on the pitch and I had often been to the same pub or party as the players the night before. I took some banter and gave some back but I was never threatened or intimidated. People kept saying that I was doing well and nothing encourages ambition like success, so I started to think seriously about climbing the refereeing ladder.

I was promoted from Class III to Class II at the earliest opportunity and upwards to Class I – again, at the first possible opportunity. There were some who said, 'He's a bit young.' When I was immediately promoted to be a linesman in the Isthmian League, the secretary of that competition, Ray Parker, said, 'Oh, you are the cocky one from Hertfordshire.' I replied, 'Yeah, and I'll be a ref in your league next year.' 'I don't think so,' he retorted. But I was.

I did 'talk the talk' but I did deliver as well. I kept getting good marks and there were plenty who took an interest, helped and encouraged me, despite my cheeky bluster. In November 1984, for instance, by which time I was a Class I ref, but still aged just twenty-one, I was the referee at an FA Vase match. My records tell me it was in Luton and that it was between 61 FC and Woodford Town. Years later I learned that Reg Payne, the Football Association's top man as far as refereeing was concerned, bought a ticket to stand on the terraces. He had heard about G Poll, a promising youngster from Hertfordshire. He did not want to declare his presence but he wanted to have a look at me. It was at the end of that season that I was promoted to become an Isthmian League referee (much to Ray Parker's surprise). I think I was probably the youngest Isthmian League ref ever.

The Isthmian League is, at the time of writing, more properly known as the Rymans Isthmian League and its premier division is in the seventh tier of English football's pyramid. It is a famous, proud old league, which was formed in 1905 and is home to some of the best known and best loved smaller clubs in and around London.

If I get no other message across at all from this book, I want to tell people that the ten years I spent on the Isthmian League list were bliss. Since then I have been to two World Cups and refereed some of the most skilled practitioners of the art of football – geniuses and giants of the world game – but the truth is that my days in the Isthmian League were probably the most enjoyable.

When people ask why on earth anyone would want to referee, I wish I could transport them to that time in my life and show them. It was a good standard of football, in decent little stadiums with floodlights, with well-cared-for playing surfaces, and stands and boardrooms peopled by folk who loved the game. I was a kid in his twenties, but doing really well and loving it. The matches were not that difficult. The odd fixture would rear up at you and pose a few problems, but mostly they went well.

I started with Hertfordshire towns along the A41 – literally towns. There was Hemel Hempstead Town, Berkhamsted

Town and Tring Town. Occasionally I strayed off the A41 into Bedfordshire and took a game at Barton Rovers. Those teams were in what was then called Division Two North but I was quickly promoted to the Premier Division, which had teams from further afield – famous clubs such as Carshalton, Kingstonian and Sutton United.

By now, I was working as a salesman and had all the patter, which I used to good effect in the boardrooms and clubhouses after the matches, when I got to know all the players and club officials. Ray Parker once told me that the marks a referee is given by the clubs can only go down in the clubhouse, never up. In other words, if you have been given a seven, your behaviour and demeanor afterwards might get you knocked down to a six. It will never get your mark increased to an eight. Nevertheless, there were plenty of refs on the Isthmian League circuit who tried to talk their way to higher marks by being especially nice to chairmen. We used to have a Mars bar before games to give us energy and the joke was that some refs saved theirs to have after the game but before they went into the boardroom – because they put more energy into flattery than football.

Anyway, I went into the Isthmian League a boy and came out a man. I had a decade of rewarding games. There were some younger players who later scaled football's heights and there were some veterans on their way down from those heights. I made myself known to one of each. I sent off a Hayes youngster called Les Ferdinand, who went on to play for QPR, Newcastle, Spurs, West Ham, Bolton, Reading and England; and I booked former Scotland striker Andy Gray, who, after a barnstorming career with Dundee, Aston Villa, Wolves, Everton, West Brom and Glasgow Rangers, spent one season at Cheltenham Town, where he was refereed by me in an FA Trophy tie. The eloquence with which Andy expressed dissent to me that day has since served him well on Sky TV – and he is still complaining about referees.

The level at which Les and Andy were playing when I showed them cards was certainly competitive, but there was not a win-at-all costs mentality. The remnants of football's Corinthian spirit survived in competitions such as the Isthmian League – and so did the opportunity to referee with some degree of flexibility. For instance, on one occasion at Saffron Walden Town, a player came out with England's most common expletive. Very loudly and very close to the main stand, he shouted, 'F*** off!' The crowd expected me to do something, wanted me to do something, but I instinctively felt that nobody wanted him sent off for a temporary lapse of control. If he had kicked someone up in the air then I would have sent him off, but he had not hurt anybody. So I gave an extravagant 'Peeeep!' on my whistle and made a big show of lecturing him sternly, but did not caution him or send him off. Then I restarted play with a free-kick to the other side.

There is no provision at all in the Laws of Football for what I did. In fact, it is completely wrong to give a free-kick for swearing unless you have shown a card. The Law gives no leeway and so a lot of refs would either have gone, 'Red card!' or have done nothing at all. I showed suitable disapproval but did not send him off. The crowd was satisfied and I think the spirit of football was honoured as well.

There are parallels with an infamous incident, decades later, involving Wayne Rooney. In February 2005, by which time I was older than the players instead of younger, I took charge of an Arsenal–Manchester United confrontation at Highbury. We shall get to the events of that game later – the altercation in the tunnel, how I tried to get Roy Keane to smile and how I managed to keep the lid on a tinder box of a game – but let's deal with Wayne's words now.

I can't remember precisely what caused the Rooney outburst. The ball was played through to him but I had to blow my whistle, either for offside or handball. The words he used were what some call industrial language. They had Anglo-Saxon roots. They were repetitive. Someone worked out that he used the f-word twenty-seven times, mostly at me. It was, apparently, an impressive demonstration of rapid-fire swearing. I say 'apparently' because, in the heat of the battle, I did not hear everything. And even if I had, in the circumstances, I would not have considered the Rooney rant worth a red card.

Despite what so-called experts keep writing and broadcasting, using 'foul language' is no longer an offence. That is because, rightly or wrongly, people swear all the time. So the football Law now bans 'offensive or abusive or insulting language or gestures'. It is up to the referee to judge whether the words or actions are offensive, abusive or insulting. So, a player can say, 'Oh, f*** off' as a way of letting off steam and mean no harm, or he can say something apparently innocuous but with venom and intend it to be abusive. The referee decides.

In Rooney's case, there were also other considerations. If I had sent him off, a volatile game might well have exploded. So, I called Roy Keane, Rooney's captain, over to us as a witness and told Rooney, 'There will be no more of this. Or else you will be sent off.' Whether Roy or his manager, Sir Alex Ferguson, reinforced my message at half-time, I do not know, but Rooney gave me no more trouble and kept his mouth more or less under control.

From my point of view, I had successfully man-managed him and had helped the game. Others saw things differently. The English Schools FA said that Rooney had set an atrocious example and many queued up to condemn him – and me for not punishing him. Sepp Blatter, the FIFA president, said the United player needed a clip around the ear – although, wisely, Sepp has never tried administering it himself.

Years later, in the months immediately after I had retired, I began to see things from the point of view of the English Schools FA. Once I had stepped away from refereeing, I began to be able to see the bigger picture and, later in this book, I will explain that altered perspective. I could see how much good it might have done to stop Rooney abusing me. But at the time, when I was in the middle of the picture, I didn't even realize the extent to which he did pollute the occasion and defile the game.

Things were more straightforward in the Isthmian League and I remained a referee in that competition for two seasons (1991/92 and 1992/93) after I had won a place on the Football League referee's list. When the time came for me to finish on the Isthmian League, they invited me to take charge of their Charity Shield match, their only major set-piece match I had not refereed. I accepted the invitation gratefully. Happy days.

When I reached the Football League, initially as a linesman, I was not sure I wanted the responsibility involved. Refereeing in the Isthmian League was far more enjoyable and far less stressful. The idea that a decision I made in the Football League would affect a result on the Pools Coupons, and so could stop someone winning a fortune, was playing on my mind.

The first rung on the ladder had been parks football, which was just for fun, really. Then came the Isthmian League, which was definitely still fun but more serious. Ascending to the third rung, and becoming a Football League linesman, involved a much greater change in terms of the calibre of matches in which I was involved. That started to faze me. It was a big step up and I thought I should give up being a linesman, give up the promotion to the Football League and just referee in the Isthmian, which I enjoyed.

I spoke candidly with my dad, who persuaded me to give it another six months before making a decision. So I did, and of course the six months turned into a long career.

I was still a wise-cracking smart alec. In my second season as a Football League linesman, I ran the line for Brian Hill, a top ref who was held in awe by his fellow officials. I put the mud from my boots in his shoes, as you do. Well, you do if you are a young buck having a laugh.

Philip Don – who refereed in the 1994 World Cup and was my first boss when referees turned professional – had the misfortune to be the ref once with me as one of his linesmen. Before the game I hid his shorts. I only gave them back at the last minute. Laugh? I don't think he did.

Nor did anyone else. My jolly japes became just too much.

The League received more complaints about me than anyone else, ever. After my first thirty games, fourteen referees had complained about my general attitude. And don't assume that I behaved sensibly in the other sixteen games. In those matches it was often a ref who had already reported me and who was too weary of my misbehaviour to complain again. I don't think there were any who happily tolerated finding mud in their shoes or 'losing' their shorts.

One assessor reported that I ran the line at Northampton 'in an unorthodox manner'. What happened was that it was a freezing, filthy night. I was at the end where nothing was happening. I was just standing near the halfway line, trying in vain to keep warm. I was hopping from one foot to another, and I suppose my movements looked a little like a Highland reel, so a few fans started loudly humming the first few bars of 'Scotland the Brave'. I played up to them by kicking one leg behind the other in a pretty poor imitation of a Scottish dance. I should not have done it because the spectators were not there to see me. I was not supposed to be a performer. The assessor mentioned my act in his report, and not in a good way.

The Football League referees' secretary, John Goggins, wrote asking me for my observations. My view was that if I wrote in response, I would have to admit what I had done. So, on one of my trips as a sales representative, I stopped off at a motorway service area and made a call from a payphone. In fact, I had to make a couple of stops and a couple of calls before getting Mr Goggins, as he was known to me.

Nervously, I said, 'What I can tell you is that you will never ever get a complaint like this about me again.'

Mr Goggins said, 'So you are not admitting it, merely promising it will not happen again.'

I said, 'I am promising it will not happen again.'

And he said, 'Make sure it doesn't.'

John Goggins did something else, something very shrewd, to straighten me out. For the last game of the season he sent me to Swindon to run the line for Neil Midgley, one of the most respected referees in the game. John Goggins gave Neil Midgley a message from the Football League to deliver to the young linesman whose antics were unacceptable. They sent Neil because he was a natural referee, the sort I aspired to be. He was certainly capable of enjoying a laugh at the right time, but he took his craft seriously.

If John Goggins had sent some straight-laced, authoritarian figure, I might not have listened. But I certainly took notice when Neil said, 'Take this as a compliment because if they didn't think you had a good future we wouldn't be having this conversation.' Then he added, 'The Football League said you must shut up or get out.'

At Football League matches, there was so much riding on my decisions as a linesman that the League wanted me to concentrate on raising my flag at the correct moment. They did not want me thinking about hiding someone's shorts. So I turned over a new leaf and quit the mucking about. But I went from one extreme to another. From being a noisy nuisance, I now kept as quiet as I could.

The new, silent Graham Poll sat in the corner of the dressing room for the first game of the 1988/89 season at Leyton Orient with my head in the *Daily Telegraph*, the largest paper I could find. Keith Cooper, the referee, asked me what was wrong. 'Nothing,' I replied keeping my words to a minimum. Keith wanted to be able to communicate with me and so made his point forcefully. 'Put that paper down or I'll rip it out of your hands,' he said. Clearly, I needed to find a happier medium for my behaviour. And so, since then, I have aimed to position myself somewhere appropriate on the scale between mad man and sad man.

As well as running the line in the Football League, I was refereeing in the tier below, the Conference. I did two seasons as a Conference ref and then, in the summer of 1990, expected to get an interview to become a Football League referee. I had the highest marks in the Conference.

But I was not called for an interview. For the first time, but not the last, football made me cry. That was the first time that Julia, who was then my fiancée, realized how important refereeing was to me.

On the day I heard that I was not getting an interview, I ran the line at a Football League match at Crystal Palace. I was in a foul mood and so, if you were there that day and think I missed all the offsides, that was why.

Given my history of pranks, the decision not to give me an interview was not really surprising, but it was probably also a test. The Football League wanted to see how I would react to being turned down.

I reacted by getting my head down and doing my absolute best. And so, twelve months later, I was, indeed, called before the Football League selection panel. The first question was, 'How did you feel last year when your friend Paul Taylor was promoted and you were not?' I replied that I was disappointed for myself but delighted for Paul. I said that the rejection strengthened my determination to reach the required standard and to join him on the League list. It was the right answer. That May, my dad presented me with that certificate.

CHAPTER TWELVE

A Tring Thing

As well as Mum and Dad, there is someone else who helped shape my refereeing, and I have not properly introduced her to you yet: Julia, my wife.

I first set eyes on Julia on Friday, 10 November 1989. No, I haven't noted it down on one of my results sheets, but it was a day and a date I have not forgotten. It was a pivotal moment of my life because Julia has provided the calm haven I have needed; the placid place to come home to, where I am just Graham, not referee Graham Poll.

We met in a pub in Berkhamsted. I was working as a salesman, I was a referee in the Isthmian League and in the Conference and was a Football League linesman. I'd bought a two-up, two-down in Berkhamsted, but didn't know many people in the town.

One friend I did have was Michael Oakley, the estate agent who had sold me the house. No wonder he liked me: he had banked a big commission. Anyway, that Friday, I had gone home after work, had eaten my microwave chilli con carne (with extra-hot chilli sauce), was doing some ironing and planning an early night before a game the following day.

That charmingly domestic scene was interrupted by a call from Michael, who insisted – obviously I needed a lot of persuading – to join him for couple of beers. Just a couple. So I met him in the pub and during the evening Julia came in with another girl and began talking to some people Michael knew. So we had an excuse to go over and chat to the two girls. At the end of the evening, I asked Julia for her telephone number. She has told me since that she never gave her number out to strange men, but she gave it to an odd one that night.

The problem was that when I wanted to telephone her on Sunday morning, I could not remember her name. She hates being called Julie by mistake, so when she had told Michael and me her name, she had stressed the last syllable of Julia. So I remembered clearly that she had a name ending in an 'a'. But I simply could not recall which name ending in 'a' it was.

I phoned my mum and asked for some suggestions. She came up with many: Tina, Vera, Sara, Rebecca, Mona, Tessa, Sheila, et cetera. No, not et cetera – you know what I mean. Eventually she suggested 'Julia' and I thought that sounded right. Thankfully, it was. Things might have been very different if I had rung and asked for Tina. That is the name of her younger sister.

I rang Julia and we went out on that Sunday night and again on the Wednesday night. Then, on the following Saturday, I drove around to her parents' house to take her out again. She worked in the John Lewis department store in Watford and had not been home long. She was upstairs, getting ready. In her mum and dad's lounge, you can see the stairs, and after a while she came down those stairs wearing a blue dress with buttons down both sides. I knew then, without a scintilla of doubt, that I loved her. And, reader, I married her. A few years passed before the wedding, and several more have passed since, but I can still easily locate among my memories that image of her descending those stairs in that blue dress.

Julia was just nineteen; I was twenty-six. Every time I took her out I gave her a little present – often a sample from the company for whom I was working. I might have been cheap, but it was the thought that counted, and the effort I put in. On Valentine's Day I looked on every floor of a car park in Watford until I found the battered old Ford Fiesta Julia used to drive. I wrote, 'I love you' on the back in toothpaste (another free sample). Then I went to her home, persuaded her mum to let me go to Julia's room and left the empty toothpaste dispenser on the bed with a single red rose. All together now, aaaah!

Julia got her own back by insisting that night that we went out in her car, with the messy affirmation of ardour message still on it. Everyone in The Boat pub – our local, by the canal in Berkhamsted – was greatly amused.

Julia was not into football at all. She just didn't get it. Her dad was a rugby chap and football did nothing for her. So I took her to a Millwall game, where I was running the line. That could have finished our relationship before it had really started but it was a big match, with a passionate atmosphere, and she found it very exciting. From that moment, she started coming to see my games. She changed jobs and began working in London, but she would make her way by public transport to wherever I was in action. That meant so much to me. And the old boys in Isthmian League boardrooms loved the bubbly young blonde who came in for a drink with me after games.

I think it helped our relationship that I was already refereeing when Julia and I met. She realized from the very beginning that it was important to me. So, in later years, when I changed jobs because of the refereeing, she understood. That was who I was.

I proposed to her in the January after we had met. She said, 'Oh! Don't ask me. Don't ask me.' It was not the response I had hoped for, but at least it wasn't a 'No'.

So I took her to Paris but the trip did not start smoothly. I thought I was a big shot, who knew his way around Heathrow airport, but I parked at the wrong terminal and we had a long trek to the right one. But we did get to Paris and when I proposed again in that romantic city, Julia said 'Yes'.

That was April 1990. We married on 13 June 1992; Graham Barber, my best refereeing buddy, was best man. The date was available because nobody wanted to get married on the thirteenth but Julia and I both thought that if you worry that a superstition might undermine your marriage then your relationship is not on very firm ground.

When I was interviewed, along with all the other referees, for the World Cup match programme in 2006, I was asked my 'favourite occasion'. Most of the refs put something about a big football match, or some occasion like that, which I suppose is what you were supposed to say. But I put 'My wedding day'. And the first match I refereed at the 2006 World Cup was on 13 June, our anniversary.

But I am getting ahead of myself again. Julia and I married in 1992. Our eldest daughter, Gemma, was born in January 1994. Josie arrived in April 1996 and Harry came along in

February 2000, well in time for the FA Cup Final. The children became part of my calm haven. To have done what I have done – to have dealt with all the controversies in refereeing, the media attention, the journeys abroad and so on – you need somewhere very stable to come home to, and someone very stable and calm. Julia is very level-headed, a fantastic mother, and can run a household when her man is away. I have been very lucky.

Refereeing has cut across family life too many times, I admit. For instance, I missed too many birthdays. So, in 2002 I asked for 24 February to be kept clear of refereeing appointments in order to celebrate Harry's second birthday as a family. But then Philip Don, who was in charge of the elite group referees, telephoned and told me he needed me for the 24th after all.

I said, 'Philip, there are twenty-four other referees on the list. Surely you can get one of them to do whatever game is being played?'

He said, 'Do I have to spell it out to you? You know exactly what the game is.'

But I didn't. He spelled it out for me. 'The Worthington Cup final.'

'Ah,' I said. 'Can you give me half an hour?'

Julia was not happy about Harry's dad working on his birthday. I recall the word 'again' passing her lips during our discussion. In fact, she said 'again' again and again. But she knew that if I turned down the appointment, it would count against me, and so we made the weekend of the final into a family event. We all went to Cardiff for the game and we did all celebrate Harry's birthday together.

Football has not been entirely unkind to Julia, however. When she came to watch the first time I refereed Manchester

United (in a 3–2 win against Queens Park Rangers at Loftus Road), I told Ryan Giggs during the game that my wife was in the crowd. I said, 'She thinks you're great. Why don't you do something special for her?' I was only joking, not demonstrating bias – and certainly not expecting what happened next. A few minutes later Giggs shimmied passed two players and scored a glorious goal. As he jogged back to the centre for the restart he asked me, 'Will that do for her?' Come on, how many husbands could ask for something like that for their wives?

When referees became professional – which meant a big change in our lives – Julia made just two stipulations. The first was that we were not allowed to move from our house in Tring, because she loves living there, and the second was that I had to promise her that every year we would have a two-week holiday, away from football, when it was just us and our family – when I was Dad, and Graham, not a referee. I used to get offered trips for the family to Milan, Barcelona and places like that by football people in those cities. Julia used to say, 'Don't you dare even think about it.'

Actually, I didn't often think about it. I much preferred a holiday in which I could forget about the refereeing for a short while. But it was not always possible. Since the start of the Premier League, and its wall-to-wall coverage by the media, my face has become very familiar to a lot of people and so they come up to me on holiday.

It might seem churlish to complain – after all, 'arrogant' Graham Poll was always seeking the limelight, apparently – but I am not moaning about any of those who approached me as individuals. They were usually perfectly pleasant and polite – as individuals. Each person who asks, 'Could you sign this, please?' is only asking once. But when a dozen different individuals ask you every day, and when that happens for fourteen consecutive days, and when it happens when you are having a quiet family meal in a restaurant, it can become a bit of a pain. I could be playing bat and ball on a beach with one of my daughters and a couple of lads would come and sit and watch. They'd say, 'All right, Pollie? We're West Ham fans,' or something. They don't mean to intrude but I just need to have some time as a husband and a dad.

The footballers I refereed could easily afford to go to the sort of place where nobody bothers you on holiday, except an attentive drinks waiter. We couldn't afford that sort of destination, but we did try and upgrade our holidays a little in pursuit of a little peace and quiet. To some of you, that will provide more proof of aloofness. To me, it was just trying to be a decent husband and father.

That is why Tring is such a lovely place to live: nobody bothers us when we are out and about. We live in Tring because it is Julia's family home town but also because it provides a sanctuary. Tring is not a football town and the good folk who live there do not feel the need to talk to me all the time about football. They are not indifferent to us. At times they have provided wonderful, genuine, warm support, but they respect our privacy and give us space to live.

Of course, if I go to a school to present prizes or give a talk, or if I dish out the medals at Tring Tornadoes (the town's youth football club) then I sign autographs for as long as they like. That is part of trying to help out at the school or football club. Sometimes they queue up for my autograph and, as I sign, they say, 'Thanks, and who are you?' But signing autographs is not a problem in those circumstances. It is an honour.

But if I am in a pub, nobody takes any notice of me and that is great. Well, they did take some notice on one occasion, but that was great as well.

I'd had a disaster of a game and had suffered a severe kicking by the media. I felt stressed and under pressure. That week was turmoil. I had to do another game, under maximum scrutiny and with minimum confidence. But, that week I went to the King's Arms with Paul Chaplin, a good mate, to help him take part in Tring Beer Festival (you can see why I love the town!). I went to the bar to buy a round, as I do occasionally, and the guy behind the bar said, 'Graham, yours is paid for. There are six Tring lads over there. They are on holiday from university and are going back next week. They don't want to bother you but they just want to show you their support. So they have bought you a beer.' Cheers lads. You didn't know how valuable that marvellous gesture was.

I am told that, after my World Cup mistake, when the *Sun* printed what they thought was a humorous jibe at me on their front page, people in Tring took umbrage on my behalf. I am told that at the newspapers section in our local Tesco store, the manager took the *Sun* off sale because so many people complained that it was objectionable. I used to be known as The Thing from Tring. Well, that remarkable demonstration of solidarity was a Tring thing. When told about it, I was profoundly moved.

I also received a letter from the town council in 2002 saying that by going to the World Cup I had put Tring on the map – as I have demonstrated with that letter from the fourteen-year-old lad, addressed, 'G Poll, referee, Tring', which managed to reach me. However, for the sake of my friend Clive the postman, I'd rather you did not test that council statement too much.

One letter I could have done without was the death threat I received from Tottenham fans after the 2002 Worthington Cup Final. It was carefully posted abroad and it said, 'You are dead.' I didn't tell Julia about it at the time and I didn't tell the police because I thought that would exacerbate the situation. I calculated that Tottenham fans probably had a few people they hated more than me and I worked out that people who are really going to kill you probably don't tell you about it beforehand.

On another occasion, a huge pair of pink, comedy spectacles were left on my doorstep. That meant that someone who didn't think much of my ability – or at least my eyesight – knew where I lived, which was a tad disconcerting. But, on balance, I thought it was probably a joke – and the kids liked the specs so much that we kept them.

Other deliveries are far less easily dismissed as unimportant. When I was a linesman, some charming fans often spat at me.

Before West Ham's Upton Park was modernized, the section of the ground known as the Chicken Run was notorious as a bear pit, if you will excuse the mixed animal metaphor. But nobody warned me about the phlegm. In my first game there as a linesman, I was assigned the Chicken Run side in the first half and, in the interval, the other linesman (an older and wiser chap) said, 'You might as well do that side again in the second half because the back of your shirt is covered in spit already.'

Similarly, at Reading's old Elm Park ground, there was one home 'supporter' who used to station himself at the front of one stand – in line with the edge of the penalty area – because he had worked out that was the most advantageous position from which to spit at the linesman. Nice.

At Millwall's old ground, The Den, a security official used to make a joke of the fact that the fans there liked to pelt linesmen with coins. He used to say, 'They do appreciate linesmen here. They make a collection and deliver it throughout the game.' When you think about it, that is not very funny. It meant spectators were throwing dangerous missiles and yet nobody was going to do anything about it.

Some referees have been victims of truly ominous, threatening behaviour. Barry Knight received an aerial picture of his house after one dodgy game, for instance. That was scary for him and his family. It meant someone had gone to a lot of trouble to demonstrate that he knew where Barry lived.

Consider also the case of Urs Meier, the Swiss referee who disallowed a goal by Sol Campbell in England's Euro 2004 quarter-final against Portugal. He was put under police protection because of death threats from England. Our newspapers were even offering one of his grown-up sons all sorts of incentives to dish some dirt on Urs so that they could use it to destroy him.

Anders Frisk allegedly had Chelsea fans turn up in his village in Sweden and thought, 'That's it. I don't need this. I am quitting.'

We are talking about decent men who have been brave enough to make honest decisions in big matches. Perhaps they did not get every decision right. They are human, after all. But we are talking about football matches, for heaven's sake.

The most frightening situation Julia and I have been in because of my refereeing was after Middlesbrough's home defeat by Arsenal in January 1996. As far as I was concerned, the game went well. I sent off Middlesbrough's

Alan Moore in the last minute for elbowing an opponent in the face but it was a clear-cut decision. Julia, who was six months pregnant, was at the game and a friend, Harry Williams, was going to drive us away from the ground. As we walked towards the car, two supporters, who had obviously been waiting for me, jumped out from behind another vehicle. One started with the 'You f***ing southerner' routine. I said to Williams, 'Just get Julia inside the car first, then get the boot open to let me put my kit bag inside.'

As I climbed into the car one of the fans put his hand inside his leather jacket, then withdrew it, made a 'gun' shape with his fingers and said, 'Bang, you're dead.' Then he threw a punch at me, missed and hit the car. Then he started to kick the car as we drove off. I said to Julia, 'He's gone, it's over.' But he hadn't and it wasn't.

The pair ran across some wasteland and were waiting as we reached the exit road. My friend was driving at around 20 mph with the 'gunman' in his sights and I said, 'Just keep going.' He did, and the two supporters jumped out of the way.

It was a horrible experience, especially because Julia was with me, but for the most part I only received the sort of ordinary abuse that fans think is OK to shout at referees. I considered that it was just one of those things that went with refereeing, like a notebook or a whistle. It was part of the deal I accepted when I first wore that shirt with the Herts FA badge sewn on by my mum.

I am not saying that abuse is acceptable. It is not, of course. The referees who take charge of games on parks pitches are the only neutral people present and it takes a degree of bravery to do that, week in and week out, for a few quid and for the love of the game.

There have been too many assaults, and too many referees who have found the abuse too much to tolerate – and I believe that the climate of constant carping which referees have to endure is encouraged by people like Neil Warnock. What managers like him say about referees at the top levels of the pyramid make blokes in parks think it is perfectly all right to abuse parks referees.

More about Mr Warnock soon, but all of us who put on referees' shirts know we are going to be insulted and, thankfully, most of the insults are not particularly inventive. It is usually just the same old stuff and the more it is repeated, the less impact it has. And so, as I went through the years and through the leagues, I became increasingly unmoved by the things people shouted, chanted, sung or wrote. As I progressed from the parks to the Premier League, I became more and more hardened. I built layer upon layer of protection.

Actually, I don't really remember much offensive stuff from my early days as a parks referee, but then, when I think back to childhood holidays, my memory tells me that it was always sunny. Yet Dad and Mum used to take us to Mablethorpe, Cleethorpes, or Skegness and so the chances are there just might have been a few spots of rain – and some wind. It is just that nostalgia paints a cheerier picture than the reality. So it is probable that I did get sworn at a lot as a parks ref, but I obviously got used to it and learned to ignore it. Then, gradually, I became familiar with bigger crowds and inured by exposure to louder criticism.

Once the crowd goes above three thousand, you seldom hear the individual, personal abuse. You might have five hundred people singing something about you, but that is not the same – not as bad, in some ways. They are just abusing the bloke with the whistle, and the role he has, not you as a person. They are booing the pantomime villain. So you shower at the end of the game, change back into civilian clothing and you are not dressed as the villain any more.

With bigger crowds, you can still hear the odd individual, or become aware of a particularly unhappy punter. In Isthmian League days, I used to answer back – in a disarming way. Once crowds became bigger still, I tried to use gestures to answer back. No, not that sort of gesture, although it was sometimes a temptation.

There was a guy at Anfield who used to stand up and bellow stuff about me and at me. So I made sure that, when a throw-in was being taken, I stationed myself in line with this wise guy, made eye-to-eye contact and blew him a kiss. His mates around him saw me do it and thought it was hilarious. They were all laughing at him and with me. Then ten minutes or so later, I made sure that I had eye contact with him again, and gave him a wink. That section of crowd thought it was highly amusing and the abuse stopped – until I gave a decision against their team.

Much of the criticism aimed at me was ill-informed because most people in this country, or in any football-playing country, do not know the Laws of the game. That comment will be dismissed as yet more arrogance, but it is a fact, and it is one with which referees live.

Let me explain. If I take someone who has never been to a football match to a fixture at say, Stamford Bridge, he or she will understand what is going on. If I take someone to a rugby match at Twickenham, lots of what occurs will be bewildering. Football is a simple game. That is its beauty and a considerable part of its appeal. But that means that, as we grow up, we do not need to sit down and learn the Laws. We just get on with playing or watching and pick up bits and pieces of the Laws as we go along. And we pick up some half-truths and myths. I won't go into them here. That is a whole other book.

However, the situation is that many journalists, broadcasters, players and managers do not know the Laws and persistently make mistaken assumptions or draw erroneous conclusions. As a referee, you just have to accept that.

You can try to inform people if you are given the chance but mostly you have to accept their mistakes. You certainly can't get worked up when Alan Hansen or Andy Gray has a go at you on TV and yet get the Laws wrong. It's just life. It's just football.

I knew that if I took big decisions in big games honestly, and got most of them right, I would get respect – not necessarily popularity, as John Gregory pointed out, but respect. So, although this will seem like even more arrogance, I knew I was doing a good job as a referee most of the time, and so the abuse was not a problem.

Insults from players or coaches? They didn't worry me, unless they eroded my ability to control the game. I was not interested in winning an argument. I wanted to end the argument and facilitate the game of football.

Fierce criticism by the media? Obviously, I would have preferred not to have been the subject of headlines such as 'Poll's a snivelling creep', which appeared in the *Mirror*, but I received praise occasionally as well. Still, that was better than a *Daily Star* headline about Paul Allcock. It said, 'Allcock no brains'.

Abuse from crowds? Well, when supporters chanted, '*You don't know what you're doing*', the truth was, I did know what I was doing. So I was not wounded by the shouts.

When they sang, '*You're not fit to referee*' I knew that I was physically fitter than most of them and that good judges thought I was one of the best referees in the country. So, again, the crowd didn't hurt me at all. When they sang, '*Who's the wanker in the black?*' it didn't hit home – because I didn't always wear black. So none of the songs and chants were accurate and none of them could penetrate those layers of protection that had built up over the years – not even the song which rhymed my surname with a coarse description of an anus. You'll have to work out for yourself what I mean if you've never sung it.

No, nothing got to me – until the season after I got back from Germany. Then, when crowds sang, '*World Cup and you f***ed it up*', it hurt. It pierced those twenty-six years of layers – because it was true.

CHAPTER THIRTEEN

Smiling at Warnock

Until the 2006 World Cup, I was immune to most of the abuse and criticism that was routinely heaped upon me. The common judgment was that I loved the limelight and sought controversy, and I had to laugh when a friend told me of a remark made by Patrick Collins of the *Mail on Sunday* newspaper. He said, 'The trouble with Graham Poll is that he enjoys being on television too much.' And Patrick said that on *Jimmy Hill's Sunday Supplement,* a Sky TV programme.

I happen to think that Patrick is a gifted writer. I don't always agree with what he writes, but it is always worth reading. I happen to know that Patrick could not referee a Premier League match, any more than he can resist invitations to appear on *Jimmy Hill's Sunday Supplement*, and, like everyone else, he was wrong about his assumption that I courted controversy. Whenever I whistled for the start of a game, I hoped that the match would pass without anything contentious happening. Of course I did. But I was frequently given high-profile matches and tried not to shirk the big decisions. I made those decisions honestly, knowing they might bring arguments and conflict, but definitely not seeking that controversy.

Perhaps one reason folk thought that I thrived on controversy was that I smiled a lot during games. Often it was because I was enjoying myself and having a laugh with the players but sometimes I smiled as a bit of a defence mechanism – my way of demonstrating a strength of will and proving that the carping, sniping and abuse were not hurting. Sometimes laughing in the face of adversity can definitely create the wrong impression, however. I got it horribly wrong in 2003, in the FA Cup semi-final between Sheffield United and Arsenal at Old Trafford. And I think it would be informative to tell that story now.

It was a turbulent match, with several flashes of controversy, and Neil Warnock, the Sheffield United manager, was his usual agitated, noisy, demonstrative self – and, as usual, most of his ire was aimed at the referee. So, as I left the field at half-time, to a chorus of vociferous criticism from Warnock and his club's supporters, I smiled broadly. It was a very big smile and a very big mistake.

My intention was to show people 'I ain't bothered.' Perhaps if they saw that they were not getting to me, they would ease up. But to Warnock, my smile signified that I didn't care, that it was all a joke. This was one of the biggest matches in the history of the club he had supported and now managed, but I was not taking it seriously. My smile infuriated him.

Now let me set the record straight about that match, which ought to be remembered for a superlative, point-blank save by England goalkeeper David Seaman. It was Seaman's 1,000th senior appearance and he crowned it with that save. Carl Asaba hooked the ball into the middle and Sheffield

United substitute Paul Peschisolido was only a few feet out when he directed a firm header away from Seaman. Yet the thirty-nine-year-old goalkeeper flung out an arm and palmed the ball up to prevent it crossing the line.

However, sadly, the match will be recalled by Warnock and some others for my part in the afternoon's drama, which began when I did not blow for a foul by Arsenal's Sol Campbell on Wayne Allison in the first half. My honest assessment was that the first challenge by Campbell was a fair one. Immediately after that, in a second challenge, it is possible that Campbell did make illegal contact. I did not think so at the time, but later on the endless television replays convinced some people that there had been a foul. Show the incident to a dozen referees and there would be several slightly different opinions. That's life, and that is certainly football. I called it as I saw it at the time, without replays.

Allison stayed down after being tackled but I did not know whether he was hurt or just making a point. I did not stop play and nobody kicked the ball out. Then, as I turned to move away from looking at Allison and follow play, Sheffield United's Michael Tonge and I collided. It was like going around a corner in a supermarket and accidentally clashing trolleys with someone – nobody's fault, just one of those things. When it happens in a supermarket, you both apologize and get on with your shopping. When it happens in a football match and involves the referee, usually the crowd hoots with laughter. Not this time.

The collision stopped Tonge getting across to make a challenge and enabled Arsenal to build their attack without much hindrance. That attack ended with Freddie Ljungberg scoring what proved to be the game's only goal. Warnock went into a vein-popping, apoplectic frenzy – and I made the mistake of smiling at half-time.

After the game, Joe Guest, from the Football Association's referees' department, told me that an FA councillor had given him stick at half-time about my performance and had said, 'If this is the best you've got, we're in trouble.' Joe Guest cheered me up further by adding, 'And you won't believe what Neil Warnock has been saying about you in the press conference.'

Yet the Sheffield United manager appeared perfectly calm when he came to the referees' room. He had put on that reasonable, avuncular smile he uses on TV. He asked, 'Graham, can you explain the incidents to me please?' I told him I did not believe Wayne Allison had been fouled. He replied, 'You will when you see it on video, Graham.'

He asked me a couple of fairly insignificant questions before he started to berate Alan Wiley, the fourth official. Throughout the game, Alan had been the target for Warnock rants, which were apparently inspired by a decision Alan had made in the League Cup semi-final, three months earlier. Alan and I both felt that it was astounding that a manager should harp on all day about another match and another incident instead of focusing intently on the job in hand – the FA Cup semi-final. Yet he was still festering about a decision made three months earlier. 'I'm glad I'm retiring in two years,' said Warnock. Alan and I immediately began counting the days.

Neil Warnock was not abusive, rude or even overcritical while he was in our changing room. When he left I wondered why he had bothered. But later that evening I received a number of calls from reporters seeking my reaction to Warnock's criticism of me at the press conference. This is part of what he had said to reporters, as recorded on the BBC's website:

> Poll was their best midfielder in the move for the goal. I thought there was a foul before the goal, but they are given at one end and not the other. Poll loved every minute of it. I don't know why they smile so much. You saw him coming off at half-time and at the end. He smiled so much, he obviously enjoyed that performance.
>
> We worked hard without the help of the ref. We lost in the semi-final of the Worthington Cup at Liverpool when their goalkeeper Chris Kirkland should have been sent off. The referee then was Alan Wiley, who was the fourth official here, and they love every minute of it.

One month later – yes, a whole month later – I received a call from the FA asking whether I thought Warnock should be charged with misconduct over his remarks. The FA wondered whether I was bothered one way or the other. I simply said that it was their decision. The FA were obviously hoping that they would be able to sweep the whole business under the carpet. But why should that happen? Warnock had been a serial critic of referees. He constantly belittled officials and, by doing so and getting away with it, he encouraged the climate of abuse and insults which every referee has to suffer.

I have said, and I believe, that everyone who pulls on a referee's shirt knows that criticism is part of the deal, but that does not mean it has to be encouraged. By letting the Warnocks of football get away with repeatedly and deliberately chipping away at referees, the authorities charged with looking after the game in England fail in their duty of care.

For instance, the sight of managers racing to the touchline from the technical area to berate a referee or an assistant has almost become an accepted part of English football. It does not have to be like that.

In Europe, UEFA take a much tougher line with managers and so, in European games, managers and coaches have a less aggressive attitude. They know that if they step out of line UEFA will hammer them. Similarly, UEFA punish any manager who criticizes an official through the media.

But in England, it is always open season on referees. I wonder how the players' union, the PFA, would react if referees started criticizing players – if we said, 'So-and-so is inconsistent. He had a terrible game. And he's a cheat.' I wonder how the Managers' Association would feel if a referee said a team's tactics were wrong, the substitutions defied belief and how so-and-so was ever selected is a mystery.

Yet Warnock and those like him routinely carp at match officials, their level of performance and even their neutrality. So I hoped that Warnock would be taught a lesson – not for my benefit but for the good of the game. Yet when he was charged with misconduct, he remained unrepentant. Now, there's a shock.

In fact, he said he did not want Premier League officials in charge of his games. He got his way on that to some extent for a few years, because his team lost in the promotion play-off final that season and so stayed in the Football League. Inevitably, he blamed the referee, Steve Bennett, for losing to Wolves in the play-off final.

And so, in August 2003, Neil Warnock was handed a four-game touchline ban and fined £300 – that's 300 whole pounds – for two misconduct charges. One related to his comments about me; the other was for insulting Steve Bennett during the play-off final.

Fast-forward three years and Sheffield United won promotion to the Premier League from the Football League. Promotion was confirmed for them before the season ended, and so their three remaining fixtures should have been party time, you might have thought. But the match immediately after winning promotion brought a home game against local rivals Leeds United. That fixture was given extra significance because Leeds were pushing for a play-off place and because their manager was Kevin Blackwell. He had been Warnock's assistant at Sheffield United and the manner of his 'defection' to a rival Yorkshire club had angered Warnock, as a lot of things seemed to do.

Blackwell and Leeds coach John Carver were aggressively vocal in the other dugout but Warnock behaved himself until just before half-time when Craig Short of Sheffield United and Leeds' Gary Kelly went for a 50-50 ball. Paul Robinson, from Hull, was the fourth official. I had told him that if there were any problems with anyone in the technical areas, he must call me over. He did call me over, and he reported that Warnock had shouted, 'Next time I hope he [Kelly] breaks his f***ing leg.'

What a viciously spiteful thing to say about any player. I sent Warnock to the stand, which was one of the easiest decisions I had to make in twenty-seven years, but he complained that the fourth official had it in for him and refused to go. He was out of control. He had lost his composure completely. I got a police officer to help ensure that Warnock left the technical area. But at half-time in the tunnel Warnock tried to have a row with the fourth official and there was another confrontation with Kelly, who was visibly but understandably angered by the comment about hoping he broke his leg.

During the interval, Warnock sent a message that he would like to see me, but I was not going to give him an opportunity to cause another scene. I sent a message back saying he could talk with me thirty minutes after the finish of the match, as the regulations permitted. And that is what happened.

At first, he tried a bit of psychology. He tried to split the team of officials by praising me and being critical of Paul Robinson, the fourth official. But I had already told Paul not to get involved in any discussion and that I would be the spokesperson for all four of us. I reminded Warnock that he could only ask me to clarify any decisions made during the game.

He said, 'I've no need to. I know why you sent me off. You told me at the time.'

I asked, 'So why are you here?'

He pointed at the fourth official and said, 'I want to ask him why he has it in for me and why haven't Blackwell and Carver also been reported for their behaviour. You've only done this because I'm Neil Warnock.'

I said I would run through the things he wanted clarified. I said, 'One: yes, you are Neil Warnock. Two: yes, you are being reported to the FA for improper conduct and your reluctance to leave the technical area when asked to do so. Three: I cannot confirm or deny whether Kevin Blackwell or John Carver or anyone else is being reported to the FA because that is confidential.'

He said, 'So are they being reported then?'

I said, 'I've just told you I cannot confirm one way or the other. It's confidential and nothing to do with you.'

He then started to round on Robinson, but I stopped him and he left. But he said, 'I know I'm going to get done.' He was right about that. I reported Warnock for his comment. He was charged and he watched Sheffield United's debut in the Premiership from the stand.

By coincidence, his touchline ban ended just in time for a game at Fulham, when I was the referee. Fulham won 1–0 thanks to a superbly taken free-kick by Jimmy Bullard but guess who Warnock blamed for United's defeat? Me, of course.

You must make up your own mind about Neil Warnock. Some of you might enjoy his nickname, which is an anagram of his real name and which begins 'Colin'. Or you might side with him in his feuds with, among others, Stan Ternant, Gérard Houllier, Gary Megson, Joe Kinnear, Nigel Worthington, Wally Downes, Gareth Southgate and, of course, Kevin Blackwell. I would only seek to sway you about one thing, and that is his abuse of referees damages the game about which he is so passionate.

CHAPTER FOURTEEN

'Robbed' of a Million

I've got that off my chest, so where was I? You've met my mum and dad. I've introduced Julia and the junior Polls. You've seen me stepping onto the refereeing ladder and clambering up the rungs. So it's time to tell you, very briefly, about my other life – my 'proper jobs' – and speak about a very good friend, Graham Barber. My work and my mate Barbs both had a big influence on my refereeing.

Very soon after leaving school I realized that I wanted to work in sales and my first chance at it was with Canon. That job brought my first company car – a beige Vauxhall Astra estate. It was all cold calling – there were no 'leads'. I used to work my way around industrial estates, chatting up girls behind reception desks. I would ask, 'What photocopier do you use? Is it reliable? Who is responsible for buying the copiers here? Can I have his/her number?' Then I would work the telephone. From fifty calls, I might talk my way to five appointments. Those might lead to two demonstrations of copiers lugged out from the back of my beige car. If I was lucky, two demonstrations might bring one sale.

Quite a few premises in the Ealing and Shepherds Bush areas of west London bought Canon products from young Graham Poll and I got even better results when my beige Astra estate and I moved to the area around Heathrow Airport.

Sales work is target-led and you have to be structured and methodical. I carried those ways of working into my refereeing life. For instance, in sales, if you have to get £50,000 of business by a certain time, that could seem very daunting. But you can break that target down and say to yourself, 'Well, I know I always get an order of at least £5,000 from that customer, and I know I have three people who usually give me £1,000 of business.' Then you look at all the other calls you are going to make and say, 'I have only got to average an order value of £200 from those.' That way, the big target seems much more attainable.

In football, I divided each game into nine ten-minute segments. That didn't mean I kept looking at my watch and taking stock at precisely ten-minute intervals. But I would have a plan for the first ten minutes – I might decide to be very strict if it was an explosive game, or I might plan to let the game flow. Then I would review things after ten minutes or so. I would think, 'Right, how is it going? Do I need to calm the play down or let the tempo develop?' Then I would do a similar mental exercise about ten minutes later, and so on. Referees always find the final twenty minutes demanding physically, but I would think, 'Seven segments done, two to go.' It worked for me.

After Canon came a job with Schwarzkopf. I began flogging shampoo. No, sorry, I began providing professional-quality hair-care products to selected retail outlets. Then after a couple of similar jobs, I landed a position with Nike sportswear – but it led to the first real clash between my football career and my life as a sales person.

The refereeing was going well. I was enjoying myself in the good old Isthmian League and as an assistant referee in the Conference. But when I had been at Nike for about six months, they called a big meeting at one day's notice. It was for the UK launch of the Nike Air shoe – a significant day in their diary – but I had a football appointment: a Conference game between Welling United and Wealdstone. If I pulled out with less than twenty-four hours' notice then questions would be asked about my reliability and my commitment to refereeing. I begged Nike to excuse me from the meeting but they said I had to be there. From their point of view, the choice between Nike Air and Welling United was straightforward. They said, 'It's the meeting or find a new job.' The choice was straightforward for me, as well. I had to find a new job. Nike were asking me to make a choice between reffing and repping, and it was always going to be football.

So I joined Oral B – 'the brand more dentists use'. They were part of the Gillette empire and were based at Aylesbury, which was good, but selling toothpaste and toothbrushes seemed like a step backwards in my career. Yet, despite using samples to write love messages on the back of Julia's car, I did well at Oral B and enjoyed the work. After six months I became regional sales manager and eventually I became national sales manager.

I left in 1991 to become national sales manager of Coty – 'the world's largest fragrance company and a recognized leader in global beauty' – and Julia and I moved to Reading. It was about that time that I started being recognized as a referee (although not, I concede, as a global beauty). A year after I joined Coty, the Premier League was formed. The new competition signed a deal with Sky TV which ramped up the coverage of football and put the hype into hyperbole.

By the mid Nineties, Coty were talking about my becoming sales director, but FIFA were talking about my being promoted to the international list. Another choice to make. The same decision. Football had to come first. I could not commit to the demanding job of sales director and keep taking time off to travel the world to referee football matches, and I had no intention of shunning the opportunities which were opening up for me in refereeing. So I asked a friend who worked in recruitment to find me a job with some flexibility but he said, 'Nobody will take you. At your level, employers want people with ambition. But all your ambition is focused on football.'

I quite expected Coty to lay me off because of my increasing football ambitions and commitments, but they did not. I stayed with them for almost a decade. But, eventually they, and I, had to make a choice. Football won again.

By Christmas 1998, there was increasing speculation that the Premier League wanted professional referees and my name was always mentioned in the stories. My boss at Coty called me in and said, 'If this happens, you are obviously going to go.'

I said, 'Well, yeah.'

Coty had to plan for the future without me and so they said they would move me out of my position but would keep me on doing project work for six months. Then I could leave and be a full-time referee. That was the plan, but then the Premier League chairmen voted by eighteen to two against professional referees. I expected to be out of work, but my boss at Coty, Ian Williamson, gave me three days a week consultancy work. That was a huge help but, like my dad before me, I wanted to provide as well as I possibly could for the Poll family, and so Graham Barber and I set up our own company to try to generate additional income. It almost made us rich – almost.

Graham Barber – Barbs – and I first met on our way to a conference for all Football League officials at Harrogate in 1986. We were not paid travelling expenses, so a group of linesmen arranged to meet at Stevenage. We left our cars there and travelled in Barbs' car – because it was the best one. He was a successful salesman and had a company Mercedes.

We hit it off straight away. He was five years older than me, but a year behind me in refereeing terms. But in his sales career, he was way ahead of me. So we had a mutual admiration and respect. We had similar personalities and shared a similar sense of humour. We had a hoot. Over the next few months we built a friendship which was to prove lasting and important. We began to meet socially and we watched each other referee. The first time I watched him referee was at a pre-season friendly at Kingstonian. I remember thinking, 'Thank goodness, he is not crap!' If he had not been any good at refereeing, it would have affected our friendship. As it was, we discussed things that happened in games and helped each other – without it ever being competitive between us.

Barbs was living in Surrey when we first became friends, but then he met Wendy, a girl from Tring, and ended up buying a house fifty yards from where I lived with Julia. He was best man at my wedding; I was best man at his. If anything happened to me he would look after my children. I would do the same for him. He is a top guy.

The company we set up together was called Arbitro (Spanish for referee). One of our schemes was for the two

Grahams to host 'Men In Black' evenings. We would wear black tracksuit bottoms and black polo shirts and we would talk, deliver a few well-rehearsed ad-libs and answer questions from the audience.

Audience? What audience? For some inexplicable reason, the public were not overwhelmed by the notion of a night out listening to a couple of referees. On our debut, at Aylesbury Football Club, as we changed in the referees' room, Tony Barrie, a friend of Barbs who helped 'promote' the event, came and warned us that business was not brisk. He said, 'There's been a bit of a slow start.'

We asked, 'How many?'

He said, 'Twelve. But that includes your families. So ten are complimentaries and only two have paid.'

That meant takings of £10. Tony's cut was a third. We were just about covering our petrol costs. We were sure it hadn't been like that in the early days for Morecambe and Wise. We decided we couldn't go on if there were fewer than thirty in the audience. So, although Tony cajoled another ten people to join the throng, we adjourned to the nearby Kings Arms and said farewell to show business.

The next scheme for the two Grahams was an internet site – and this one would have worked. It was inspired by driving home from matches, listening to radio phone-ins and realizing that fans often completely misunderstood refereeing decisions and issues. So why not have a website on which referees explain and discuss? Our idea was to persuade top referees, from England and abroad, to write exclusively for our site. We signed up Pierluigi Collina, Anders Frisk and leading Premiership officials and we received a letter from the FA giving us permission to pursue the plan. Then we pitched our idea to companies with existing football websites.

TeamTalk, based in Leeds, liked the idea of adding RefTalk to their portfolio. The deal they offered us would have meant Barbs and I sharing £1.45 million. They were offering us £250,000 each up front, £250,000 each in shares and a salary of £75,000 each per annum for a minimum of three years as consultants.

All that remained was the final and formal blessing from the Football Association, the Premier League and Football League. But Ken Ridden, who had given us the go-ahead to pursue the idea, had been replaced by John Baker as the FA's head of refereeing. He and Joe Guest, another FA official, sat down with us at a meeting. The others there were Mike Foster, secretary of the Premier League, Brian Philpott of the Football League and Philip Don, who was pencilled in to take charge of the soon-to-be professional referees.

Joe Guest and Philip Don backed us; the others did not. They could not stop us launching the website but we were reminded that our position as National List referees was reviewed every year – we got the message. When Barbs and I had set up Arbitro we had agreed that we would not let it jeopardize our refereeing, so we backed down. When we got home from that meeting, the contracts from TeamTalk had arrived in the post that day: we could not sign them.

That was so frustrating. We had worked so hard developing the idea and selling it to other referees and to TeamTalk. Richard Scudamore, chief executive of the Premier League, and Nic Coward, company secretary of the FA, agreed to pay us £20,000 each as compensation. It was a gesture, but it was not the £1 million-plus we had been promised.

Then, on Monday, 13 June 2001, the BBC website reported:

Referees in England will be professional from next season, the Football Association confirmed.

The FA, working alongside the Premier League and Football League, will overhaul the management, training and development of all match officials.

The new scheme will enable officials to go full-time as a result of the financial incentives on offer, and they will also be more accountable regarding their performances in matches.

The referees' National Review Board is to be replaced by a new organization, called the Professional Game Match Officials Board.

The group will consist of the three governing bodies' chief executives and refereeing managers in addition to the FA's head of refereeing.

The restructuring, aimed at improving the overall standard of refereeing in the professional game, will see match officials categorized into two groups.

The select group will officiate in the Premier League and other competitions and comprise of 24 referees and 48 assistant referees.

Referees in this group will receive an annual retainer of £33,000 plus match fees of £900 for their commitment to training and development over several days each month in addition to their match commitments. Assistant referees in the select group will receive an allowance for their time dedicated to training.

This group will be the responsibility of referees' manager, Philip Don.

Outside of the Premiership, the national group will officiate in the Football League and other competitions, with 50 referees and 188 assistant referees.

> Referees manager Jim Ashworth will supervise this group, which will also receive increased training and development.

The revolution had begun. If I am honest, most of us would-be Ché Guevaras had doubts and misgivings. I was among the leading advocates in the campaign to go pro, but there were real benefits about having an 'ordinary' job as well as refereeing. It meant that you could not think too much about football matches beforehand or afterwards. You would referee Arsenal against Manchester United, starting at 4 pm on the Sunday, and then by 6 am on the Monday you would be up, showered and ready to drive off to manage a big sales force. The Sunday game had to be cleared from your mind. You did not have time to get bitter and twisted if someone else was appointed to referee the match you wanted. You had your job to think about and it was good to focus on an interest outside football.

On the other side of that coin, however, I can remember driving home from Liverpool after a night match and pulling into a service station for an hour's sleep because I was so tired. I needed to get home because of work commitments the next day.

The switch to full-time professionalism meant that referees got more training, more feedback and more analysis. Then again, they got more stick.

CHAPTER FIFTEEN

Lost Identity

Philip Don, who did so much to convince English football that it needed professional referees, knew only too well how difficult it had been to be a top official while holding down a 'day job'. He was a leading referee whose ability was rewarded when he took charge of the FA Cup Final in 1992, the European Champions League Final in 1994 (when Milan thrashed Barcelona 4–0 in Athens) and two games in the 1994 World Cup, including a quarter-final. But he retired prematurely so as not to damage his other career, as a head teacher. Then when the Premier League chairmen eventually voted to have professional refs, there was a job too for Philip – as our manager.

Twenty-four refs were called to London for a meeting and offered our new, professional contracts. We were like kids in a sweet shop, looking around at each other and grinning. We had all started in parks football, refereeing for a hobby, and none of us had ever imagined that our hobby would become our job. I felt particularly well-prepared for my new life as a pro because, the previous summer, I had been to my first major tournament, Euro 2000. For five weeks I had lived like a full-time ref.

I was told I was going to Euro 2000 at a UEFA course in Malta, and the moment had its element of farce. Scottish referee Hugh Dallas and three Englishmen – me, Graham Barber and Paul Durkin – were the Brits with a chance of being selected and all four of us were called to see Ken Ridden, the Football Association's representative on UEFA's referees committee. Ridden said, 'We have four referees in the room. Two will be happy and two won't be. Graham and Hugh – you're going. Graham and Paul – unfortunately you've not been so lucky.'

I said, 'Ken – can you tell us which Graham please?'

He explained that I was the Graham who was going. Barbs was not, and we both knew that, at forty-one, he would probably not get another opportunity. Paul Durkin had refereed at the 1998 World Cup. My selection for Euro 2000 ahead of him effectively meant that he was no longer England's top referee. Yet, to his immense credit, Durks was the first to shake my hand, wishing me all the best. Barbs and I went back to the room we were sharing but he left again immediately to let me have some privacy when I telephoned Julia. When he returned a little later, the first thing I saw was his genuine and generous smile. The second thing I spotted was that he had bought a bottle of champagne for me. He is a class act.

I cannot tell you anything else about that UEFA course in Malta because I was focused completely on that decision about Euro 2000. I had gone from parks football, through the leagues to the top competitions in England. I had become an international referee. Within two years I had been elevated again to the group of the top fifty refs in Europe.

Now, with selection for Euro 2000, I could consider myself among the top dozen or so.

Euro 2000, or 'The 2000 UEFA European Championship', was co-hosted by Belgium and the Netherlands. The chosen few referees went out for a course at Easter and stayed at the modern hotel just outside Brussels which was to be our base for the tournament that summer. I can remember boarding the Eurostar train to travel to that course and feeling so proud.

Then, after returning from that trip, I was told I was going to referee the European Champions League semi-final second leg between Bayern Munich and Real Madrid and my mind went to all those nights when my mum had got me back up out of bed to watch great European games on *Sportsnight with Coleman*. Bayern and Real Madrid – two of the biggest clubs in world football. Incredible. The game was at the Olympic Stadium and I remember being taken up to the top of the BMW tower which literally overlooks the entire Olympic park. Way below, in the stadium, groundstaff were giving the pitch its final cut. I was too far away too see the staff or their mowers, only the changing geometric pattern on the turf as they went about their job methodically and with precision. It is something that has stuck in my mind – and so has the atmosphere at the game, which was like nothing I had ever experienced. Bayern won 2–1 but Real went through on away goals.

That was on 9 May. Twelve days later I refereed the FA Cup Final, and despite the nastiness of the false allegation about my supporting Chelsea, it was a memorable month in an unforgettable season. When the time came to travel to Euro 2000 – this time by plane instead of train – my excitement far outweighed any apprehension.

There were thirteen referees at our base outside Brussels – twelve Europeans and Egypt's Gamal El-Ghandour who had been invited as a guest referee. I was very much the rookie and knew I was there to learn. The others included the giants of European refereeing: Pierluigi Collina and Anders Frisk of course, plus men like Kim Milton Nielsen, Dick Jol and Urs Meier. I hope you can understand what it felt like to see the list and to see, included in it, the entry 'Graham Poll, England'.

It was relaxed and friendly and hugely enjoyable. There was a tremendous sense of camaraderie – a shared sense of how long and hard we had all worked to get there.

My first appointment was as fourth official to Portugal's Vitor Manuel Perreira for Slovenia versus Yugoslavia, a game with plenty of political needle and some controversy. Then I was due to referee reigning world champions France versus the Czech Republic – and things started to go wrong before kick-off.

Phil Sharp, like me from Hertfordshire, and Eddie Foley of Northern Ireland were my assistants. Hugh Dallas was the fourth official. We attended the stadium in Bruges the day before the match to look around and on the morning of the tie we went back for a security briefing, at the end of which I took off my photo ID and went for lunch with friends and family. Julia and my parents were there, along with Graham and Wendy Barber, my brother-in-law Tony, Keith Hill (a referee and a close friend) and Phil Sharp's wife Debbie. They had all driven to Bruges.

We had a leisurely, relaxing lunch and I was unhurried and unflustered when I returned to my hotel. In my room, I opened my briefcase to take out my photo ID, which I would need for the match. It was not there.

I told myself not to panic and then immediately ignored the instruction. I knew I'd had the ID that morning, yet it was not in my briefcase, nor in any of my pockets. Phil Sharp knocked on the door to say we had to leave. I told him what had happened and he double-checked my case for me and came to the same conclusion: I'd lost it. The only explanation I could fashion was that I had put the ID in a bag of washing I had given to Julia.

We were now fifteen minutes behind schedule. In the car taking the match officials to the stadium, the referee's match observer, a Romanian, looked on with increasing incredulity as I telephoned Barbs on his mobile. He was with Julia and the others. We arranged for our two cars to meet on the way to the ground. Somehow, we managed to arrive at a set of traffic lights at the same time and, while the lights were red, I jumped from our car, ran to the other vehicle, threw open the boot and rummaged through my dirty washing. There was no sign of my ID.

In what was a wonderful example of both improvisation and Anglo-Scottish co-operation, Hugh Dallas found a spare length of the purple cord to which the IDs were attached. I put an empty loop of cord around my neck and tucked the front into my jacket, as if the pass was in the top pocket of my shirt. Then I breezed into the stadium and ambled passed the security checks with studied nonchalance.

International football is very different from club football. That might sound obvious, but the difference, although profound, is a subtle one. The pace is slower but the intensity is greater, for some reason. The match is the focal point of ardent national attention, of course, and the players certainly understand that. At Euro 96, for instance, it seemed like the whole of the country watched every England match, and there was this collective will centred on the game. In the 2006 World Cup in Germany, when the home country played, it felt as if the entire nation was thronging the streets of every city and filling every fan park urging their kinsmen on.

I did not, however, find international matches as enjoyable as club games. Perhaps I was always aware of the magnitude of international matches and found it stifling. Certainly I refereed at my very best in fast-moving, high-tempo contests – and internationals were not like that. I think as well that in Bruges the business of the lost ID made my head in a mess – and probably occurred because it was already in a mess. I was inexperienced and covering my anxiety with my usual bravado.

But to understand why things went awry in the France–Czech Republic game, you need to know about a UEFA instruction for the tournament. The officials were all told that if there was a foul or handball close to the edge of a penalty area, the assistant referee should give a secret signal to indicate whether the incident was inside or outside the box. If he was sure it was inside, he should run briskly towards the corner flag. If he was certain it was outside, he should run sharply away from the corner flag. If the assistant's 'signal' was ambiguous, the referee should not give a penalty. The thinking was that the referee should make his decision, whatever it was, without going to talk to the assistant. The decision would then look less debateable and there would be no risk of players mobbing the assistant.

That was the theory. But, not long after Thierry Henry had given France the lead, the French captain, Didier Deschamps, shoved Pavel Nedved to the ground as the Czech Republic player closed in on goal. It was a foul, but was it inside the area? I looked across at assistant referee Eddie Foley, who ran a little way towards the corner flag but stopped and seemed to dither. I sensed uncertainty on his part.

What I should have done, according to UEFA, was give a free-kick outside the box. If it had proved the wrong decision – if the offence had been inside the area – I would have been absolved from blame because of the assistant's ambivalent 'signal'. But I wanted to get the decision accurate, not to satisfy a UEFA directive. I also wanted to help my assistant, who looked like a rabbit in the headlights, so I ran over to him. He said, 'In – definitely in.' I awarded a penalty. There were no serious protests from France. Karel Poborsky beat Fabian Barthez with the spot-kick.

However, when we came out for the second half, the France and Arsenal midfielder Patrick Vieira said to me, 'Graham, you have a problem. The penalty was outside. We've seen it on television.' He was not being confrontational. He knew I had acted on the word of the assistant and he was sorry for me. Yet, because substitute Youri Djorkaeff struck another goal for France, they won 2–1 and so the penalty did not affect the outcome.

The penalty apart, the game went well and there were handshakes all round at the end, so I was fairly sanguine when I joined my family and friends for a meal in a fine restaurant in the centre of Bruges. While I was there, my sister Susan telephoned me from England. She told me that the 'penalty' foul was inches outside the box. She had seen it on TV and wanted me to know in case I was asked about it. She was being supportive, but, although I kidded everyone that it didn't matter because it had not influenced the result, I knew it would matter.

I said goodbye to my family and friends that night, went back to my room and began to realize that, by ignoring the UEFA directive, I had probably guaranteed that I would be going home early from my first major tournament. Still, that night I found the ID – it had slipped down a pocket at the back of my brief case – so it wasn't all bad news.

On the following day there was a video debrief of the game. Eddie Foley took the heat off me by telling the UEFA referees committee, 'I told Graham to award the penalty.' His error cost him his place in the top group of assistants. It was costly for me, too. The observer – who had seen my attempt to recover my ID from the dirty laundry in an adjacent vehicle – gave me a mark of 7.5 for the match. It was nowhere near good enough: I would be going home after the first round. I went to my room and sat there, devastated.

Later that night I shared a few beers with some colleagues and my mood continued to improve the following day when I was in the crowd for England's victory over Germany in Charleroi. And I was given one last fixture: Slovenia versus Norway in Arnhem. It proved to be an extraordinary game.

The score was 0–0 when the crowd and the two benches received the news that Spain were losing 3–2 to Yugoslavia. If the scores in both matches remained like that, then Norway would go through. Slovenia were happy with a draw as well, because they had lost both their previous group games. So for the final twenty minutes of my match, the teams knocked the ball about without much intent and nobody put in a serious tackle. At the final whistle, Norwegian players and officials partied on the pitch.

But, unknown to me as I relaxed in the officials' dressing room, seven minutes of added time were being played in

Bruges. And in that time, Gaizka Mendieta equalized for Spain with a penalty and then Alfonso Perez scored again. Spain had won 4–3. That meant Yugoslavia and Spain were in the second round; Norway had been edged into third place in the group.

When Norwegian delegates came into my dressing room to say 'thank you' – and present me with a pewter cheese knife for which I was very, very grateful, honestly – I asked them why they looked miserable. They told me about the result from Bruges and said, 'We're going home.'

I replied, 'If it is any consolation, so am I.' I don't think it was.

Paul Durkin had told me that he was affected badly by learning he was going home from the 1998 World Cup. He told me to learn from his mistake if the situation arose for me. So I was determined to be courteous and professional. The next day, after training, Ken Ridden, the FA's man, was looking for me. I spotted him first and said, 'Don't worry Ken, I know I am going home. I have already phoned Julia to tell her.' I watched the remainder of the tournament on television at home.

Although I left Euro 2000 worried that I had damaged my chances of going to future tournaments, I don't want to leave it here, in this book, without putting my disappointment into perspective. This narrative, my story, is punctuated by the landmarks of my refereeing life, and some of those conspicuous moments in my career were low points – but if you plotted the graph of my career, most of the line would be very high up in the area representing happiness and excitement, and there would be some real peaks. I had more than a quarter of a century of fantastically joyous times as a referee. I went to places and experienced things that I never dreamed of when it all started in Division Five of the North Herts League. I loved it.

I am proud and delighted to say that people who mean a lot to me also derived immense pleasure and satisfaction from sharing my adventures. In the final weeks of my final season, my mum was in tears as I drove back from a game at Liverpool. She said, 'It has been such a long journey.' I thought she was complaining about the blooming M6, but she meant she'd been with me for twenty-seven years. The 'journey' had started with her driving me to matches, but then, in later years, she'd been around the country and around the world as my guest at amazing places and for astounding events.

CHAPTER SIXTEEN

Red Wine and Blue Tank Top

Let me tell you about the first few seasons as a professional referee because they were, in the main, blissfully happy. That feeling we had all shared and enjoyed when we were called down to London to be offered our contracts – kids in a sweet shop looking around at each other and grinning – was never far away.

What Philip Don, our manager, and others realized was that the new, improved, professional referees had to demonstrate that they were better than the old, amateur, part-time refs – although we were the same people. The clubs were committing money to pay us and they wanted to see something for their investment. Philip believed – we all did – that the better preparation and the intense level of scrutiny we were putting ourselves through would lead to big improvements. But better decision-making and match-management would be impossible to quantify or prove. Philip calculated, correctly in my view, that the most tangible thing he could deliver was better fitness. And so, particularly in the first year, we were 'beasted'. We were worked really hard but because we were all so thrilled about our new lives, and were extremely well motivated, we loved the training. In fact, we trained harder than ever before. Matt Weston, our fitness instructor, had worked with all sorts of sports people, including rowers and table tennis players, and he said we were the easiest group he'd ever had because we just wanted to get fitter and quicker.

We had fortnightly get-togethers in Northamptonshire but for the rest of the time, because our homes were spread around the country, we all had to continue to train on our own. We strapped on heart monitors when we exercised and detailed information was recorded on special watches on our wrists. We then uploaded that information onto our new laptop computers and emailed it to Matt Weston. He devised individual, daily programmes for every one of us.

It was suddenly very different from forcing yourself to go out for a run in the evening after work. Now the physical preparation was relevant and appropriate to the task you were preparing for, and you had time to train properly. We were given carefully considered advice on diet as well. That made a difference because the correct fuel helped us work harder and train better. I loved running anyway and now I could run at a decent time – at eleven in the morning when I was fresh and keen. The fitter I got, the better I felt about myself and the more I enjoyed the training.

A typical week without a midweek game, when we were not having our get-together in Northamptonshire, went like this:

Wherever I had been officiating on the Saturday – working, as I could now call it legitimately – I drove home during the evening after the match. I would try to get back to Tring in time to watch *Match of the Day*, but the first job was to put my kit in the washing machine and turn it on. Then I telephoned the Press Association news agency with the details of cautions and sendings-off from my match. The FA had arranged for the Press Association to collect and collate that information for them.

On Sunday, I sometimes went for a short run to break up the lactic acid in my legs. But, if I am honest, I usually didn't bother. I just chilled out, spent time with my family and watched more football on TV.

On Monday, I would receive Matt Weston's exercise schedule by email. Before starting training, however, I would sit down and read the sports pages of a couple of newspapers. Some referees avoided them. Steve Bennett, for instance, said that he never read newspaper reports because they would bring negativity. But I regarded the sports pages as the equivalent of a trade journal. Football was now my business and I needed to know what was going on.

Then, at 11 am, I'd do my training. Monday's workout, which involved proper warm-ups, stretching and warm-downs, usually took about two hours. Then, at about lunchtime, I would receive the email telling me my fixture for the next weekend and I would exchange emails with the two assistant referees to make arrangements.

On Tuesdays, the training was usually a harder session. By the time I returned home from it, the post had normally arrived, including a ProZone disc with the computerized analysis of my match the previous Saturday. ProZone had up to twelve cameras positioned around every top stadium, capturing the action on the pitch. A computer programme plotted the coordinates and movements of every player every tenth of a second. All the top clubs used the data to investigate their own performances and get details of opponents.

I was one of the refs who found ProZone really useful. For example, there were videos clips of specific incidents, shown from four different angles at three different speeds. They gave me the definitive answer to whether I had made the right decision. If I'd got it wrong, why did I get it wrong? Could I have improved my positioning to get a better view? Should I be working on getting more width to provide a better angle. Tuesday's emails included a copy of the report on my performance compiled by the assessor. I would read that carefully – although it was sometimes contradicted by ProZone.

Wednesday was normally a rest day. Thursday would involve a reasonably high-intensity training session. Friday's was a light session, concentrating on speed work – short, sharp stuff. Then on Friday afternoon you would leave for the game.

Match weekends were very different once we had become full-time pros. On one occasion before we were professional, we had a meeting and were addressed by a psychologist. He asked us what was our biggest fear – and you might be surprised by the answer. It was not that we would make a big mistake, not that we would get abused horribly and not that we would be beaten up in the car park. Of the twenty refs in the room, eighteen said that their biggest fear was that they might not get to the game on time – that they might get caught in traffic and be too late. I was one of the eighteen who put my hand up and owned up to that fear.

For midweek games before we were professional, for instance, I would be working in the morning and say to myself, 'Right, Pollie, you have got to leave the office by one o'clock.' Inevitably, it would be a quarter to two before I would run out to the car thinking, 'If I get a move on I might still have time to stop at a service station for a sandwich.' Making a journey in that frame of mind, and arriving at the ground flustered, was far from ideal.

We did stay overnight at hotels before some games when we were amateurs, but, because we only had a £60 allowance, we would stay at a Travelodge, or somewhere equally cheap. And, of course, we had to find our own way to the ground, which was not always straightforward. The first opportunity we had to get together with the assistant referees and the fourth official was in the guests' lounge at the stadium. They had probably suffered a fraught journey as well.

My Mum and Dad loved the old system. They came with me, came to the guest lounge and met other mums, dads and family members. It was a nice, social occasion – but it was not the correct way for a referee to prepare to take charge of a major match.

Once we had become professional, if a game was more than 120 miles from home, we stayed overnight in a decent hotel which was booked for us. I drove everywhere, because public transport meant the chance of being with fans of one of the teams you were refereeing. The two assistants also stayed at the same hotel, and we would meet the night before the game and catch up with news and have a bit of a laugh.

When I was professional I always planned my routine backwards from kick-off time. In other words, it did not matter whether the match started at 3 pm, at one o'clock or at 5.45. I would always have the same routine.

But let us assume we are talking about a Saturday game kicking off at 3 pm. In those circumstances, at 11 am I would meet the two assistants in a pre-booked meeting room at the hotel and have another chat. Then, an unmarked people carrier took us to the match in plenty of time. The driver knew all the routes to the ground and so a lot of stress was taken away. The people carriers were introduced for all the Select Group referees as a direct result of the incident when the car I was in with Julia was attacked at Middlesbrough.

Anyway, I normally liked to leave the hotel at midday. I didn't have any lunch at the hotel but made sure I'd had a good breakfast. I liked to conduct the pitch inspection at about 12.30 and then sit and watch the first half of that day's 12.45 match on television. Probably, at that stage, I'd have a sandwich. At 1.30 I would go back out onto the pitch and give my instructions to the two assistant referees. I liked to give my briefing on the pitch because I could refer to specific areas of the field of play and we could all visualize situations we were discussing.

At a quarter to two it would be the security briefing. The home club's safety officer and a senior police officer – either the match controller or his deputy – would arrive at the referee's room together with the police officer who was going to be on duty in the tunnel. The safety officer explained the circumstances in which I should stop the game and get the players off the field. He told me the codes and procedures for bomb scares, fires, crowd evacuation and so on. The senior police officer then announced how many away fans were expected, where they would be in the ground and whether any known troublemakers were among them. Sometimes, the officer would say, 'The police have no intelligence today.' I found the best policy was not to make a joke reply, like, 'That's why the country is in such a state then.'

One hour before kick-off, the team sheets arrived. Some were brought by managers, some by assistant managers.

Both were fine by me. For instance, Pat Rice, the assistant manager at Arsenal, always brought their team list and so if there was any point Arsenal wanted to make, or any remark I needed to deliver, then we could do so. Chelsea always sent Gary Staker, their player liaison officer and administrative manager. He was a nice guy but he didn't go into the players' dressing room, and so referees could not make any point to the players or manager via him. I think, as well, that the issue of who takes the team sheet to the referee involves the question of respecting each other. The Premier League should insist that it is the manager or assistant who brings in the team sheet.

Once you have the teams, you check the colours and decide what kit you will wear. We used to have three different shirts in our bag – a black one, a green and a yellow. I preferred the black (because it helped me look slimmer!) and I loathed the yellow one. In fact, I only wore yellow once. If you have a yellow car, the insurance premium is lower because it is so highly visible that other vehicles are unlikely to drive into it. A yellow shirt on a referee makes him too visible. When you look at the pitch from the stand, your eye is drawn to the bright yellow ref, but the ref should merge into the background and only emerge when he has to take some action.

Refs had twenty-five minutes to put on their kit and needed all that time once we became professional, because of the microphones, earpieces, heart monitors and so on. The heart monitor was introduced in the year 2000. It was on a strap which the ref put around his chest. The monitor fed information to a special wrist watch which the ref could look at during the game and from which data was downloaded later for Matt Weston, the Premier League's fitness expert.

By looking at how the heart performed during a game, Matt could devise training programmes which replicated the physical demands of a match.

The microphones and ear pieces were connected to a battery pack which was on a neoprene strap which went around the waste. I am not entirely sure the mikes and earpieces were a good idea. Before we got the mikes, I had always gone and talked to an assistant or a fourth official when I had needed to anyway. If an assistant wanted me, he got me. Introducing the communications system changed the dynamic of the way people refereed, because they were talking to assistants and the fourth official more than they needed to. Sometimes being miked up inhibited the banter between the referee and players. That banter was part of a referee's management technique, but players were sometimes wary of saying much once the mikes were introduced.

Another piece of kit a ref had to put on was an armband which vibrated when an assistant pressed a button on the handle of his flag. The idea behind that was that the assistant pressed the button when he raised his flag for a foul or offside – or pressed the button if the ref did not respond to his raised flag. So referees had so many straps and wires to put on before a match there was no time to sit about. I always found that the time flew by.

I would put the players' numbers in my notebook and then I was ready, half an hour before kick-off, to go out onto the pitch to warm-up. I had a set, fixed routine which lasted eighteen minutes. As well as working all the appropriate muscles, the routine was part of my process of focusing on the job ahead.

In the years in which I was professional, I was completely calm in the final moments before a match. There were no nerves – not because I was professional but because of the years of experience I had banked. Some referees like to pump themselves up. The match ball was usually in the ref's dressing room when he arrived for the match and some got ready for the game by repeatedly bouncing the ball up and down. Some said things to psyche themselves up. I was the opposite. My mantra before and during the game was, 'Cool, calm, collected'. And the other 'c' was 'concentrate'. I knew that, during a game, if I was watching a throw-in and someone in the crowd behind the player started to do something noticeable, I needed to ignore the fan and focus completely on the football.

After finishing the warm up, we'd return to the dressing room with twelve minutes to go before kick-off and I would give a few last words of encouragement to the assistants.

Then, in the tunnel before kick-off – once the assistants had finally persuaded the teams to come out, and they were invariably late – I would turn and face both teams and exchange a few smiles and nods. I wanted to appear completely at ease and in a good mood, so that the players knew I was confident.

And I was confident. I always knew I would not referee badly. That is not saying I would not make mistakes – that is not the same thing – but I would not give a poor performance in terms of being afraid to make big decisions or failing to keep control. I expected and accepted that I might make mistakes – human errors which I hoped would not affect the match – but I was not afraid that I would referee badly.

Over the years I learned not to say stupid things to players in the tunnel – not to be the old class clown from Thomas Alleyne's School – but I only learned that from making the mistake of doing it. I once said to Roy Keane in the tunnel, 'I've already got your name, Roy. I just need the time.' So during the game, when he committed a bad foul and I went over to him, he snarled, 'Well, you've got your time for me now.' My stupid aside had given him reason to believe I already had it in for him, that my mind was made up before the start that he would be cautioned. I stopped saying daft things after that.

The referee goes out ahead of the players from the tunnel onto the pitch and, for me, that was a special, magical moment. In the Premiership, the stadiums were nearly all magnificent and often jammed completely full. The colours, the noise, the intensity of the occasion made the hairs on the back of my neck stand up. I know that is a well-worn expression, but that is precisely what happened. So, I repeat: when people ask me why I refereed my answer was, 'Why wouldn't I?'

A major change once we became professional was the introduction of our fortnightly group get-togethers. We went to Staverton Park, a conference and training centre in Northamptonshire, about ten miles away from the M1 motorway. The centre had a hotel, a swimming pool, a gym and a golf course. It did not have a football pitch, however. At first we did most of our training on a public park, with fairly Spartan facilities. There were a few grass pitches, which we used to ruin, and an Astroturf area. It was like being back at Ridlins Wood Playing Fields in Stevenage. Later Staverton Park took over a cricket ground and put a couple of football pitches there.

There were twenty-four pro refs. Most of us reported in at Staverton every other week – and we had a hoot. We were fit, youngish and, for the first time in our lives, were being

Left Susan, Deborah, Graham and Mary: the four Poll children in our garden in Stevenage in about 1968.

Right My big moment on stage, playing Fat King Melon (pictured astride horse, inspecting troops) at Ashtree School in 1973.

Above 'The comrades'. Alan Crompton and me, right, on stage at Thomas Alleyne School. We are still comrades all these years later.

Right Mum and dad, Beryl and Jim, at a family wedding in 1992.

Left My Football League debut as an assistant referee in 1986. The match was Leyton Orient against Peterborough United, the ref was Jeff Lovatt and the other 'linesman' was Mike Bullivant. I was just 22.

Above The Aubrey Cup Final (the Herts Senior County League's top cup competition) in 1984, with referee Alan Mitchell and the other assistant, Paul Taylor (who later became a Football League referee).

Right Another cup final, six days later, in 1984 – and this time I was the referee. It was the Stevenage Sunday League Challenge Cup Final at Stevenage Borough's ground, and a big day for me – although I should have worn the same socks as my assistants.

Stages (and haircuts) of my career, captured in cuttings. *Left* The Stevenage Comet marks my promotion to become a Football League linesman in 1986. *Below* The local Reading paper records my arrival as a Premier League ref in 1993. *Bottom left* The Daily Telegraph reports my FA Cup Final appointment in 2000.

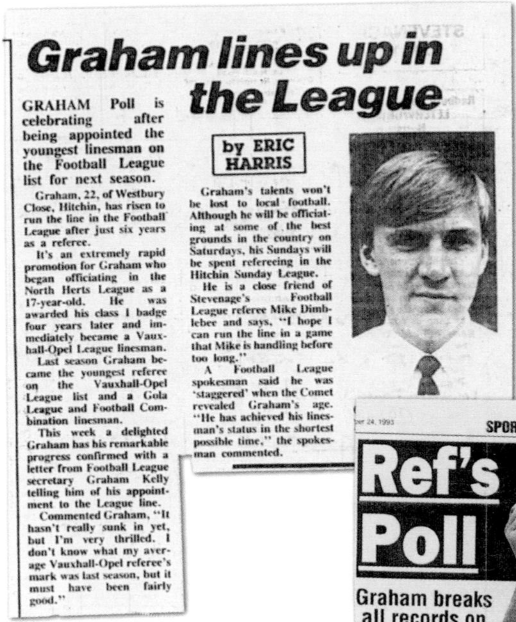

Graham lines up in the League

by ERIC HARRIS

GRAHAM Poll is celebrating after being appointed the youngest linesman on the Football League list for next season.

Graham, 22, of Westbury Close, Hitchin, has risen to run the line in the Football League after just six years as a referee.

It's an extremely rapid promotion for Graham who began officiating in the North Herts League as a 17-year-old. He was awarded his class 1 badge four years later and immediately became a Vauxhall-Opel League linesman.

Last season Graham became the youngest referee on the Vauxhall-Opel League list and a Gola League and Football Combination linesman.

This week a delighted Graham has his remarkable progress confirmed with a letter from Football League secretary Graham Kelly telling him of his appointment to the League line.

Commented Graham, "It hasn't really sunk in yet, but I'm very thrilled. I don't know what my average Vauxhall-Opel referee's mark was last season, but it must have been fairly good."

Graham's talents won't be lost to local football. Although he will be officiating at some of the best grounds in the country on Saturdays, his Sundays will be spent refereeing in the Hitchin Sunday League.

He is a close friend of Stevenage's Football League referee Mike Dimblebee and says, "I hope I can run the line in a game that Mike is handling before too long."

A Football League spokesman said he was 'staggered' when the Comet revealed Graham's age. "He has achieved his linesman's status in the shortest possible time," the spokesman commented.

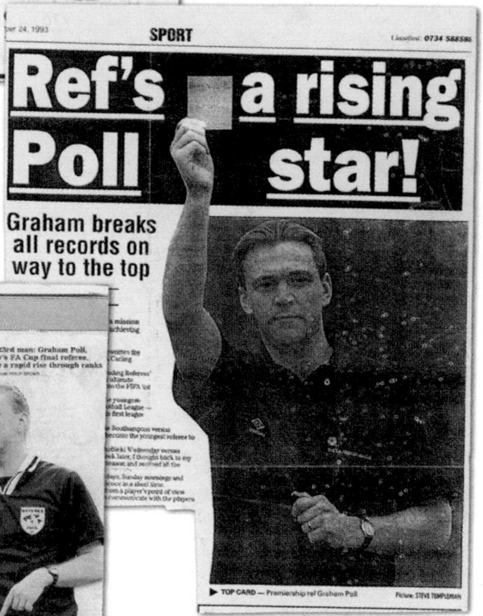

SPORT

Ref's Poll a rising star!

Graham breaks all records on way to the top

▶ TOP CARD — Premiership ref Graham Poll

THE DAILY TELEGRAPH

The 23rd man: Graham Poll, today's FA Cup final referee, made a rapid rise through ranks

Cup final fan Poll takes the middle way

AXA
THE F.A. CUP
Presented with compliments of
The Football Association to
commemorate the last F.A. Cup Final
at the 'original' Wembley Stadium
20th May 2000
THE FOOTBALL ASSOCIATION

Right The pennant commemorating the last FA Cup Final at the old Wembley.

Above Ruel Fox of Norwich is having the blood wiped off his face, Francis Benali of Southampton is receiving my red card and Dave Beasant is restraining Mickey Adams. It was 1994, in my first Premier League season.

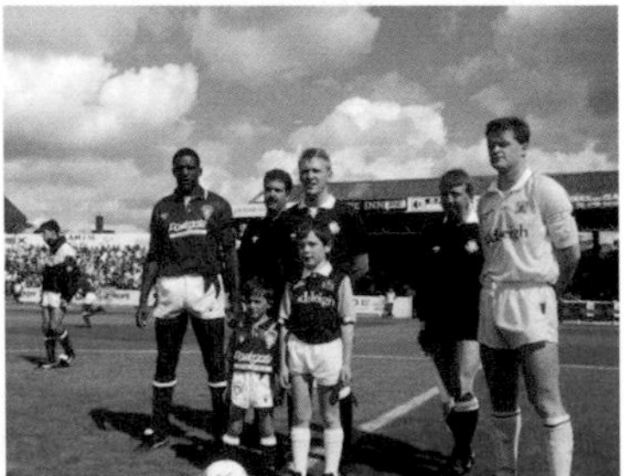

Above My first Football League 'middle', Rotherham United against Burnley, in 1991.

Left The certificate made and presented to me by my dad. See page 105.

Above I have to take avoiding action as Manchester United captain Steve Bruce objects to my awarding a penalty for QPR at Loftus Road in 1994. Paul Parker can't believe it.

Above The picture Pierluigi Collina sent me for my 40th birthday. It shows us at the 2002 World Cup in Korea.

Right Holland against Argentina in the Amsterdam Arena in March 1999. It was a friendly – but I had to send off Edgar Davids.

Left World Cup 2006 fitness test in Frankfurt. I am setting the pace for Lubos Michel (Slovakia), Eric Poulat (France) and Roberto Rosetti (Italy).

Right Free time at Euro 2000 in Brussels: with Anders Frisk (far left), Hugh Dallas (brown jacket and a pint) and Kim Milton Nielsen (front right).

Left The 61st minute of Croatia versus Australia and I am cautioning Josip Simunic (for the first time!).

Right The crucial page from my notebook from the 2006 World Cup: my mistaken recording of Croatia 3's second caution. The letter C appears, wrongly, against the yellow (Australian) 3.

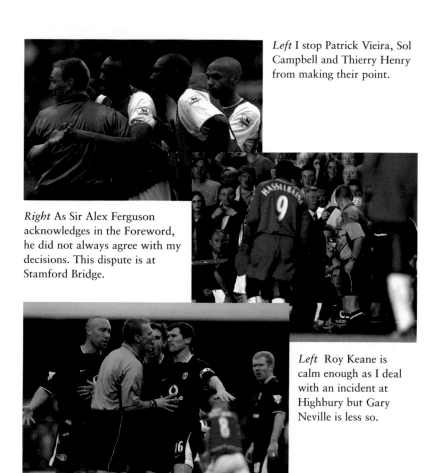

Left I stop Patrick Vieira, Sol Campbell and Thierry Henry from making their point.

Right As Sir Alex Ferguson acknowledges in the Foreword, he did not always agree with my decisions. This dispute is at Stamford Bridge.

Left Roy Keane is calm enough as I deal with an incident at Highbury but Gary Neville is less so.

Right Real Madrid have just lost 3-0 to Bayer Leverkusen in the Champions League in 2004. Perhaps I should not have looked so happy, but David Beckham gave me that shirt for my daughter.

Right Before a match at Portsmouth in the 2003/04 season.

Below The start of my last match as a professional referee – Derby County v West Bromwich Albion at Wembley in the 2007 Championship play-off final.

Above My family. Josie, Gemma and Harry with me and Julia in our garden in Tring.

supplied with proper, coordinated training kits and living the lives of professional athletes. It was a magnificent time. Our hobby had become our job and, like any group of blokes doing the same tasks and sharing difficult experiences, we built a camaraderie. The only people who really understood what it was like to referee in the Premiership were others who were doing it, and there we all were together. You didn't have to explain anything about your world to your peers and contemporaries. There was a special, unspoken understanding and we laughed together at some of the abuse and criticism we received from outsiders as a way of dealing with it. Strong, lasting friendships were formed.

Philip Don wanted us there on Wednesday evenings for dinner to have a relaxing, sociable time and be ready for serious training on Thursday morning. On Thursday afternoon we had a session with video recordings of match incidents and refereeing talking points. Then we'd train again on Fridays and have a motivational session before lunch. You could either stay for Friday lunch or disperse before lunch.

The golfers among us used to book in at Staverton Park by Wednesday lunch time and play a round of golf in the afternoon before the others arrived. Peter Jones was appointed social secretary and on Thursdays we had quiz nights. We went out tenpin bowling occasionally. We just enjoyed ourselves as a group.

There was always blokey humour going on. It was like twenty mates at a holiday camp. The funniest man in the group, without a doubt, was Paul Durkin. He had our total respect, because he was a top, top referee, but he was always larking about and was easily the most popular of the group. On one memorable occasion, when Matt Weston was giving us a hard time about a training session, Durks found a kid's scooter and started riding around us, weaving in and out between us in the dressing room. We were all laughing so much we were hurting. He fitted on the scooter as well, because he was only five feet five inches tall but he joked about that as well, telling us that short was the new tall. He refereed in the same way – not on a scooter, admittedly, but with a smile on his face and with a wicked sense of humour. Fans and players understood that and appreciated it.

Steve Dunn was another good, solid bloke to have around. He was a bit too solid, if truth be known. He had owned a newsagents in Bristol and should have sold the sweets and chocolates instead of eating them. The fitness tests were sometimes problematic for him, but he was good to be around at Staverton and he was a much better referee than he perhaps believed himself to be. Dunny and I were mates before we started going to Staverton. In fact, in the week before Dunny took charge of the 2001 FA Cup Final between Arsenal and Liverpool, Graham Barber and I went down to Bristol to help him prepare.

We had our in-jokes and, for some long-forgotten reason, we used to do an Arthur Askey impersonation, saying, 'Aye thang yow' and miming doffing an imaginary hat. When I was refereeing a Real Madrid Champions League game, with Dunny as the fourth official, I was particularly pleased with myself when I spotted a foul. So, turning to Dunny by the halfway line, I touched my imaginary hat and mouthed, 'Aye thang yow.' Dunny laughed of course, but anyone else among the 80,000 crowd in the Bernabeu Stadium who noticed us must have wondered what on earth was going on.

During one pre-season, the refs all went away to a hotel for a break from Staverton. The referees' rooms were all on the second floor, in a rectangle overlooking the flat roof of a function room on the ground floor. The weather was warm and so most of us left our bedroom windows open and there was some banter shouted between rooms. Steve Dunn invited Mike Dean over to his room and so Deano climbed out of his window to walk across the flat roof to Dunn's room. But before Deano could get in, Paul Durkin, who was sharing the room with Dunn, closed the window. Deano made his way back to his own room but his room-mate, Phil Dowd, closed that window as well. Then another light went on, and out of one of the windows popped Philip Don's head. Deano was caught, literally, out on the tiles.

At Staverton, one running gag was the presentation of a light blue tank top jumper to the referee who did something to deserve it – if he had a nightmare at training or did something clumsy at meal times or said something daft. It was the sort of thing footballers do, although they usually do it with some sort of hideous training top. We got the hideous bit right. The tank top was appalling and if you were 'awarded' it, you had to wear it all day. The others were all trying to get Graham Barber or me, and if we were 'awarded' the tank top of shame, we wore it. Nobody ever said, 'No, I am not doing that.'

Nobody missed the Thursday quiz night either. You might not fancy it one week, but at 8.30 pm you'd be upstairs in the York Suite, ready to try to answer questions on the subject of the night – music, sport or whatever. There were bingo nights as well, which were very rude and very funny.

Four of us who were particularly close mates – Durks, Dunny, Barbs and Pollie – became founder members of an unofficial 'Red Wine Club' which convened in the evenings. We would discuss refereeing matters over a bottle of hotel red, and were often joined by some of the younger refs such as Mike Dean, Andy D'Urso, Rob Styles and Phil Dowd.

During the second Christmas get-together at Staverton, Barbs had to referee a Carling Cup tie between Aston Villa and Liverpool. The plan was that, after dinner at Staverton, the rest of us would adjourn to the bar to watch the game and then the Red Wine Club would convene in my room for a cheese and wine party. The kick-off at Villa Park was delayed for a quarter of an hour and Barbs was interviewed on Sky Sports by Clare Tomlinson. She said, 'Disappointing that the start has been delayed, Graham.'

He replied, 'Not half. There will be no cheese left at the cheese and wine party back at the hotel.'

Back at Staverton, Philip Don joined in the laugher and said, 'He's funny. Good joke.' Our manager was blissfully unaware that Barbs was speaking the truth. We made sure the prophecy was fulfilled by eating all the cheese before Barbs eventually showed up at my room.

Thinking back, I am moved with affection for some of those guys from the first few years at Staverton. Eddie Wolstenholme – 'Steady Eddie' – was a lovely chap. Dave Pugh, a Scouser who had an ad-hoc double act with Mike Dean, was a scream. Steve Bennett was our conscience, who tried to make sure we did things correctly, and we respected him for that. Uriah Rennie, who was a magistrate, was always getting us involved in fundraising for various charities. They were good people and those were good days.

But the good days didn't last. After a few years, the exciting novelty of Staverton began to wear off. We were all starting to take our new lives for granted. Instead of being overjoyed about having free training kit, we started complaining about the fit or the cut. Instead of being excited by each other's company, the all-embracing camaraderie started to fragment. Cliques started forming.

I can see that to some of the other refs, it appeared that the Red Wine Club was a clique. That was not what we intended. Nobody was barred. But we couldn't have twenty or so blokes sitting about in one bedroom, and now I can see that those who did not join in might well have felt excluded. To add to that problem, Barbs and I were both in the top refereeing rank in Europe and regarded as the top two in England. To the refs who had not joined the unofficial Red Wine Club, we could well have seemed a self-appointed elite. That was not how we felt about it at all – we were just mates having a natter – but I can understand how it must have looked.

I also believe, looking back, that I overdid the mickey-taking, or perhaps didn't get it right. I was still being the class clown, but at school I had been the joker to win acceptance. At Staverton, I had some status from being a top referee and so, although I didn't know it, when I ribbed any of the younger referees, it had a different effect to the one I intended.

If I said to Graham Barber, 'I saw you on the telly. You missed a penalty. Again,' he would reply, 'Yeah and you missed two bookings and a sending off.' But if I said to someone like Mike Dean, 'You missed a penalty,' he would laugh but later, alone in his room, he might think, 'Graham Poll thinks I made a big mistake.'

There are very few things I would change about my life, given the opportunity. I have made errors, but they are part of who I am. Yet I would change some aspects of my refereeing career if I could. I don't mean I would go back and award a particular penalty or anything. I mean I would alter the way I behaved in some circumstances – including my demeanor in those days at Staverton. I didn't deal with the situation I was in as well as I should have. Some felt shut out from the Red Wine Club and when I took the mickey out of those refs outside our little group, it was not a comfortable experience for them. I did not recognize that then. I regret it now.

I was by no means the only one getting the dynamics of Staverton wrong and as the team spirit started to fracture, as the quiz nights and bingo sessions ran their course, perhaps the managers should have acted to change things and freshen them up again. Then again, perhaps it is unreasonable to hope that we could all remain best buddies for ever. In any company or organization in which twenty people work, they will not all be lifelong pals who want to socialize together.

So rivalries emerged. Some referees started to think, 'I am a professional now and I should be getting this game or that game.' Jealousies took hold. We were all competitive by nature, and all dedicated, driven people. Without those qualities, we would not have scaled the refereeing ladder. But with those traits, there were bound to be frictions and frustrations, and a lot of the frustrations were because of me, or rather, because I got the most games and the best games. Philip Don wanted me to referee as often as possible, because I was getting the top marks. When he was replaced by his deputy, Keith Hackett, he too kept giving me the best matches and lots of them. Joe Guest at the FA was giving me plenty of work as well and I was also getting European and international fixtures. In my final seasons as a referee, the number of UEFA and FIFA games I did meant that I missed most of the Staverton sessions but some of the guys there did not miss me. Some of them resented my success, but what was I supposed to do? Should I have rejected some appointments to salve their egos? I once asked Hackett, jokingly, if he wanted me to be the least popular referee ever. He replied, 'I don't care. I want you to be the best referee. If you're unpopular it doesn't matter.'

John Gregory had been right all those years before.

CHAPTER SEVENTEEN

An Offer I Had to Refuse

The first season of professional referees brought some of the most extraordinary events of my career, but before recounting them here, I want to explain a little bit more about why one of the changes that was introduced – the increased security for referees – was so welcome. It is sad that referees going to a sporting fixture need to be driven there in an unmarked people carrier but every referee can tell you stories about occasions when fans definitely regarded football as more than a game – and the match officials as fair game.

Before we went pro, I had a few unpleasant brushes with fans. One came in October 1998 after I sent off Stuart Pearce. He was playing for Newcastle at home to West Ham in the Premiership. He struck Trevor Sinclair with his arm and it was an obvious red card. Obvious to me, that is, but the 'Toon Army' did not agree and their mood towards me was not helped when West Ham went on to win 3–0.

Julia and I had arranged to meet some friends for a drink in the Vermont Hotel where we were staying. I went to the bar while Julia freshened up. I had barely touched my drink when four Newcastle fans came over to me and one said, 'You are not welcome here.'

I said, 'Sorry ...?'

'You heard what I said,' was the reply.

I tried to defuse the situation with a joke that had worked before: 'Don't tell me you've mixed me up with my brother. Bloody referee. He's always getting me into trouble.'

The class clown's act did not work. One of them said, 'We know exactly who you are. Leave.'

I asked, 'Can I finish my drink?'

He said, 'No.' I put down my bottle of Bud and left.

Of course, people like that are not representative of Newcastle fans. So to redress the balance I should tell you that on another occasion a supporter of that club demonstrated a very different attitude. On the night before a Newcastle versus Sunderland game, I was having dinner with Graham Barber, who was my guest at the game, when a couple at the next table recognized us. The guy asked, 'Which of you two is doing the game tomorrow?' When I told him it was me, he said, 'Right. I'm a Newcastle fan and if Newcastle win you can sleep with my girlfriend.'

We all laughed, even his girlfriend. Then, later, when the guy left the table to visit the toilet, she said, 'Yes, for the right result you can sleep with me – no problem. But I am a "Mackem". So it's only if Sunderland win.' I often wonder how that couple got on with their relationship. They were engaged when we met them. I wonder if their mixed marriage lasted. By the way, Sunderland won 2–1, but not, I hasten to add, because I accepted the offer.

Throughout my career I was never offered a genuine, monetary bribe, although my name was mentioned in the corruption scandal in Italian football just before the 2006

World Cup. At the heart of that scandal was the suggestion that certain clubs selected the referees they wanted for specific games. My name came up because I took charge of a Champions League game involving Juventus. The police tape recorded a telephone conversation in which Luciano Moggi, the Director General of Juventus, complained that I wasn't the ref he wanted!

It is worth emphasizing that, whatever the English media say about our referees, they are regarded throughout Europe as incorruptible. That is not to suggest that lots of other countries have problems, but there have been allegations involving Portuguese, Greek, Italian, Polish and German officials.

Anyway, let's get on to my first season as a professional referee, 2001/02, because when I took charge of a World Cup qualifying game between Slovenia and Russia, some Russians did wonder if I had taken a backhander. Perhaps their suspicions were partly due to the fact that bribery was not unheard of in Russia. Alex Spirrin, who refereed in that country for a long time, once told me, 'The hardest game to referee is the one when you've already been told what the result will be.'

My game, in the Slovenian capital of Ljubljana, brought me into contact for the second time in my career with Srecko Katanec, the Slovenia coach. I'd had dealings with him at the Euro 2000 game against Yugoslavia when I was fourth official and when he applied psychological pressure throughout the match. If any free-kick was awarded against his team, he was up on his feet in the technical area, complaining and telling all the officials to be fair to Slovenia.

You can steel yourself against that sort of thing but subconsciously, does it influence you? Do you try too hard to be seen to be fair? For instance, after a sending-off, four of the next five free-kicks are usually awarded to the side who are down to ten men. I defy any referee who has officiated at the highest level to say, hand on heart, he has never been affected by a clever coach or a hostile crowd.

In that game in Ljubljana, Katanec was at it again all through the first half and so, at half-time, I warned him about his antics. He apologized and calmed down in the second half, but I can't pretend that I was not aware, at some level, of his insistence that Slovenia were a tiny nation who did not get a fair deal from officials.

During the game, the Russians kept holding opponents at corners. I warned one Russian defender, who had been particularly guilty of shirt-tugging, that if he did it again I would award a penalty against him. In the final minutes, with the score 1–1, a Slovenian corner came over and the Russian defender was at it again. I blew my whistle and pointed to the penalty spot. Did the pressure get to me? Was I 'looking for it' because Katanec had sowed seeds of doubts about unfairness? Did I see more in the shirt-pull than I thought?

At the time, I made what I believed to be an honest decision. But now, with twenty-twenty hindsight, I know it was the wrong decision. Two things were confirmed for me by that penalty in Slovenia. The first was that referees are remembered for the things they give and not the things they miss. The second was that the timing of the decision robbed it of credibility. By that I mean it was too late in the game to resolve the issue of shirt-pulling. I should have dealt with it long before I did. And, because I had let a lot of it go, when I finally reacted to one offence, the decision caused uproar because it was not consistent with what had gone on before.

The shirt-tugging, wrestling, holding, blocking and general free-for-all at corners and set pieces is a problem for referees – but it is not a problem for players. They accept it as part of the game. They practise it every day in training – both doing it and negating it – and regard that as part of their job. But that doesn't mean it is right.

For referees, the difficulty is that there are at least three or four offences at every corner and every free-kick. Both sides are at it, so who do you penalize? What we were encouraged to do, in my last few seasons as a ref, was to intervene before the corner was taken. We were supposed to signal that the kick should not be taken yet, and then lecture the worst offenders. But that didn't really stop anything – penalty areas still looked like a barn dance, with everyone taking their partners.

Then what tends to happen with referees is that they think, 'I've got to do something. Next time, I'll have to give something.' Yet the next time, you are watching someone holding an opponent but he lets go just before the corner is taken, and so you don't give anything. So you think, 'Next time.' Then you penalize someone during the rough and tumble at the next corner, but it is probably nowhere near as bad as half the tugging and shoving that has gone on before. The easiest thing for me to do, now that I am retired, would be to deliver a stern sermon to my former colleagues and say, 'You should sort it out.' Yet the truth is that I didn't solve the problem when I was refereeing.

In Slovenia I gave one penalty, too late in the game to have credibility. Milenko Acimovic scored from the spot and Slovenia won 2–1. Only one country would qualify automatically. Russia were the group leaders, Slovenia were in second place. It was a massively important victory for them and potentially a very damaging defeat for Russia.

At the final whistle, the Slovenians were too busy celebrating to worry about the referee. No police, security staff or stewards came to help me as I left the field. The Russians were incensed about the penalty and Alexander Mostovoi, their creative midfield player, was even more infuriated than his team-mates. I believe Mostovoi thought I had been 'got at'. I also think he might have assaulted me if Phil Sharp, one of the assistants, had not used his flag as a barrier.

Once we had battled our way back to the dressing room, we learned that Horst Brunmeier, FIFA's Swiss match observer, was giving me a good mark. He said the penalty was controversial but that I had 'such a good game previously'.

The Russian newspapers did not agree. *Sport-Express* said, 'In Ljubljana, referee Poll acted like a big-time bandit.' *Sovietsky Sport* called my decision, 'Murder in the eyes of millions.'

The next morning I went for a walk with the assistants (Phil Sharp and Dave Babski) and fourth official Andy D'Urso. We stolled through a park and went past a huge church. The service had finished and the congregation were talking among themselves outside the church. Most of them turned to stare at us, because we were conspicuous in our FIFA tracksuits. So we all acknowledged them, in a friendly fashion, as you do. We went, 'All right?', smiled and nodded. Nothing. Just stony stares in response, which struck us as odd.

Later, an official drove us on a little guided tour. He showed us the park and we commented that we had been there that morning. We mentioned the fine church. He said, 'That is the Russian Orthodox Church.' And the rouble dropped. The congregation had been Russians who did not feel much like smiling at me.

I reported to FIFA that I believed Mostovoi had tried to assault me but I do not think any action was ever taken. In the end, Russia won their group and Slovenia reached the World Cup finals through the play-offs. My concern was that the controversy would damage my own prospects of reaching the finals. That was how I viewed every game: would it help or hinder my progress to the next target in my career?

The postscript to the Slovenia game came in the summer of 2003 when I was invited to referee a friendly in Moscow as part of an anti-racism campaign. I got through the match without showing any cards and Nikolai Levnikov, the former Russian ref who was on UEFA's referees committee, said I would be welcome to return to Russia any day. That particular slate had been wiped clean.

But back in 2001, a week after the Slovenia versus Russia match, I was scheduled to referee Roma's home Champions League tie against Real Madrid. In my hotel room on the afternoon of the match, I turned on the TV and saw a plane crash into a building. My initial reaction was that I was watching a movie channel but I wasn't. It was the news. This was 11 September 2001. Like billions around the world, I watched in a state of devastated, shocked disbelief as the horrific events of 9/11 unfolded live, on television.

I rang the match delegate and said, 'The game will be off, I presume.'

He said, 'You have to prepare as if the fixture will go ahead. We will meet as arranged at 6.30 and I will let you know of developments.'

It felt fundamentally wrong to pack my bag for a football match. New York's twin towers had been reduced to rubble and yet I was checking to see whether I had a spare watch and whistle. Of course, assistant referees Dave Bryan and Phil Sharp, and fourth official Andy D'Urso all believed fervently that the tie could not, and should not, go ahead.

The police contingent due to escort us to the match was half an hour late because, understandably and correctly, they had other priorities. The city of Rome, like other major cities around the globe, was on a high alert in case more terrorist attacks were planned. From what we could gather, there were discussions going on between the governments of the United States and European nations about whether the Champions League ties that night should be played. A factor for consideration was that the various stadiums were mostly sold out and fans were milling about. Airports were closed, so travelling supporters could not fly home.

I learned, several years later, that mine was one of only two matches which the authorities concluded really had to go ahead. They believed that the safest thing to do at these two games was to play them. And, because they needed to play two of the games, they decided to go ahead with all that night's fixtures, although it was not until an hour and a quarter before my kick-off that it was formally agreed that we would try to stage a football match.

At Roma's Stadio Olimpico, the dressing rooms are in a corner of the ground but you walk along a concrete passage, out of sight of spectators, along the back of half of the main stand before emerging onto the pitch near the halfway line. That night, the long walk with the teams just added to the sense of unreality; the feeling that it was not right. Gabriel Batistuta, Roma's Argentine striker, and Luis Figo, Real Madrid's Portuguese forward, were walking side by side and I talked with them. It felt surreal to all of us. None of us could believe we were about to be part of a game of football after what we had watched on our TV screens.

In England the players would have stood in the centre-circle for a minute's silence but in Europe, football shows its respect in a different manner. The players lined up as usual but, at the kick-off, the ball was moved only half a metre and then all the players stopped and held their positions. We gave one minute of the match to the memory of those who had died in New York. During that minute, the 82,000 crowd clapped in a restrained, respectful manner. It was an inadequate gesture, of course, but it was heartfelt and moving. As I stood there on the pitch, listening to that crowd of people making a quite eerie noise with that subdued clapping, I was not alone in fighting back a tear or two.

After a minute had passed I made a signal for play to resume and a game of football took place. Real won 2–1 and afterwards the match officials went for a sombre dinner. Telephone networks around the globe were in meltdown and so we could not speak to our families. We did not know how or when we would get home. We felt dislocated and isolated, and, of course, all the time, there was the sense of appalled shock about the attack on New York.

Unexpectedly, the airport reopened the following day and we were able to fly home more or less as planned. I still have the commemorative pennant from the game in Rome, dated '11-09-2001'. It is among the most evocative items of my football memorabilia.

The following month I headed to France for Olympique Lyonnaise against Barcelona. If Lyon lost, they were out of the Champions League. It was an important match – and I believed it was particularly important for me because my assessor was to be Volker Roth, chair of UEFA's referees' committee and a member of FIFA's refs' committee. He is a German with a great sense of humour and I always got on well with him, but I calculated that he was coming to see whether I was good enough to referee in the World Cup. In my head, I thought he was coming because I had made that penalty decision in the Slovenia–Russia game. I thought, the top man in European refereeing wanted to see how I handled pressure in a big Champions League game and to consider whether I should go to the 2002 World Cup.

That was how I was. I believed I had to get the key matches right. I can think right back to refereeing the Hertfordshire Centenary Trophy Final match at Boreham Wood in 1985. All the Herts FA dignitaries were there in the blazers and badges. It was Pirton against Welwyn Garden City, and I had just become a Class I ref. I knew that if I refereed well, the people who mattered in my county Football Association would stop thinking of me as 'that young man' and consider me to be a good ref. Incidentally, Mark Halsey, who went on to be a Premiership ref, was in goal for Welwyn – and did not concede a goal. Welwyn won 2–0.

I'll be honest and admit that I had to look up that result on my sheet for that season but I remember very, very well without any prompting that Freddie Reid, one of the referees who had used a Subbuteo table football game to examine me five years earlier, came up to me after the game. He was with his wife, while I was with my mum and dad. Fred said to my parents, 'He is very, very good and he could go all the way, but he has got to keep his feet on the ground.' His wife added, 'And his cloth cap on.' She meant that I should not get any airs and graces.

Fast forward again to October 2001 and Olympique Lyonnaise against Barcelona. For European games, we were not notified of the actual match we were doing until the week before the fixture and we were told it was confidential. UEFA said that if the news got out before they announced the appointments, we would be taken off the fixture. This was to ensure that we could not be 'got at' and could not have pressure heaped on us by the media. Final confirmation, with flight details and so on, arrived on the Monday of the week of the match. That was when I noted the name of the assessor: Volker Roth.

We flew out on the following day, Tuesday, and I trained in the stadium as I always did – to run off the effects of the flight and get a feel for the place. That evening we were all taken out for a meal in a very good restaurant with views over the city of Lyon. That was when Herr Roth told me, in an off-hand way, that I was going to be given a World Cup qualifying match in South America. He said, 'I can't remember which one, but it doesn't matter at this stage.'

Doesn't matter?! I couldn't believe the news or the way it had been delivered. The reason he said what he did, and in that manner, was to indicate that he was not at the Olympique Lyonnaise game to see whether I was good enough for the World Cup. That decision had been taken: I was good enough; I was going to the World Cup.

On the day of the match, as was the routine at European matches, I performed a 9.30 am pitch inspection and, although you would not think it was necessary, checked the pitch markings, the goals and so on. It's not as daft as it sounds. In 1997 a tie was replayed because Sion of Switzerland successfully appealed that the goals had been the wrong height at Spartak Moscow. So now, after the referee's pitch inspection, he meets representatives of each team at 10 am and says to the away team, 'You have trained on the pitch.

Do you have any complaints?' That is the last opportunity they have to challenge anything. Then the referee checks that the two kits do not clash and so on.

The remainder of the morning was taken up by sightseeing. I had a pasta lunch and then, as always, went back to my hotel room for a sleep. With the travel and the training, I did not tend to sleep well the first night of a European trip, and so found it easy to nod off for a nap of up to two hours on the afternoon of the fixture. Then I used to have a relaxing bath before meeting up with the assistants and fourth official at the hotel to get my instructions to them out of the way.

Then it was time to travel to the stadium – at a stupid speed. It was always ridiculous on the continent. For the police on motorbikes escorting you to the game it was an opportunity and an excuse to drive as quickly as they could. You flew through the streets, going on the wrong side of the road, screeching round corners and generally being terrified. The police were trying to beat their personal bests and if they set a new record, they all gave each other high-fives. It was crazy. In England we would just have left a quarter of an hour earlier from the hotel.

I used to give little FA pin badges to the police at the ground, to thank them for not killing me. Once, in Belgium, a motorcycle cop lost it in the wet on the way to the ground. He put his bike over on its side and skidded along the road, but our vehicle just ignored him and kept going at this crazy speed. The officer left behind on the floor didn't get his pin badge.

In Lyon, the score was 2–2 with a few minutes left when the home side had a corner. They sent their goalkeeper up in search of the winner, but the ball was cleared, Barcelona broke upfield and there was a big appeal for offside. Glenn Turner kept his flag down, Barcelona continued and scored.

The French team refused to kick-off. They were staging a formal protest – and I was thinking, 'Not with Volker Roth watching, please!' I cautioned their captain. I said, 'You are the captain. You are delaying the restart. I am showing you the yellow card.' And by my mannerisms I was saying, 'Who is next?' We kicked off. The match finished with Barcelona winning 3–2 and we went off.

There was a steep ramp in the tunnel away from the pitch and as Jacques Santini, the Lyon coach, approached me aggressively, I stepped back suddenly, as if startled by him. It was a technique I had used before. It made it clear to everyone that Santini's belligerent demeanour was wrong. He looked horrified, realized he could be in trouble and calmed down.

In the dressing room, Volker Roth told us he had seen a video replay. There was no offside, Glenn Turner had been absolutely correct not to flag and Roth was delighted with the way I had quelled the protests. The top man in European refereeing finished by saying to me, 'Enjoy South America.'

Ah, but by the time I went to Paraguay for their World Cup qualifier against Colombia on 14 November, I was thinking, 'I have got to do this game well or I might lose my place at the World Cup.' Again, that was how I was – I could never just enjoy individual matches on their own merits.

Before leaving for the game (with assistants Tony Green and Phil Sharp plus fourth official Graham Barber) I did as much research as I could about South America in general, Paraguay and Asunción, where the match was being played. I telephoned Hugh Dallas and Pierluigi Collina for advice but nothing could have prepared me for the experience.

For a start, on the first leg of the flight we flew Business Class with British Airways to Sao Paulo in Brazil. Now, when I was a kid, my mum and dad had never been able to afford to take the Poll family on foreign holidays. We'd gone to Mablethorpe, Cleethorpes, or Skegness. So when I received the travel documents to South America for the four officials, and spotted that the cost of the return air tickets was £22,500, it struck me as extraordinary.

On the flight, I kept playing with the buttons on my reclining seat, like a naive kid. We travelled in tracksuits for comfort but changed into suits on the plane to make a good impression on arrival. Yet once we had made the second flight, from Brazil to Asunción, the protocols and procedures were bewilderingly different. For instance, the referee was not expected to speak at any of the meetings, which was just as well, because they were conducted entirely in Spanish.

The grinding, abject poverty we witnessed travelling through Asunción was a jolt. I had seen some poor conditions in the former Soviet Union and other countries in Europe, but here people were living – just about – in shanties and shacks.

We visited the national stadium, where we trained in stifling heat and oppressive humidity. We ate alone in our hotel and, having been advised not to go out unaccompanied, all had an early night.

The next morning we woke to find a ferocious storm turning the streets into rivers. On the way to a meeting at the brand new offices of CONMEBOL (Confederación Sudamericana de Fútbol), the South American equivalent of UEFA, Tony Green opened the window of our vehicle to take a photograph of the incredible scenes – and a four-by-four went past, sent up a wave of water and deluged him.

With Tony's clothes still soggy, we had an audience with Nicholas Laoz, the president of CONMEBOL. He struck us as a remarkable, impressive man. It was an honour to be there. We were 6,500 miles from England and felt we were representing our country.

Later, as we were warming up at the stadium, I was taken aback to hear someone shout, 'Good luck, Pollie.' I looked round and there was a flag of St George with 'AVFC' on it. No, it was not John Gregory. A knot of Aston Villa fans had travelled, hoping Juan Pablo Angel would play for Colombia. He had not been selected, so I suppose I was a very poor second in terms of someone to cheer.

Neither national anthem was played because there had been too many previous disrespectful incidents at games between the two countries. The match itself began accompanied by a stunning and deafening display of fireworks and firecrackers let off by supporters. I couldn't see Barbs in the technical area and did not know he was being harangued by the television producer who wanted the match delayed until the smoke cleared. Too late.

Paraguay had qualified already for the World Cup while Colombia needed to win 5–0 to earn a play-off against a country from Oceania. I thought that was an unrealistic target and so expected that the game would not be all that tense. I was wrong on both counts.

Tino Asprilla, who had a spell at Newcastle, was playing for Colombia and was utterly outstanding. With the help of a penalty for a foul on Asprilla – correctly awarded, of course, but hugely unpopular with the home crowd – Colombia managed to grab four goals. Then they hit the bar. They hit the post. They did everything except collect goal number five.

Everything was happening off the pitch as well. There was a baton charge by police at one point and, at the finish, police with riot shields formed a phalanx around the officials as we left the field. In the dressing room the Argentine assessor's debrief consisted of giving me a hug, and I took that as confirmation that we had done well.

That evening we were taken to the Paraguayan referees' centre – a facility the referees had paid for themselves. They held a barbecue in our honour and you have never seen so much meat in one place. After that, the four amigos went to a salsa bar because we did not want to go to bed. We did not want the evening to end.

Refereeing? Why did I do it? Because of occasions like the trip to Asunción.

CHAPTER EIGHTEEN

Savage 'Humour'

That first season as a professional referee, 2001/02, saw one other unforgettable event – and I do not mean my refereeing of the Worthington Cup Final at the Millennium Stadium, Cardiff, between Blackburn and Tottenham, although that was the last big, domestic appointment I needed to complete my set. It was Harry's birthday, and a great occasion for the Poll family. The actual football also went well enough. The only contentious issue, as Blackburn won 2–1, was when Tottenham's Teddy Sheringham tumbled in the area after a tackle by Nils-Eric Johansson – I waved 'play on'. As I was leaving the stadium, Spurs manager Glenn Hoddle got into the lift with me. I like Glenn. He was always prepared to listen to referees and discuss things. We had a jokey exchange in that lift. He said, 'It was a nailed-on penalty, Pollie. You'll be embarrassed when you see it.'

I said, 'I have seen it. I am not embarrassed. It was not a penalty.'

He said, 'So you've seen it on TV?'

I said, 'No. I was there.'

Unfortunately I was also there, at Filbert Street, on 20 April 2002. That was when Robbie Savage visited the referees' toilet and earned himself a fine. I know there are some who still think that it was officious to report him, so here, for the first time, is the full account. It is not for the squeamish, because although reports summarized his offence as using the referee's toilet, 'using' does not tell the story of what he did.

Robbie's team, Leicester City, were already doomed to relegation from the Premiership. This was their penultimate game at their old Filbert Street stadium where they were playing Aston Villa. I had finished my warm-up and so had the players. It was the final period before we all went out again for the match. Suddenly, Savage burst into the officials' dressing room. I asked him to leave but he said, 'I've got to use your loo. I'm busting for a shit.' With that, he went into our toilet, sat down and, with the door wide open, he gave a running commentary as he defecated.

We could not believe what was happening. I saw his team-mate Matt Elliott in the corridor and asked, 'Are the toilets in your dressing room working okay?' He thought it was a weird question but confirmed that the plumbing was functioning normally.

While Robbie was in the cubicle, Dennis Hedges, the match observer, entered the dressing room and according to Robbie's account of events I said, 'You'll never guess who is in our loo' as if it was all a hoot. I might well have said that, but if I did so, it was in appalled astonishment and when Robbie finished, I told him his behaviour was unacceptable. He laughed and said, 'I'll leave it floating so you can see it for yourself.' And he did.

Now I was almost lost for words but managed to remark that he should at least consider washing his hands. He replied, 'No need.' With that, he turned to Dennis Hedges and wiped his hands down the lapels of Dennis's jacket. He said, 'Mr Hedges won't mind. He can take a joke.'

Now, I am not a prude. I have spent a lot of time in football and around footballers. I am used to language and behaviour which, in other walks of life, would be considered crude. They don't bother me at all, normally, but Robbie Savage's behaviour was just horrible. I wouldn't report a player for using my loo but the moment Robbie wiped his hands down Dennis's jacket meant that he was being deeply disrespectful.

At the subsequent disciplinary hearing, he maintained that he had an upset stomach. But the Leicester dressing room was less than twenty yards away from ours. Was what he did an attempt at a joke, as he has always maintained? Was it an attempt to belittle me or destabilize me before the game? I don't know, but I knew I had to report him.

After the match, Micky Adams, the Leicester assistant manager at the time, spoke to me about an incident on the pitch. I told him about what Robbie had done and that I was reporting it. Adams apologized and promised action would be taken against the player. Four days later, Leicester announced that they had fined Robbie two weeks' wages, the maximum financial penalty they could impose.

The FA charged Robbie with improper conduct. Gordon Taylor, chief executive of the Professional Footballers' Association, represented him at the hearing and said the matter should have been dealt with in a more sympathetic, less official way. He added that it was common for players not to wash their hands after using the toilet before games, because they are so focused on the football.

Robbie produced a doctor's certificate to prove he was on antibiotics at the time of the game, and said he had been overwhelmed by his upset stomach. He conceded, however, that he had managed to play a full ninety minutes and then attend a supporters' club function, but did not seem to notice any inconsistencies in that account. He also said that the mood in my dressing room during his visit was jovial and that I could not have been offended because I had demonstrated a friendly attitude to him during the game. My answer was that, as a professional, I did not let any misconduct before the game affect how I approached a player during the match.

Finally, Barry Bright, chairman of the hearing, asked the player, 'Do you understand you have been charged with improper conduct? You may want to consult with Mr Taylor before answering this but, having heard all of the evidence and understanding the regulations involved, do you think there is anything you did which could be interpreted as improper?'

Savage replied immediately, without consulting Gordon Taylor, 'Yes.' With that, although he didn't understand, Robbie had made the entire hearing pointless. He'd admitted his guilt. If he'd done it in a letter, he could have saved all our time. But then paperwork was not his strong point. He was fined £10,000, subsequently appealed but lost and eventually paid up. I believe he successfully appealed against Leicester's club fine, however, and I know that he considered it a bit of fun and still feels hard done by over the incident.

There is another tale to tell about Robbie Savage and this is an appropriate moment to do so. At the end of the 2002/03 season, West Ham went to Birmingham fighting for their Premiership lives. Robbie had moved on to Birmingham and before the game I chatted to him in an effort to let him know that what had happened at Leicester was in the past and we must move on. He felt the only reason the FA charged him was because of the involvement of the assessor, Dennis Hedges. Robbie thought I should have, 'stood up to the assessor' about the toilet incident. I was disappointed that he still could not see that what he had done was abominable.

And, during that game against West Ham, I was disappointed again by Mr Savage. He had been in the Leicester side that had suffered relegation and so knew what an empty feeling that is for players and yet he revelled in West Ham's plight. When Birmingham took the lead, he leaned over a West Ham player who was on the floor and said, with real venom, 'Now you're going down.' What a nasty thing to say and do. I cautioned Savage for adopting an aggressive attitude towards an opponent and he told me I was only doing it because of the past.

When I bumped into him after the game, he asked me why he'd been cautioned. He said, 'I didn't use foul language. It was just a laugh. People misunderstand me.' I explained why I had booked him, but changed the subject and he gave me a bit of banter about my clothes. He was wearing a long, light-coloured coat which was covered in creases.

I said, 'How can you give me stick when you've got this bit of creased old cloth?' And I put my hand on the shoulder of the offending garment.

At that moment, Steve Bruce, the Birmingham manager, appeared from round a corner and said, 'I saw that, Pollie, You've wiped your hand on my player's jacket.' It was a reference to what Savage had done to the assessor's jacket and, to my mind, it was a lot funnier than any of his player's gags or stunts.

I had one more laugh at Robbie Savage's expense during my career. He had fouled someone, and when I was dealing with him, I said that I was in charge of the game, not him. He said, 'Yeah, but I've got more money than you.' After a pause, he added, 'Loads more money.'

Towards the end of the match Savage asked how much time was left to play. I said, 'Sorry Robbie, I can only afford a cheap watch and it's broken.'

After Robbie's attempt at toilet humour, season 2001/02, my first as a professional, ended for me at Manchester United versus Charlton. I stayed the night before the game with the assistants and fourth official at the Radisson Hotel in Manchester and we went to breakfast in our tracksuits. An American guest told us we 'looked sporty'. We fell into conversation. He said, 'I am here for the United game. Can you tell me what time it starts?'

I said, 'When I blow my whistle. I am the referee.'

He said, 'If you are the referee, I'm the King of Spain.'

After the match, Julia and the children joined me at the hotel and we bumped into the same guest. I resisted the temptation to address him as 'Your Majesty', but he said he felt 'a Goddam fool'. He had not thought much of the game, which had been goalless, but I enjoyed myself because the Poll family made a weekend of it and stayed in the Lake District. It was good to have some time with them, because the World Cup was looming.

CHAPTER NINETEEN

Sleepless in Japan

So we have arrived at my story of the 2002 World Cup. I learned that I was going in January in a telephone call from a journalist, Christopher Davies. He was disappointed that I had not rung him to tip him off – but I hadn't heard. He had spotted it on the FIFA website. I ran to my computer, waited for what seemed like eons for it to boot up, found the site ... and, sure enough, there it was: the official list of thirty-six referees and thirty-six assistants for the World Cup. Five referees came from the South American confederation and five from CONCACAF (North and Central America, plus the Caribbean). Africa and Asia provided five each. There was just one, my Aussie friend Mark Shield, from Oceania (Australia, New Zealand and the Pacific Islands). The rest – fourteen referees – came from Europe. On the official announcement, the European contingent was named first and listed in alphabetical order. And so the first name on the entire document was 'Pierluigi Collina (ITA)'.

Already, you can see the seeds of resentment and jealousy. Not towards Pierluigi – the whole world knew he was the best – but the other confederations resented the overwhelming influence and success of UEFA. That was particularly true of the Confederación Sudamericana de Fútbol.

None of that concerned me. What mattered to me was name number eleven on the list: 'Graham Poll (ENG)'. People say moments like that are the realization of a dream, but that does not capture how I felt. This was something I had not dared dream about when I started refereeing; an achievement way beyond anything I had contemplated. It was the seventeenth World Cup, but the first outside Europe or the Americas, the first in Asia and the first to be jointly hosted by two countries – and I was going.

The kid from Stevenage, who had been so insecure at school that he had been the class clown, had worked his way up the refereeing ladder and gained recognition in his own country. He had gone on to become recognized as a top official within Europe. Now, that page on the FIFA website meant that he was one of the top referees in the world.

I know good old Freddie Reid had told me, back in 1985, always to keep my feet on the ground, and his wife had said I should retain my metaphorical cloth cap. Well, sorry Mr and Mrs Reid, at that moment in my study in Tring, if I'd had any sort of hat on I'd have chucked it in the air. And feet on the ground? No, I was flying.

The next few days were a wonderful time of celebrations with friends and especially with my family – my mum and dad and Julia, who had shared so much of my career, and my lovely kids, who were just happy their dad was pleased.

In March, the World Cup referees – and I never tired of reading that phrase – went out to Seoul, in South Korea, for a week on a course. It was like nowhere I had ever been before. Of course, the Koreans do not use our alphabet but, unlike the Japanese, they do not have any signs for shop names which are at all comprehensible to Westerners. When I walked around I could not understand a single word. And, I have to admit, I inspected every morsel of every meal because I didn't know what any of it was and did not want to eat dog. If that is ignorant, then I am sorry, but I was entirely ignorant. I was in a completely different environment and culture to anything I had ever experienced.

It was a great week, however. It began with a speech by George Cumming, the Scot who was FIFA's director of refereeing. He sat us down and said, 'Summa Petenda – aim for the highest. One of you thirty-six here will referee the World Cup Final.' As I have already recalled, most of us looked at Pierluigi Collina.

During that week in Seoul, our sleep patterns were all over the place and I taught some of the others an English word, 'knackered'. When I got home, UEFA rewarded my selection for the World Cup by awarding me with the UEFA Cup semi-final second leg between AC Milan and Borussia Dortmund in the San Siro Stadium – a ground I had always wanted to add to my list. Marvellous.

Then I received an email saying that the referee appointed for the first leg could not do it, so I was being switched. Instead of the second leg, I was now due to officiate at the first leg, in Dortmund. Milan played dreadfully, Dortmund played exceptionally and the Germans won 4–0. So I thought, 'Now the second leg will be a non-event, and so I have been lucky.'

It seemed to me that everything was going really well. Robbie Savage did his best to ruin my mood, but not even that disgusting episode quite managed it. Graham Poll (ENG) was going to the World Cup.

The seventy-two officials flew out two weeks before the tournament. We assembled in the same, massive city centre hotel which we had used for the course in March. The police closed the motorway for us every day when our coach carried us to a huge stadium for our training and there was a real sense of occasion and importance. We had fitness tests and some team-bonding and then the early appointments were announced.

We congregated in a big room and the appointments were projected onto a screen. By that quirk of the senses that occurs on occasions like that, I spotted my name immediately. I was down to referee Russia against Japan. But within seconds, the projector was turned off, the acetate sheet was taken away and hurried consultations took place while the refs sat around wondering what was going on. I subsequently discovered that because of my adventure in Slovenia, the Russian representative had objected to me. Eventually we were told to go to dinner and when we returned two hours later to see the appointments again, I had been reassigned to Italy versus Croatia.

As I now know, that game did not go well. So the badly-awarded penalty in Slovenia really did cost me. If I had not given that penalty, the Slovenia match would have passed without incident and I would have begun World Cup 2002 by refereeing Russia against Japan instead of Italy versus Croatia. Who knows how events might have unfolded subsequently? It is possible that Russia–Japan would have gone well and I would have had a successful World Cup. That would have made it impossible for me to be kept away from Euro 2004.

When God made us, he only gave us eyes in the front of our head. We can only look forwards. And so I completely accept that there is no point in saying, 'What if ...?' No point at all ... but then again, what if?

Anyway, the reassigned appointments were announced in that room in Seoul. Half the officials were staying there in South Korea but I was in the contingent flying to Tokyo, Japan. As soon as we landed, we were taken to the imperial palace to meet the crown prince. He believed it was an honour for him and his country to be our hosts and that attitude characterized the entire World Cup.

After trying to avoid eating dog, and so consuming nothing much other than boiled rice for a week, I had lost weight and was starving. At the palace in Tokyo, there was a huge buffet laid out and Peter Prendergast, a referee from Jamaica with whom I had become friendly, cajoled me to start being a little more adventurous and to actually try various foodstuffs. I had just persuaded myself to put a portion of raw jellyfish in my mouth when I heard a perfect, clipped, Oxbridge English accent enunciate, 'Where is this English referee I would like to meet?' It was the crown prince. So I gulped down the jellyfish – which was probably the best way to deal with it – and shook hands with the prince.

The reason we had gone straight to the reception became apparent when we left – and made the two-hour journey to the referees' base which was in the middle of the countryside. In Korea we had been able to walk out into shopping areas or get a free bus to other areas of the city. We were in the middle of bustling city life. In Japan we were in the middle of nowhere. But we were there together and I made some really solid friendships.

I was lucky enough to be a spectator when England played their opening game, a 1–1 draw against Sweden in Saitama – and I do mean lucky. The nation was watching at home, half way around the world, but I was there. All the referees who were not involved elsewhere were given tickets for the England game, and I kept thinking to myself, 'I am watching England in the World Cup!' It was extraordinary to see so many Japanese people, who had 'adopted' England as their team, wearing England shirts with either of 'Beckham' or 'Owen' on the back.

My first appointment was two days later in the same stadium – as fourth official for Japan's first match, against Belgium. The stadium was built especially for the World Cup and had been open less than a year. It held 63,000 and because of the home country's involvement, most of them had Japanese shirts or flags. The atmosphere was tremendous, although somehow it was completely unlike a British crowd. All the goals came in the second half. Japan fell behind, equalized and then grabbed the lead before conceding a goal sixteen minutes from the end. It finished 2–2.

On the Thursday, two days before I was due to have my first 'middle', I sent this email home to friends and family:

> I hope you are well and enjoying this wonderful World Cup tournament at least half as much as I am. First the most important news ... my weight! Things have settled down at my usual fighting weight.
>
> Yesterday evening I went to the Germany–Ireland game which was very exciting and nice to see a team giving everything after England's poor showing in the second half against Sweden. What about tomorrow night? Can England do it against Argentina? Of course not, but it's good to dream isn't it?
>
> I am sitting in Collina's room using his PC to type this message as he's in Sapporo for the England game. I have

promised him a nasty surprise in his room if I'm not pleased with his performance.

My first involvement here passed without incident in what was one of the best games so far ... fourth official at Japan v Belgium. A fantastic second half.

Tomorrow I leave for Ibaraki for my game and was really impressed with the stadium when watching the Irish match. Having been here for two weeks, I am pleased to be able to get my whistle out and pleased that there has been no pressure applied as to how we are to referee. Just express yourselves and give clear decisions is the message.

Given this and my preparations I am quietly confident for Saturday evening.

Regards, Pollie.

When I re-read that, I can recapture the feelings I had of excitement and anticipation. I was thrilled to be a part of the World Cup. After twenty-two years of refereeing, I had climbed the ladder from taking charge of Woolmer Green Rangers Reserves and here I was making myself at home in Pierluigi Collina's room, for heaven's sake! And I was looking forward my own first game. 'Quietly confident'. Yep, that summed up how I felt.

One of the reasons I had gone to watch Ireland's 1–1 draw with Germany in Ibaraki was to have a look at one of the assistant referees, Jens Larsen of Denmark. He was going to be part of 'my team' for my game, with Phil Sharp from England. Jens had run the line at the Euro 2000 final and was regarded as one of Europe's leading assistants. But he was poor in the Ireland match. When I discussed his performance with other refs and assistants who were at the game, most of us thought he was too intrusive: he looked like he was trying too hard to make his mark.

That was the view as well at the FIFA debrief for the game. Jens was criticized heavily by the match observer, Carlos Alarcon of Paraguay, in front of all the other refs and assistants at our rural Japanese base. The bad news for Jens was that Senor Alarcon was to be the observer at our match. That was bad news for me as well, because it put pressure on Jens and I did not want him trying to demonstrate what a good official he was. I did not want him making a big, dramatic decision just to show that he was up to it. I needed him to feel positive and part of the team – not someone desperate to prove something.

As we travelled back to Ibaraki in a people carrier on the Friday, the day before the match, we listened to a CD of party music Jens had compiled. The three of us sang along and built up a rapport. At our hotel we watched Paraguay lose to Spain (which did not improve the mood of Senor Alarcon) and then watched England beat Argentina with a David Beckham penalty. Phil Sharp and I tried, without a lot of success, to keep our celebrations restrained.

I went to sleep easily enough, still quietly confident. I woke at 6 am because I thought I'd heard a noise in the room. I even asked, 'Who's there?' There was no answer and no more noise, so I went back to sleep. In the morning I discovered that it had been Phil pushing good luck cards from home under my door.

Jens was nervous as we left for the stadium. So we put his CD on again. It seemed to do the trick – until we got out at the ground. There, Carlos Alarcon, who had travelled separately, came over. He shook my hand and wished me luck. He did the same with Phil Sharp. He did the same with the fourth official, William Mattus of Costa Rica. But to Jens, he said, 'Be strong.'

I rolled my eyes in disbelief and dismay. Of course, Alarcon thought he was doing the right thing, but Jens's mood changed straight away. He was nervous again. All the painstaking confidence-building Phil and I had done had been wiped out by one misguided remark. As I believe subsequent events proved, Jens felt he now needed to prove that he was a top assistant. He believed, subconsciously no doubt, that the way to do that was to make a big, brave decision. So, subconsciously again, he started the match waiting for a big decision. Over the years I had learned not to look for them – they come along without you seeking them.

Five minutes into the second half, Italy's Christian Vieri scored with a header from close range. Jens stuck up his flag for offside. There was no way I could go against his decision or ask him about it. I had to disallow the goal.

Vieri scored a legitimate goal five minutes later with another header and Italy sat back, content that they could hold onto the lead instead of pressing for another goal. Yet, after seventy-three minutes, Ivica Olic got in front of the Italian defence to reach a Robert Jarni cross and equalize. Three minutes later, Milan Rapaic's volley was deflected into the Italian net by Italy's substitute, Marco Materazzi. Croatia were winning 2–1.

Four minutes from time, Francesco Totti took a free-kick from thirty yards. It thumped against the inside of one post, bounced along the line, brushed the other post and went out for a goal-kick. The drama was building and the Italians kept pressing.

In stoppage time, a long-range free-kick eluded everybody and bounced into the net, but Jens had his flag up. I thought at first that he was signalling offside, but then he indicated that he had seen a shirt-pull. Again, I had to accept his decision and disallow the goal without going over for a discussion with him. The Italians were outraged. For the second time they had managed to get the ball into the net only to have the goal disallowed – and this time, the decision had condemned them to defeat.

I expected protests at the finish, and when I blew the final whistle a minute or two later I was surrounded by Italian players. I had a good relationship with most of them because I had refereed them in Champions League matches. Vieri said, 'Graham, it's not you ... he has killed you.' I shielded Jens from the furious Italians, but their body language told me they thought they had genuine grievances.

In the dressing room I asked Jens if he was certain about disallowing the stoppage-time goal. He said he had seen Filippo Inzaghi tug a defender's shirt. He was adamant it was the correct call. He said, 'I would not have flagged otherwise.'

What none of us knew at that stage was that disallowing the fiftieth-minute header by Vieri was a huge mistake. The striker was clearly onside. The assessor, Carlos Alarcon knew, because he had seen all the crucial incidents on television. When he came into our room, his face told us all we needed to know. I went to have a shower and Phil Sharp was in tears for me. He only managed to say, 'You poor bastard.' He knew that I would carry the can for the errors made by Jens.

I telephoned Julia and we both cried. She said, 'They won't blame you. All the TV pundits are saying how well you refereed and how the linesman let you down.' I kept telling myself that was right. I kept saying to myself that I had not done anything wrong, that they were Jens's mistakes. I knew and accepted that, as the referee, I was ultimately responsible for every decision during a game, but the mistakes had not been mine.

After a sleepless night I spoke to Volker Roth (chair of the UEFA referees' committee and a member of the FIFA referees' committee). He said, 'The World Cup is over for Jens. For you, we'll have to wait and see.'

We did not have long to wait. Carlos Alarcon led the debrief that afternoon and, for the first time, I saw the video replays of the disallowed Vieri goal. It was not even a close call. When the ball was played forward, Vieri was about a yard onside. He timed his run perfectly and headed home from close range. It was a shocking mistake to flag for offside. Jens told the debrief, 'Graham had no alternative than to accept my signal. It was my mistake.' But, to compound the mistake, I cautioned Vieri for the way he gestured at Jens in protest.

The Vieri incident was shown over and over again. I felt the South Americans were making a point about shoddy European officials. Eventually they moved on to another incident where it was felt I'd missed an Italian player leading with an arm as he challenged. Then the stoppage time incident was shown. It began when I awarded Italy a free-kick near the halfway line. The Croatia players were trying to delay the restart to use up time and so I stayed close to the halfway line instead of moving towards the penalty area where the Italians were obviously going to play the ball. I should have ignored Croatia's time-wasting tactics and positioned myself closer to the ball's 'drop zone'. From where I was, I had seen a bit of pulling and pushing from both sets of players in the crowded penalty area but nothing excessive.

Jens stuck up his flag, but the South Americans at the debrief were very critical of my positioning.

The inquest, covering three or four incidents, lasted three-quarters of an hour. I knew I was beaten long before the end. The South Americans were like a dog with a bone. They had found a way to blame me as well as Jens. Eventually I said, 'We're going round and round in circles here. Can we just accept I did my very best in the game? I don't think I have anything to blame myself for. You've said what you've said, you've marked how you've marked and what will happen, will happen. Can we just leave it at that?' I added, 'If anyone in this room feels I have let them down I will apologize here and now.'

All around the room, referees and assistants shook their heads. Someone said, 'No, you have not let us down.'

Jens maintained he was correct about the stoppage-time shirt-pulling, but he had no defence about the Vieri 'offside'. He couldn't have. After the debrief he said to me, 'I know I've finished my World Cup. I feel bad about that but I feel even worse because I think I've also finished yours.' We both suspected I was not going to referee again at that World Cup. I had toiled so hard for so long to get to my second major tournament but I was probably going home early again.

I was told that the next day I needed to have a telephone conversation with George Cumming from FIFA. At the appointed time I went to the function room that FIFA had commandeered as an office and took the call. I can still remember taking the phone into the corridor and can remember details of that corridor. I can remember all of the phone call. George Cumming said, 'I am really sorry, Graham, about what has happened.'

I said, 'So am I. But this wasn't my fault.'

He said, 'Unfortunately in refereeing, as you well know, the referee takes responsibility for what happens during a game. That is life. I am afraid that you can have no more games at this World Cup.'

I said, 'Is that fair? Is that right?'

He said, 'No. Welcome to FIFA.'

At that point he told me to stay strong and that I was still young enough to referee in the 2006 World Cup. He insisted that I was very highly thought of, et cetera et cetera. I may have laughed; I very probably swore. I definitely thought that was all complete nonsense. I was being dumped from one World Cup so I was hardly likely to be called up for another.

It cannot have helped that Italy, a major football power, were involved but FIFA did not want me to tell anyone that I had been axed because of the controversy over the Italy–Croatia game. They wanted me to keep that little secret to myself. I was expected to stay strong and positive, remain with the other referees – and then go home when the cut was made for the officials for the knockout stage. If I went home before the cull, the focus would be on me and the reason for my being sent home – perhaps the unfairness would be remarked upon. If I went home at the same time as everybody else, I would just be another referee who had not survived the cut.

I went back into the FIFA office and said I wanted to go home. They told me to take some time out, play some golf, go into Tokyo. They didn't say 'But don't go home' but that is what they meant. Although I was at a very low ebb, I knew that, if I said the wrong thing, or did the wrong thing, I could damage all my future prospects with FIFA. I remembered again, as I had at Euro 2000, that my friend Paul Durkin had hurt his international career by reacting badly when he was sent home early from the 1998 World Cup.

Not for the first or last time at a major tournament, I was in turmoil. But, in that room in Japan with the FIFA men, I started to pull myself together. I said I'd go for a walk to clear my head and let them know what I was going to do in an hour or so. My family and close friends had been incredibly supportive and I told myself I was also at the finals representing all of England's referees. I returned to my room and telephoned one of them: my dad.

He analysed my game blow-by-blow, suggesting where I could have done better. That was the last thing I needed, frankly, but then he said, 'It doesn't matter though. We all love you. Don't come home. I've brought you up to fight and be strong. When you eventually come home you can hold your head high.' I knew he was right about needing to show that I was strong. I went back to the FIFA officials and told them, to their obvious relief, that I'd had a change of heart. I said I would be training with my colleagues the following morning.

So, the next day, I tried to slip back into a normal routine. As usual I went for a short, brisk ride on a mountain bike as soon as I got up. After breakfast I talked to Volker Roth. He was unhappy with what was happening to me and told me that, if he thought it would make a difference, he would offer to resign. We both understood that it wouldn't make a scrap of difference and so he said, 'It is better that I stay and fight to get you another appointment than walk away.'

I appreciated our talk, but it lasted longer than I realized and I arrived in the lobby at 9.02 – two minutes after the coaches had left for training. I got back on the mountain bike and sped off and was almost killed by one of our buses that had been sent back to pick me up. As I pedalled around a corner, it forced me into the side of the road and I fell into a bush.

I picked myself up and finished the three-mile bike ride to the training ground. I arrived as the other referees were starting their warm-up lap – so I did it on the bike. The class clown was back and everyone had a smile on his face. Word later reached me of how impressed FIFA were with my attitude. And, thanks to Roth's influence, I did get another appointment – as fourth official to Pierluigi Collina at Japan versus Turkey. Just as I had picked myself up off the floor after my cycling accident, I felt that I was managing to end my World Cup positively. But it was definitely ending.

The time arrived when it was announced who was staying and who was going. Perhaps there were one or two were borderline cases but most of the officials knew in their hearts whether they were staying or going home. I knew I was heading for Tring.

My bag was packed but, before I could get away, all the referees were taken out for dinner on a boat in Tokyo. I felt real sympathy for Japan's Toru Kamikawa, who was a victim of FIFA politics. The South Korean official Kim Young-joo had suffered a nightmare in the Brazil versus Turkey game so he could not survive into the next stage of matches. FIFA felt that it would be incorrect to let a ref from the other host nation continue, hence Kamikawa was rejected.

There was a karaoke machine on the boat and Kamikawa sang a Japanese folk song with tears in his eyes. A sense of honour is a central strand of Japanese life. He felt he had let down his country. Of course he had not, but seldom can a song have been delivered more mournfully. I gave a terrible rendition of 'Delilah' – with special emphasis on the line '*Why, why, why?* ...' – but it had far less effect on the room.

The next day those of us who were going home were paid our fees – in cash. I received $22,000 in notes, which I then carried in my hand luggage all the way home. Well, not all of it – I handed over a sizeable amount to pay for the excess weight of my cases, which were stuffed with souvenirs for my family and friends. I was too weary and deflated to argue or put the souvenirs into my hand luggage. I just paid up and then flew home alone. It was a long, long journey.

There is one more observation to make about the 2002 World Cup. When Jens flagged for a foul, and forced me to disallow Italy's late goal, it was because he had seen Filippo Inzaghi tug the shirt of a Croatian defender. That defender was Josip Simunic – the man I was to show the yellow card to three times at the 2006 World Cup.

CHAPTER TWENTY

Gerrard, Zidane and a Full Set

By now you will see that my final years as a referee were punctuated by the big, set-piece tournaments: the World Cups and European Championships. After the 2002 World Cup, there came two seasons in which I was building towards Euro 2004 – or so I believed. But 2002/03 did not start well.

Footballers often suffer 'hangovers' after European or World Cup finals. So do some referees. A major tournament takes its toll on players and officials. Whether they perform well or badly at the tournament, whether luck is with them or deserts them, the vast physical and mental commitment involved makes it a draining experience. Inevitably, once the tournament is over, they relax and try to recuperate. Then, when they return to domestic action the following season, it is difficult for them to pick up the pace again. The summer 'break' is never very long, of course. England's professional referees are only allowed two weeks of complete inactivity before starting training again – gently at first. In week one of pre-season training, I only did a bike ride and a jog. In week two I did three activities and made them more strenuous. The amount of exercise built up and I expected to be fit by the second week in July, because that was when we normally went away somewhere for a training week and usually underwent the fitness tests.

I never got the opportunity to build my momentum and form in 2002/03 because, after one game, I knew I could not finish top of the English refereeing rankings. Well, more accurately, after two games. Because of my commitment to my local clubs, I refereed a friendly between Tring Athletic and Tring Corinthians, but I shouldn't have. I was due to take charge of my first 'official' fixture – Nottingham Forest versus Preston – the following evening and should have cancelled my local fixture, but I did not want to let them down. So we got home from two weeks' holiday in Puerto Pollensa, in Majorca, on the Sunday, and on the Tuesday I did my Tring thing and on the Wednesday I took charge at Forest.

I still maintain that I had a decent game at Forest, and yet the assessor stuffed me. He gave me such a poor mark that I knew my average for the season would not be, could not be, high enough to make me number one. If a football team lose their first game, they don't think that their season is over, but for a referee, one bad mark in August can put him in a position from which he cannot recover.

Let me explain about this business of wanting to be number one. George Cumming's motto for referees at the World Cup was 'Summa Petenda – aim for the highest'. When I was growing up, the adage that was drummed into me by my dad and mum was, 'Good, better, best. Never let it rest, until your good be better and your better best.' Perhaps because of that little verse, or because of something in my own character, I had to strive to be the best at refereeing. When I was working my way up, I would look at those who were getting better marks and think to myself, 'What are they doing better than me? How can I improve my performances to overtake them?'

That was competitive, but it was striving to improve myself, not to damage them. That was a very different attitude to the one I encountered once I was number one. Then some of those ranked below me thought, 'What can we do to undermine Pollie? How can we knock him down?' I hope you can understand the difference in the two attitudes, because I believe the difference is profound.

Anyway, in 2002 I had been England's World Cup referee and by then I knew that, if I performed at my best, I would continue to be the number one referee in England. The marks are not published, and so I cannot tell you accurately how often I was top of the ranking, but referees always had a good idea who had the top average and I wanted it to be me. I wanted to have that number one position because anything less meant that I was not performing at my absolute zenith.

Although I felt hard-done-by about my mark at Nottingham Forest's City Ground, as the 2002/03 season progressed I knew I was not refereeing to the standard I had set myself. I could, and should, have asked for some low-profile matches at the start of the season so that I could build up my form, but that wasn't my style. Like the kid who used to burst into rooms at school, I met the challenge head-on and relished being given big matches.

So, just before Christmas, I was really pleased to be given Liverpool against Everton at Anfield, one of the 'golden games' referees look out for when the fixtures are announced. The game was goalless and went well enough –

until the eighty-seventh minute. I was aware of Liverpool's Steven Gerrard making a challenge on Gary Naysmith but, although I was in a good position in terms of keeping up with play, it turned out to be a poor position to see what happened. An Everton player – I think it was Mark Pembridge – ran across my line of vision at the crucial moment. The assistant referee on that side, Phil Sharp, was watching for an offside or whether the ball was out of play and did not get a good look at Gerrard's challenge either. The fourth official, Neale Barry, later said he saw nothing untoward.

But in the *Guardian* the next day, Kevin McCarra called it a blood-curdling challenge and when I saw the incident on video, it was, indeed, horrific. Naysmith slid in and took the ball. Gerrard, realizing he was about to lose possession, lunged in with both legs outstretched, and both his boots hit Naysmith's legs. I had missed a red card foul. Fortunately, I had not even shown him a yellow card. If I had, I would not have been able to ask subsequently for it to have been upgraded to a red.

On the Monday morning, I sent an email to Joe Guest, at the FA. I said, in part, 'Having viewed the video of the game I can confirm that, had I seen the incident, I would have sent Mr Gerrard from the field of play for serious foul play. Mr Gerrard did come to my dressing room after the game to offer an apology.'

Incidentally, it was very unusual for a player to come and say 'Sorry' like that and I respect Gerrard for doing it, but because of my email the England international was charged with misconduct. He asked for a personal hearing, which was held at Bolton. The video evidence was clear. Gerrard was given a three-game suspension, as he would have done if

I had sent him off during the game. I'd had a twelve-hour day, with nine of those hours spent driving through snow flurries to and from Bolton's Reebok Stadium, and I think Liverpool only went through the charade to show Steven Gerrard how much they cared about him.

There was certainly no residual resentment between Gerrard and me. In fact, in my last season as a referee, he gave me one of his Liverpool shirts, which he signed and on which he added the message, 'To Graham, top ref'.

I have quite a collection of shirts. I have one each from Fabio Cannavaro, Patrick Vieira, Steve McManaman and Luis Figo, among others. Most of them were offered to me by players without my asking. In fact, I never targeted any player until Pierluigi Collina, an avid collector of shirts, told me that he usually decided which one he would like before a match and then set about getting it.

Before Collina refereed England versus Argentina during the 2002 World Cup, he said, 'Which shirt would you like?' I picked David Beckham's shirt, as you do. Sure enough, he returned with it and I was delighted – until I realized that he had not acquired it for me. The purpose of his question had been to show that he could get whichever shirt he wanted – and he wanted the Beckham souvenir for his own collection.

During that 2002/03 season, as I gradually shrugged off the World Cup hangover, I successfully persuaded Zinedine Zidane to give me his shirt. His team, Real Madrid, were away to Borussia Dortmund in the European Champions League. After four minutes, Dortmund took the lead. Then, on the half hour, Ronaldo was sent scampering away by a pass from Zidane. Inside the Dortmund area, the Brazilian was tackled. From my angle it looked a clean challenge, but as we left the field at half-time Ronaldo was waiting for me, shaking his head. He said, 'Very bad referee. Very bad. Penalty.' Players are usually honest in such circumstances so I asked Andy D'Urso, who was the fourth official, about it. He said he had seen a TV replay and that it should have been a penalty.

The tunnel at Dortmund is narrow with a tight staircase and, as we all came out for the second half, I made a point of getting alongside Ronaldo so that I could talk to him. I said, 'I owe you an apology.'

He said, 'Ah, the penalty. So now you owe me a favour.'

I replied, 'Up to now I have made one mistake. If I give you something you don't deserve it becomes two mistakes.'

Zinedine Zidane was listening to our chat and smiled. He said, 'That is the right answer.'

So I said, 'Thank you. At the end of the game is it possible to have your shirt?'

He said, 'If you are good.'

Thirty minutes into the second half, as Real Madrid prepared to take a free-kick, I talked to 'Zizou' again. I asked him, 'Am I good yet?' He made a gesture with his hand – maybe, maybe not. Roberto Carlos was extravagantly off target with the free-kick (which Zidane might have taken if I had not distracted him) but, in stoppage-time substitute Javier Portillo equalized. As the relieved Real players trotted back for the restart, I said to Zidane, 'Chemise?' He smiled, possibly at my French.

Of course I would not have done anything partisan in favour of Zidane or his team. The exchanges between us were just banter – part of the rapport with players which I felt was important and useful. But I did want that shirt, so at the end of the tie I 'just happened' to be next to Zidane. He started to take off his 'chemise' in full view of the spectators, television viewers and the UEFA delegate. I said, 'Not now. In the dressing room.' He gave a Gallic shrug and, to my horror, swapped shirts with Jan Koller, of Dortmund. I thought to myself, 'You are no Collina, Pollie.'

After the match we were actually given replica shirts by Real Madrid. I was given a 'Figo'. But later, after I had showered and changed, there was a knock on the door. In walked Zinedine Zidane and he handed me a shirt. It was the one he had worn in the first half. He'd given his second-half shirt to the Dortmund player. He said, 'Thank you very much. Excellent referee.'

I gave the Figo replica to Peter Dahlgren, the Swedish UEFA delegate and an ex-referee, for his son – but I like to think that was not why he gave me a good mark. He asked me about the conversation he had seen me having with Ronaldo at half-time. I said that I had been told that I had missed a penalty and that I managed the situation by speaking to Ronaldo. I explained to Dahlgren that I was telling Ronaldo I knew what had happened and that he appreciated my honesty. Dahlgren said, 'That is exactly what I had hoped was happening. It shows me what an excellent referee you are, as well as being a good communicator.'

As season 2002/03 progressed, the recovery from my World Cup misadventure continued. The season finished with me refereeing that special anti-racism game between Russia and a team of players from the Russian League which I mentioned in Chapter Seventeen. That fixture helped me wipe my slate clean with Russia, and the season had helped me recuperate from the World Cup. By the time season 2003/04 kicked off, I was flying again – on top of my game and 100 per cent motivated. I was making my good better, and my better best.

Yet halfway through that 2003/04 season, I learned that Mike Riley would be the only English representative at Euro 2004. I will deal with that crushing, devastating disappointment, of course. But, to put it into perspective I need to tell you about another landmark moment in my life and my career which was not a low point.

The 2003/04 season ended with my refereeing what is said to be the most valuable club fixture in the world: the play-off final which determines who is promoted from the Football League to the Premiership. In some ways, being awarded the play-off final in 2004 was a consolation prize for missing out Euro 2004. If I had been selected for the European Championship, I would not have officiated at the game in Cardiff between West Ham and Crystal Palace. It is true, as well, that the play-off final led to some nasty moments, but overall, I would still rate it as a positive experience and a definite highlight of my domestic career. At the age of 40, I had achieved everything I could domestically. I had refereed the Community Shield, FA Cup final, League Cup final and now the Football League's top play-off final. That was a full set.

One of the best things about play-offs in Cardiff, while Wembley was being rebuilt, was that the stadium was almost entirely filled with genuine fans. There was a buzz in the city and the noise inside the stadium was so loud that you could almost feel it as well as hear it.

It did not matter to me who won, but I had a suspicion that Palace would triumph because I sensed a tension among the West Ham players and staff. When the manager, Alan Pardew, came into the referee's room at 2 pm with the team sheet he looked anxious. In noticeable contrast, Palace manager Iain Dowie was relaxed and chatty. I'm sure this confidence communicated itself to his players.

Before the national anthem, Pardew said, 'Don't fall for the old Tomas Repka trick, will you?' Loosely translated, this meant that I should not assume every tackle the Czech defender made was a foul, despite opponents giving that impression.

I said, 'Alan, don't try that one on me again.'

'Well, he's not as bad as they say,' he replied.

Perhaps not, but Repka was bad enough to be the first player I cautioned. My game plan was to let the match flow within the Laws, and to avoid any cheap cautions. Players were aware of the importance of the occasion and that led to a few mistimed early tackles, but nothing nasty and so I man-managed these situations. However, after about half an hour, Repka took a poor throw-in that went straight to a Palace player who headed off towards the West Ham goal. Repka set off in pursuit and felled him with a bad challenge. I cautioned him. In all, I took eight names – three from Palace and five from West Ham.

Neil Shipperley scored for Palace and then, with about ten minutes to go, Palace defender Mikele Leigertwood put in a tired challenge on Michael Carrick inside the penalty area. I was only five yards away, and my first instinct was that it was a foul but, to my surprise, nobody appealed. Under those circumstances a referee will start to doubt his initial, gut reaction. I am not saying penalties are only given when players appeal. If someone handles the ball on the goal-line or commits a blatant foul, then there is no waiting period – it's a penalty and the referee gives it. But, throughout a game there are always marginal, less clear-cut incidents and, on those occasions, a referee will always hesitate momentarily. That is when the genuine, instant reaction of players – or their lack of reaction – can provide a guide.

The other point worth making here is that, as fans and players know, some challenges which are always seen as fouls outside the penalty area are not always punished when they occur inside the penalty area. UEFA talk about referees having a good feel for the game, a good gut reaction. And sometimes, the feeling in your gut is that you should not give a penalty. Referees reading this will understand what I mean, some fans won't. Some people will probably think it is an outrageous statement, but it is the truth. It doesn't accord with the Laws of the Game, but it is right in terms of the spirit of the game.

At the Millennium Stadium that afternoon I paused imperceptibly to wait for West Ham players to turn and shout 'Penalty!' None did. The ball broke away and I let play continue. My assumption was that I had misjudged the challenge and that it had been legitimate. At the final whistle not a single West Ham player, nor any member of the coaching staff, made any comment about the incident.

The fourth official, Neale Barry, came onto the field with some water at the end and I asked him about the penalty incident. He had seen it on a television monitor in the technical area and felt that it was a foul and should have been a spot-kick, but he also said that neither Alan Pardew nor any of his staff had complained. The West Ham supporters in the stadium did not chant 'You don't know what you're doing' at me. Rarely can an incident like that have passed by without a dissenting voice raised. I think that was because it was a close call and it was difficult to tell whether Leigertwood had fouled Carrick or not.

However, there are two matches these days: the actual contest on the field and the match as seen on television. All a referee can do is take charge of the actual match – the one played on grass – and make honest, brave decisions in real time, based on what he sees with one set of eyes. You get one view at one speed and one chance to get it right or wrong – the same as the players do.

But there are twenty-four television cameras at Premiership games, and TV coverage includes instant replays from different angles, with 'super slo-mo'. And when 'experts' in the commentary box, and fans at home, have seen something enough times from enough viewpoints, whatever has happened looks obvious to them. If the ref has got it wrong, then they think he is incompetent.

Although the mistakes made by footballers – all the miss-kicks, the poor passes, the poor positioning, the slowness to get a block in, the miscued headers, the wrong decisions and so on – are sometimes highlighted on TV, the players are seldom subjected to the same level of criticism. People shrug at the mistakes that players make. People get angry about mistakes by referees.

After the Worthington Cup Final, West Ham fans became very angry with me. The after-match analysis on TV showed the 'penalty' incident scores of times and convinced West Ham supporters that they had been robbed. Back at our hotel, I received some abrasive comments from some of them, but I had been hardened to this type of situation over a twenty-four-year career – although family and friends were often upset by the more aggressive remarks.

After dinner, we went into the bar for what we hoped would be a sociable finish to the day but a group of West Ham supporters started to make noisy comments. They had been in the stadium and had not thought it was a penalty at the time, but now TV had told them it was. So they kept up the deliberately provocative, X-rated banter for fifteen minutes, despite the fact that Julia, my wife, was with me.

I decided to speak to them, reasoning that if I gave them my honest account, they might ease up. I told them that yes, with the benefit of slow motion replays from different angles, it probably was a penalty. But there had been no appeals and so I had assumed that I had misjudged the challenge and that it was legal.

As it had in the past in different hotels after different games, the open approach worked. The West Ham lads said they appreciated the time and trouble I had taken to explain things. They thanked me. They said West Ham had not played well and did not deserve to win. I returned to continue my nightcap with Julia.

We skipped breakfast the following morning but as we were preparing to leave a West Ham supporter in the lobby held up a newspaper with a photograph of the tackle – which proved nothing. The enormous headline read, '£25 million error'. A Palace supporter asked me to sign his autograph book, which I did. The West Ham supporter then thrust the paper at me and, in front of Julia, asked, 'Do you want to sign that, you f***ing w***er?'

Unlike the reasonable West Ham supporters from the night before, this one did not look as if he was prepared to listen to an explanation – nor were his six pals who came over. One said, 'You're coming with us in a minibus to east London.'

Laughing, I said, 'I've got my car, thanks.'

One said, 'It wasn't a choice.'

But Julia and I did go home in our own car, and I reflected how unfair and irresponsible that '£25 million error' headline had been. I'd made a difficult, honest judgement in the heat of the moment, based on the evidence in front of me. If I had given the penalty, there was no guarantee that West Ham would have scored. If they had scored, there was no certainty that they would have won.

Who'd be a referee? Well, I would. At age forty I had completed the full set of big domestic games. I had earned them by getting consistently high marks, by being number one. Okay, I was not going to Euro 2004, but there was nothing I could do about that. I had got my head down, driven myself on and had pulled myself up from the disappointment of the World Cup. I had made my best better and proved something important to myself. Who'd be a referee? Me, definitely.

CHAPTER TWENTY-ONE

Not Bitter but Angry

Despite the fact that season 2003/04 ended with me thoroughly satisfied with my form, I do have to tell you how depressing it was to spend the following summer at home instead of in Portugal at Euro 2004.

Throughout my career, I set myself target after target, like a sales person. I was always thinking of the next milestone to reach and pass. And so, naturally, the big international tournaments were the major targets. I had come home early from Euro 2000 and from the 2002 World Cup, but my reputation had survived those setbacks and I had every reason to believe I could aim for Euro 2004 in Portugal.

The first seeds of doubt were sown in January 2003. That was when Graham Barber and I had coffee with Ken Ridden of the FA at a UEFA referees' course. We were pumping him about our chances of big European matches and then Barbs asked, 'What about Euro 2004?'

He was retiring from the international list at the end of 2003 so it was a question asked on my behalf. Ken replied, 'Obviously it will either be Graham or Mike.' He meant

Mike Riley. It was not the answer I expected. In fact, it was a bombshell. I was way ahead of Riley in marks and tournament experience.

Barbs said I was being paranoid; that Ken Ridden was just being cagey. Other people scoffed at the idea that I might not go to Portugal as well. In October I rang Yvan Cornu, UEFA's referees' manager, on another matter and, in the course of our conversation said, 'I know my European marks have been good ...' Cornu interrupted. He said, 'No, they've been exceptional.'

That was reassuring and at the end of our chat I felt more upbeat. But the doubts gnawed away and I learned that Ken Ridden was upset about me. I was very active in the Select Group in England, and was trying to assist Philip Don as the manager of the Group. Someone misinformed Ken that I was manoeuvring to get Philip a top job – Ken's job on UEFA's referees' committee. This was not true. So I telephoned Ken. He said, 'Graham, I do have to tell you at this point there are some committee members backing Riley and not you.'

I asked, 'So how does it look?'

He said, 'As ever, Graham, the criteria will be marks. It's as simple as that. Marks will determine whether you go or not.'

Mike Riley had received a low mark in a Champions League qualifying tie. Given my sequence of marks, that meant it was impossible for him to have a higher average than me. So I said to Ken Ridden, 'I don't think I've got anything to worry about then.'

I was wrong. In December, the UEFA referees committee discussed the appointments for Portugal. My mobile was off and when I turned it on there was a message telling me to ring UEFA. My first thought was that I had been given another European club fixture. I was not expecting any call about Euro 2004. That announcement would be made through the normal, formal channels. But when I telephoned, I was told Yvan Cornu wanted to speak to me. At that moment, I knew.

When Yvan came on the phone, I said, 'It's not good news, is it.' It was a statement, not a question.

He replied, 'No, I'm afraid it isn't. Unfortunately the decision has gone against you and you've not been selected for Euro 2004.' Mike Riley had been chosen ahead of me. Yvan said, 'The criteria used to select the match officials for Portugal were marks, age and previous tournament experience.'

My marks were ahead of Mike Riley's. He was a year younger than me, which was not significant because, in international terms, we would both retire between the same tournaments. I said to Cornu, 'So it must be based on previous tournaments.'

He replied, 'That's the only conclusion I can come to.'

He told me I should not be too disheartened, which was easier said than done. But he said to keep going because there was always the 2006 World Cup in Germany. He added that, given how well I was refereeing, I would have every chance of being selected for Germany.

Somehow I packed my football bag and left for the following day's match: Newcastle against Liverpool, live on Sky. I missed another Steven Gerrard two-footed tackle but, frankly, I don't know how I managed to do the game at all.

I learned later that, at the UEFA meeting, Ken Ridden had proposed Mike Riley instead of Graham Poll. When challenged, he had reminded the others that they had an agreement not to interfere with another country's nominations.

I would have understood if Ken had sat me down and said, 'I know it was not necessarily your fault, but Euro 2000 and the World Cup 2002 did not work out for you and I'm not going to put you forward as England's representative for Euro 2004' – but we did not have that conversation. The only time we talked about my not being selected for Euro 2004 was a long time after the tournament finished. In November 2004, Ken was the assessor when I refereed Everton against Fulham. He asked me to talk to a delegation of Norwegian referees after the game and I travelled back with him to his hotel. He said, 'Everyone is remarkably impressed by the way you have dealt with the situation [of missing Euro 2004]. You have come back stronger and you are refereeing extremely well.'

I let my frustration overflow. I said, 'You always said the selection for Portugal would be on marks. I know this was not the case and so do you. I can move on and I can work with you but I will never, ever forgive you for hurting me and my family.'

He said, 'I know. I was wrong.'

I never did and never could hold a grudge against Mike Riley. He did nothing to influence Ken Ridden or push himself for Euro 2004 at my expense. When he was chosen he was stunned and embarrassed but naturally pleased.

Disappointingly, but not surprisingly, some referees at Staverton could not hide their glee when I was not selected. Graham Barber, Paul Durkin, Steve Dunn, Alan Wiley, Rob Styles, Andy D'Urso, Mike Dean, and Steve Bennett were the most supportive and Riley showed genuine empathy, which I appreciated immensely. Others enjoyed the fact that I had been kicked in the teeth.

It was hard to watch Euro 2004 without an agenda. I thought I would simply be an England fan, cheering David Beckham and the boys from my armchair, but I took as much interest in the refereeing as the progress of my country and I found myself with too many negative thoughts, almost wanting referees to make mistakes.

I did not like discovering that trait in me, especially after others at Staverton had wallowed in my misfortune, so I spoke on the telephone to Craig Mahoney, the Select Group's sports psychologist. I asked if I should continue to watch the Euro 2004 matches.

He said, 'Of course you should. You should keep in touch with top-level European refereeing and international football. You are going to be refereeing games like these so it is important you watch them. But the emotion you should have and continue to feel throughout the tournament is anger. You should be angry that you aren't there. Not bitter but angry.

'Going into next season, you should harness that anger to referee really strongly. You will need a motivation so use this anger to raise your own game. You are already at the top, but great sportsmen find something to make them kick on and become even better. Use your anger to make yourself better.'

He told me to go and see him. So I did. At our meeting, I said that, despite his words, I had no chance of going to the 2006 World Cup. He said, 'Well which English referees do have a chance?'

I replied, 'Mike Riley, obviously. He is in pole position, or Poll's position. And Steve Bennett. He is going well.'

He responded, 'Well, what if Riley has an injury and Benno loses form? Who else from England is in the top group of European referees?'

I replied, 'I am.'

Craig drove the point home, saying, 'So you must have a chance. How big a chance would you say you and the others have got?'

I said that I thought Riley was 80 per cent, Benno maybe 15 per cent and me 5 per cent.

He said, 'Right. When you arrived you said you had no chance. Now your own estimate is a 5 per cent chance. How can you make that 10 per cent?'

Craig got me to talk about my routine before matches and I mentioned, in passing, that I usually had a couple of glasses of wine on the night before a European match.

He said, 'Right. Cut out the wine. Show people you have made a change; are making a special effort. Make the people in UEFA think, "Look at Pollie – he is so determined." Make them think that they cannot ignore you.'

I had my target. I would raise my game. I would aim for Germany 2006.

So I kept viewing Euro 2004 on TV and watched Urs Meier rule out what England thought was a winning goal in the quarter-final against Portugal. Sol Campbell thought he had scored but my friend Urs ruled that John Terry had fouled Portugal goalkeeper Ricardo. I can understand why Meier made the decision. It was a subjective call, but it was an honest call. It was an unpopular one in England but referees should not shirk decisions because they are unpopular. And without Terry's suspect challenge, Meier would not have had a decision to make.

England lost on penalties. David Beckham slipped as he took his kick and scooped the ball up over the crossbar. But, of course, the English media decided the referee was the man responsible for England's exit. In Switzerland, Urs Meier's fourteen-year-old son was approached by an English tabloid newspaper who asked whether his father ever hit him or mistreated him in any way. Reporters and some supporters camped outside the Meier home and so Urs stayed away. He only had six months to go as an international referee and I know that it took tremendous strength of character for him to see out his remaining time and not allow the mob to beat him.

A year later Meier was a guest of the Football Association when Arsenal beat Manchester United in a penalty shoot-out to win the FA Cup. When his face was shown on the big screens, boos rang out at the Millennium stadium. Sometimes it is difficult to be proud to be English.

CHAPTER TWENTY-TWO

Arsenal, United and That Game

The 2004/05 season saw seismic events in English football, but they involved a Portuguese, a Russian, a Frenchman and a Scot. An Englishman based in Tring was involved in some key moments, and I would like to tell you about them.

The Portuguese, of course, was José Mourinho. The Russian was Roman Abramovich, the billionaire owner of Chelsea. Together they set about making Chelsea champions for the first time in fifty years. The Frenchman, Arsenal manager Arsène Wenger, and the Scot, Sir Alex Ferguson of Manchester United, seemed more concerned about their own enmity than about the newcomer. We all soon learned that we could not ignore Mourinho, however.

Just before the start of that 2004/05 season I was invited along to Chelsea's training ground, which was then at Harlington, to the west of London. I was asked to brief the players about changes in the Laws of the Game and some new interpretations.

Mourinho welcomed me into his office and we talked about the two European ties I had refereed when he was coach of FC Porto in Portugal. He said, 'I want you to tell us what we need to do and how we can get through the season without upsetting referees.' Recalling that remark now in the light of what has happened since, I am surprised that he kept a straight face.

Mourinho was complimentary. He said, 'Chelsea want to be the best so we wanted the best referee here.' He was helpful: when I pointed out that I had a flight to Switzerland later that day, he brought the players' meeting forward a little. He was restrained: he took a back seat as I ran through the law changes and answered questions from the players.

It went very well, I thought, and there were no problems a couple of weeks later when I refereed Mourinho's first Premiership match, in which Chelsea beat Manchester United.

But, in December 2004, I was in charge of Chelsea's visit to Arsenal. That was when Mourinho ceased to think I was the 'best referee' and when my opinion of him changed. The game was an epic. It ended 2–2 and was full of good football, but the next day's headlines highlighted a controversy over a goal scored from a free-kick by Arsenal's Thierry Henry. Well, the media thought it was a controversy, and so did Mourinho and his players – I just applied the Laws.

I penalized a foul, about five yards outside the penalty area, in line with the left-hand post. Thierry stood over the ball as the Chelsea players shuffled into position in front of him. Thierry asked me, within earshot of some Chelsea men, 'Quick or slow? Can I take it, please?'

I replied, 'Yes.' I stepped aside and gestured with my arm that the kick was about to be taken. Petr Cech, the Chelsea keeper, was still standing by the left-hand post (his right), making sure that part of the goal would be covered by the defensive 'wall' of players. Chelsea's Eidur Gudjohnsen realized what was about to happen and tried to get his goalkeeper to move to the middle of the goal. At the moment Eidur turned his head to shout at Petr, Thierry clipped the ball towards the unguarded side of the goal. It went in and Chelsea went potty.

Thierry's goal made it 2–1 to Arsenal, but Eidur equalized later and Chelsea remained at the top of the League. That did not appease Mourinho. When he addressed the media, he said, 'If you can forget the way Arsenal scored their second goal – if you can call it a goal – the result was correct. But it's difficult for me to forget Arsenal's second goal, so I don't think the result was fair. If I speak about it maybe I would have to go to the FA and be sent to the stands for a few weeks or pay a large fine, and I should keep my money for Christmas presents. I am more than unhappy, but I cannot say the words in my heart and soul. I just cannot do it.' Then he added this quite extraordinary postscript: 'In pre-season, we had a top referee at our training ground who showed us all the rules of football. So I have no doubts about it. One of the things he explained to us was walls, distance, whistle – everything was clear. I have a lot of respect for Mr Poll. He is a top referee. But the rules of the game are the same all over the world – in China, Japan, Mexico or England, in the top league or under-15s.'

Mourinho did not bother to tell anyone that the 'top referee' who had explained the Laws to Chelsea was Mr Poll. And if he honestly thought that I had talked about 'walls, distance, whistle' at that briefing, then he was not listening. I did not deal with the subject of taking free-kicks because nothing had changed, and I was only dealing with new Laws and new interpretations. The situation with quick free-kicks was exactly as it had been two years previously when I had allowed Jimmy Floyd Hasselbaink to score for Chelsea in an FA Cup replay before West Ham had organized their wall. Arsène Wenger commented, after Thierry's goal against Chelsea, that the players should know the Laws and the goalkeeper should remain alert. Hear, hear!

What was instructional from my point of view was that Mourinho used me as a scapegoat for his team's lack of awareness – and that he produced a version of my visit to the training ground which was not what I knew had happened. Mourinho's version suited his message, but it was not accurate.

A couple of months after that game at Highbury, my friend the Swedish referee Anders Frisk was the recipient of even more unacceptable criticism by Mourinho. Again, the Chelsea manager's version did not tally with the facts. Anders sent off Chelsea's Didier Drogba in the second half of a Champions League match against Barcelona at the Nou Camp stadium. Afterwards, Mourinho claimed that he had seen Barça manager Frank Rijkaard enter the referee's room at half-time. That was against UEFA regulations and the implication was that Rijkaard had influenced Anders in some way, and that had led to the sending-off of Drogba.

The irrefutable truth is that Rijkaard did not enter the ref's room. We know that for certain, because Pascal Fratellia of UEFA was in the room with Anders. But Mourinho had a version which suited his purposes, and Chelsea fans believed their manager. Anders retired prematurely from refereeing, FIFA announcing that it was because of 'death threats against his family'.

When I missed out on Euro 2004, Anders had been wonderfully supportive. He told me, 'I feel someone has wronged you, so do what you can to make it right. I think you are a fantastic referee. The best ship is sitting at the harbour. You must sail again.'

When Anders decided he did not want to risk going to sea again, to use his metaphor, I was personally saddened for him as a man and a friend. I was also saddened for refereeing and for football.

With his abilities as a motivator, organizer and tactician, José Mourinho does not need to target referees – to use them as diversions when his team does not win and to put them under pressure to try to affect their decision-making. He had some success doing just that when he was working in Portugal, and so he imported the tactic with him to England. I also believe, fervently, that he made Chelsea players think it was acceptable – desirable even – to blame referees for their own failings. Because José produced inaccurate accounts of events to fit his indignant view of the world, the Chelsea players thought that was the correct way to behave as well. After I sent off John Terry against Spurs, the Chelsea captain had no qualms about implying that I and the other three match officials were part of a conspiracy. The Chelsea captain was just taking his lead from the Chelsea manager.

Don't forget that in my last match at Chelsea, when they played Manchester United and Senhor Mourinho used atrocious foul language, I learned exactly what sort of behaviour the Chelsea manager thought was acceptable towards match officials. José Mário dos Santos Mourinho Félix is a truly great coach, but as a human being his methods are open to question.

So, let's leave him. Let's move on to two other managers near the top of the English League in that 2004/05 season – Arsène Wenger and Sir Alex Ferguson – and let me tell you about refereeing the match between their teams at Highbury which I consider one of my best performances of my career.

To put the fixture in context, we need to know about a game in which Mike Riley was the ref. That was in October of that 2004/05 season, at Old Trafford. Arsenal went into the game hailed as 'The Invincibles'. They had put together a sequence of forty-nine unbeaten games in the Premiership. But in match number fifty, Sir Alex's men won 2–0.

It was a bruising, bitterly contested encounter, and long-standing hostilities between the clubs were bubbling just below the surface throughout the game. They erupted afterwards in the tunnel and in the dressing rooms area. In a scuffle between players and staff on both sides, slices of pizza were hurled.

So when the season reached the return fixture, at Highbury in February, the game did not need any hyping-up. That did not stop Sky from doing just that, of course. The satellite TV company showed endless repeats of previous red card incidents between the teams. I took it as the highest possible compliment that I was appointed to take charge of a game which newspapers predicted would be 'unrefereeable'. I understand that both clubs asked for me to be in charge, which, again, was a tremendous compliment. I had earned the respect of two clubs with whom I had a fairly chequered history.

Sir Alex Ferguson is not exactly known for praising referees, but he is well known for complaining if referees do not add on enough time (if his team are trailing) or when they add too much time (when his team are winning!). At one game at Old Trafford, at the start of the 1996/97 season, United fought back from 2–0 down to level the scores but because I 'only' allowed five added minutes, Fergie raced towards me at the finish of the match. Brian Kidd, his assistant at the time, got hold of one sleeve of his manager's coat but Fergie was so determined to get to me, he wriggled out of the coat. Thankfully, his assistant managed to grab his other arm and keep him away from me.

Managers had to send their own match reports to the Premier League. Usually they harped on about one specific incident about which they felt aggrieved, but on one occasion Sir Alex made a more general point. He said of me, 'This is supposed to be the future of English refereeing. He's good but he makes too many mistakes.'

On yet another occasion – before the start of the second half of United's game at Liverpool in November 2003 – United's Rio Ferdinand asked me, 'Are you going to give us something this half?'

I said, 'Did the gaffer tell you to say that? You wouldn't have thought of it yourself.'

I spotted Sir Alex Ferguson, who had overheard the exchange and had a broad grin on his face. He said, 'Well, I've seen you have better halves.'

Gradually, over the course of many seasons involving many controversies, I earned the grudging respect of Sir Alex. In my last season, he was asked at a media conference about Howard Webb. Sir Alex remarked that it appeared Howard was being groomed to 'take over' from me as the country's top official. He then added that, in his opinion, I had been 'the best referee in England over the last ten years'. That short phrase is locked away in my memory banks because it meant such a lot to me.

My relationship with Arsenal had been much more fraught. I had endured problems with them ever since February 1998 when I cautioned four of their players and sent off

Patrick Vieira for a second yellow card offence during the Coca Cola Cup semi-final at Chelsea. Gary Lewin, the Arsenal and England physiotherapist, came to see me after the game and told me the players were 'confused' over a number of my decisions.

So I contacted Arsenal a few days later to tell them I was willing to talk to the players and manager Arsène Wenger. They could raise anything they wanted about the match. But the request was rejected out of hand. I was told, 'We have our job to do and we'll do it our way. You do your job. That's it.'

So we went about those jobs without building any bridges. My job was to referee their games fairly and to make honest decisions. Many of those decisions upset them. I got many of those decisions right, but I accept that I got some wrong. That is life. That is football.

I certainly got some things wrong when I refereed Arsenal against Liverpool at Highbury in the first Monday night live TV game of 2000/01. Because Euro 2000 had not gone well for me, I was not in the right frame of mind for such a big match. It was probably my worst refereeing display, not so much for decision-making but in terms of my mental approach to the match. If I could change one game in my entire domestic career, it would be that one. I sent off Liverpool's Gary McAllister and Didi Hamann, plus Arsenal's Patrick Vieira; I booked four players. But, although I was not happy with my performance, when I looked at a recording of the game, the only really poor decision was to send off Hamann. I had already cautioned him and was convinced that he then pulled back Robert Pires by grabbing his shirt. When I looked at the incident again, however, the Liverpool player did not touch Pires. So I successfully asked the FA to withdraw that second caution. We did have a procedure to do that, and it meant that Hamann was not suspended for being sent off.

I was also in completely the wrong frame of mind before another Arsenal match. That was in December 2001 when I had just heard that Gerald Ashby had died. He was just fifty-two.

When I first became a Premier League referee, Gerald was a top ref and, although our personalities were very different, I gravitated towards him and was always pleased to listen to his advice. Once refs became professional, we each had a refereeing coach appointed. Gerald had retired by then and became my coach. That meant that I spoke to him on the telephone after every game to discuss issues and so on. I also telephoned him at other times and he was wonderfully encouraging, but then Gerald was a wonderful man; thoroughly decent and utterly honest. He was one of the biggest influences on my refereeing. He helped me work on my composure; he set me standards; he ensured I never became complacent. The moment I heard of his death was the first time my children saw me stifling tears.

I was struggling to control my emotions again in my car before the game. I went into Brent Cross shopping centre and bought a black tie, which I wore instead of my Premier League tie. I wore a green top for the match to accommodate a black armband on my sleeve. But my request for a minute's silence was turned down – because it was 'not really a football matter but a refereeing issue'. Instead, the four officials held a minute's silence in the dressing room before the game. Again, I broke down.

Clearly, I should not have taken charge of the game, which was against Newcastle, but somehow I did. I refereed by instinct. I had to send off Craig Bellamy of Newcastle and Arsenal's Ray Parlour and I did not have a good game. I wrongly awarded a penalty against Arsenal's Sol Campbell. It was a poor decision. But the only reason I got through the game at all was that Gerald had taught me well.

Arsenal lost 3–1 and Thierry Henry led the protests at the finish. I had enjoyed a good relationship with Thierry up until that moment but he was apoplectic and absolutely castigated me. Incredibly, he confused me with Steve Dunn, who had handled Arsenal's FA Cup Final against Liverpool the previous May. Thierry thought Arsenal should have had a couple of penalties in the Cup Final, and now he was screaming at me on the Highbury pitch. He said, 'You've cost us again!'

The Arsenal supporters knew nothing of my grief about Gerald Ashby. They did not know that Thierry was abusing me, in part at least, for decisions Steve Dunn had made seven months earlier. They just saw their hero confronting a referee and so it was not difficult to work out which side they would be on. The crowd gave me more abuse than I have ever suffered before.

Later, when I was in the welcome sanctuary of my dressing room, Patrick Vieira arrived and said that he was conveying apologies from Thierry. But a month after that, Arsenal's David Dein, who was the Arsenal vice-chairman and a big name at both the FA and the Premier League, had a pre-arranged meeting with the referees' Select Group at Staverton. He made a presentation about refereeing abroad. He felt it was better in Italy than in England. We did not agree. We told him that if he saw their referees week in and week out, he would see all their mistakes. More importantly from my point of view, I took the opportunity to have a private word with Dein. I wanted to confront him about a rumour that Arsenal had asked that I should not referee any more of their home games.

I had gone to Staverton armed with a printout of all the matches I had refereed there – thanks to those results sheets my dad had persuaded me to start all those years before. The printout showed that everything about those games was normal – an average number of bookings and sendings-off, no statistically abnormal results. Dein, however, had his own view. We spoke for about twenty minutes and, finally, he said, 'We don't think you're a bad referee. We think you're a good, strong referee. But we just don't think you can referee at Highbury.'

The Premier League did not ban me from Highbury – but I did impose my own ban after that meeting with Dein. I felt that it would be unwise to referee there with the home team so convinced I was about to have a bad game.

So I stayed away for three and a half years, until 28 March 2004, when Arsenal were at home to Manchester United, when I reckoned that everyone would be more focused on the football than the referee. In the tunnel before the game, Roy Keane was his usual surly self and I tried to lighten the atmosphere by saying, 'Come on Roy, give us a smile.' Patrick Vieira joined in the banter but Keane's expression did not change. We kept on saying, 'Come on Roy. Smile.' Eventually he turned to the Arsenal captain and said, 'If we were nine points clear, like you, I would be smiling too.' And with that, his face did crack into a grin. The tension was broken.

The game went well. Thierry scored just after half-time, and Louis Saha equalized for United just before the finish. I had a good match. The 'ghost' of previous visits to Highbury had been laid. Hence, when it came to the 'unrefereeable' game the following season, 2004/05, both United and Arsenal wanted me to take charge.

Not for the first or last time, I used some advice from Pierluigi Collina. He always refused to speak to coaches or players before a game because he felt it might suggest a lack of confidence, a weakness. So when I was offered the chance to address the Arsenal and Manchester United managers, or club officials, in the build-up to the match, I said, 'No thanks.'

Instead, as I always did, I tried to assess the mood of the players by observing them as they warmed up. If they were relaxed, I could adjust my refereeing accordingly. If they were tense or aggressive, I could plan to referee in a different way. To me, that made more sense than having a cup of coffee with a chief executive or manager and asking him to ensure good behaviour from the players.

But that day at Highbury, the mood during the warm-up was not much of a clue as to what was about to unfold. As the players did their stretches and jogs, there were plenty of smiles, but later there were none at all.

The 'mind games' started as soon as I pressed the bell for the teams to leave their dressing rooms. Neither team emerged, because neither wanted to be first. Each wanted to leave the other standing about in the corridor. I pressed the bell a second time. Again nothing happened. Arsène Wenger and Sir Alex Ferguson were keeping watch by their dressing room doors, each waiting for the other to blink first in this stand-off.

I then decided on a personal approach. I walked to the Arsenal dressing room. As I passed United's room, Sir Alex let me know in three, chilling words what he expected of the game. He looked me in the eyes and said, 'Good luck tonight.' The '... and you will need it' was unspoken but implied. I reached the Arsenal room, asked Arsène, politely, to let his team out, and he did.

I walked along the tunnel, next to Arsenal's Patrick Vieira and tried to lighten the atmosphere. I said to Patrick, 'Remember this fixture last year when we made Roy laugh as we waited to go out on to the pitch?'

Patrick replied, 'That will not happen tonight.'

As we walked past the United dressing room I asked Sir Alex to send his team out. He answered, 'Roy's not ready.'

I said, 'OK. No problem. He can join us in a minute.'

So the Arsenal line of players and the four match officials made their way towards the end of the Highbury tunnel.

Patrick dropped back and almost as soon as I had realized that he was not at the head of the Arsenal line, I heard raised voices further back in the tunnel. Patrick and Gary Neville were in each other's face. Patrick was saying that he wanted to break the England defender's legs.

At that moment, Roy arrived. He said, 'Pick on someone your own size.'

I thought then, and have always thought, that was a brilliant comment, with six foot four inches Vieira squaring up to five foot eleven Gary Neville. But I did not have time to admire the playground taunt because now Patrick was squaring up to Roy.

Patrick said, 'I'll break your legs as well.'

Roy replied, 'If you were that good, you'd be playing for Real Madrid.'

It was another clever riposte – Patrick had been courted by Real the previous summer – but I could not stand about admiring Roy's repartee.

I could have 'sent them off', although we had not even made it to the pitch yet. Some disciplinarians will tell you that is what I should have done; that I should have dealt severely with them there and then. But I needed the Frenchman and the Irishman on the pitch. I knew that if I could manage them during the game – and I felt sure I could – then the two influential captains could help me control a volatile game. I also thought that sending them off before the kick-off would ramp up the tension.

So I split them up, and we went out onto the Highbury pitch. When the time came for the toss of the coin, I pointed to their captains' arm bands and told them I expected their help and co-operation during the game. Patrick and Roy refused to shake hands. Neither was willing to call 'heads' or 'tails' so I assigned the sides of the coin for them.

The testosterone was still coursing through the players' veins when they kicked off. Tackles went flying in. I awarded six free-kicks in the opening two minutes as I stuck to my game plan of keeping a lid on everything at the start.

Ashley Cole, then still an Arsenal player, claimed an early penalty after going down with what looked to me like a comically unconvincing dive. In fact, it looked so bad to me that I thought he might have been trying to make a point about an innocuous tackle on Wayne Rooney by Sol Campbell at Old Trafford in the previous meeting which resulted in a penalty. I did not award anything in this match but made a point of running close to the Arsenal full-back and saying, 'Careful Ashley ...' I did not want to caution a player so early in a powder-keg game for a technical offence.

A few minutes later, Gabriel Heinze became aggressive when I awarded a free-kick against United. He thought, or perhaps pretended he felt, that I had reacted to the crowd. I put out my hand, palm outwards, as a 'calm down' gesture, but Gabriel was barging forwards and almost bounced off my hand. Roy joined in the protests, and a little posse of players formed. I told the United players I was not going to be intimidated by them, or the Arsenal crowd – I was going to be impartial.

As I continued to clamp down on anything looking like a foul, Roy came over and said, 'You're making it worse.'

I replied, 'Give me two more minutes and the game's yours.'

I hoped that my rigorous opening gambit would tell the players I was in charge and that, after that, they would have confidence in me and not try to settle their own feuds.

And, immodest or not, it worked. The 'unrefereeable' game was an absolute epic, with some magnificent, high-tempo football. Patrick scored and Ryan Giggs equalized. Denis Bergkamp put Arsenal ahead again just before half-time but nine minutes after the break, Cristiano Ronaldo equalized again. Four minutes later Ronaldo got another and, a minute before the finish, John O'Shea grabbed a fourth for United.

I handed out six cautions and one red card. The red was when Mikael Silvestre headbutted Freddie Ljungberg. As Silvestre left the field, Sir Alex, who had not seen the off-the-ball incident, asked him what had happened. Mikael replied, 'He pissed me off so I butted him.'

The only other contentious issue was the outburst of profanities from Wayne Rooney, which I have dealt with elsewhere. I shall return to the subject later in this book. But on that day, in that difficult match, I dealt with it by involving Roy Keane in calming down young Wayne. So I think I was right not to send off Roy in the tunnel and correct not to send off the hot-headed Rooney. Gordon Taylor, chief executive of the Professional Footballers' Association, thought so as well. He wrote thanking me for the way I had handled the match.

If I had let the game explode, it could have done terrible damage to the image of football and the English Premiership. Instead, we had a fixture which enhanced the reputation of both.

CHAPTER TWENTY-THREE

Betrayed but Selected

The 2004/05 season ended with one of my top ten games. It is impossible for me to pick the best match of my career, the most satisfying achievement or the favourite highlight – although that doesn't stop people asking me. But if I had to give some games back – to have them erased from history and from my memory – then I would definitely keep matches like the FA Cup Final, World Cup games, European Championships, play-off finals and so on. Despite the fact that there were disappointing circumstances surrounding some of them, the big, prestigious, memorable appointments probably comprise the ten or so high points of my refereeing career. And right up there, near the very pinnacle of that top ten, would be the 2005 UEFA Cup Final.

Remember how difficult it was for me to sit and watch Euro 2004 in Portugal the previous summer; how unfair and political it was that I did not referee in that tournament? Yet, instead of becoming bitter and demotivated, I remained completely professional, 100 per cent focused and utterly committed. I had lifted myself to referee as well as I possibly could.

In acknowledgement of that, UEFA, who had not selected me for Portugal in 2004, picked me for one of their top two appointments at the end of the following season. They could not give me the Champions League final, because Liverpool were involved, but they gave me the next best thing, the UEFA Cup Final – and it was in Portugal. There was a nice symmetry about that. It felt like redemption.

Given a choice between Euro 2004 and the UEFA Cup Final the following summer, I would have taken the Final. Honestly. Going to Euro 2004 would have meant recognition as one of the top dozen referees in Europe and would have probably involved doing a couple of group games at best. Getting the UEFA Cup Final in 2005 meant they thought I was one of their top two – and some of the committee men told me that I would have been given the Champions League final if Liverpool had not been participating.

There is a maxim about the important thing being not how low you drop but how high you bounce back. I don't care if it is a cliché or not. It was pertinent for me because I knew I could not have bounced back any higher. I had recovered from the dismal disappointment of missing Euro 2004 with a successful, thoroughly enjoyable season and I was rounding it off with the biggest appointment UEFA could give me.

Some of the credit had to go to Craig Mahoney, the referees' sports psychologist, who had found such apposite words when there was a danger that the poisonous feelings about missing Euro 2004 could corrode my attitude and belief. Some of the credit should also go, as always, to my family, for providing unstinting and unquestioning support. Whenever I was with my family, I remembered what was really important but I also gained the strength and resolve to work harder and referee at my very best.

So, in May 2005, when I headed for Portugal, Julia, Mum, Dad and Graham Barber came with me. Mike Tingey and Glenn Turner were the assistants; Steve Bennett was the fourth official. It was particularly good having Benno with us because he and I could reminisce about the fact that we did one of the Isthmian League Cup Finals together years earlier, with me as ref and him as fourth official.

By a quirk, the UEFA Cup Final was at the home stadium of one of the competing teams, Sporting Lisbon. They were playing CSKA Moscow, and although Russian teams were not followed by huge crowds away from home, the fact that the match was at the José Avalade Stadium ensured that it was a 45,000 sell-out.

The Portuguese fans, however, did not have a great evening. Their team took the lead, through Roderigo, but Brazilian midfielder Daniel Carvalho set up three goals for Moscow, scored by Alexei Berezutskiy, Yuri Zhirkov, and Vágner Love.

Neither did I have a great summer after that Final. During the 2004/05 season I had been getting pains in one leg which I thought were a hamstring problem. They were actually referred pain from back damage and the real problem was in the sacroiliac joints, which are on both sides of the base of the spine. The sacroiliac joints are part of the pelvic girdle – I know, because I have had to become an expert on them. In the summer of 2005 I had to have injections in the base of my spine, without analgesic. Ever since then, I have needed to have the sacroiliac joints 'cracked open' every few weeks by Gary Lewin, the Arsenal and England physiotherapist.

After the injections, which were the week after the UEFA Cup Final, I set about losing some weight and getting super fit. I had been fit enough to take charge of a European Final but I wanted to be fitter still – because I hoped that the 2005/06 season would culminate in my going to the World Cup. But because I was recovering from the injections in my back, I could not do 'impact work' – anything that involved my legs thumping down onto the ground. I still worked my plums off for six weeks, however. I went swimming and cycling and used a step machine. Because I was doing exercises with which I was not familiar, I could not gauge how hard I should work, and so, to be on the safe side, I did too much. I used to cycle as fast as I could up a hill near my home, freewheel back down and then pedal like fury back up again – and again and again. When I got home, my legs were wobbly and I needed to sit down to stop myself fainting with exhaustion.

For the swimming, I went to Hemel Hempstead sports centre, but I did not actually swim. I put buoyancy aids around my waist and 'ran' across the deep end as fast as I could. I waded across, upright in the water, with my arms pumping and my legs going up and down some distance from the bottom of the pool. Some would say that it was not the first time in my life I had been out of my depth. Some would also say that when I refereed I looked as if I had a buoyancy aid around my waist. I certainly looked very odd to the other pool users when I turned up nearly every day at about 11am. Two lanes were roped off for 'serious swimmers' and I restricted myself to the other lanes. So I only disturbed the 'leisure swimmers', most of whom were elderly ladies at the time of day I went, but I imagine I did look fairly disturbing.

I had to do this tough exercise work through the entire summer. I did it because I was driven by the knowledge that the following summer I hoped to be at the World Cup.

The first impact work I was able to do was at the referees' pre-season training week at an army base in Aldershot. I was really looking forward to that training camp because I would be with my mates and because the physical workouts would help my fitness campaign. Yet that week at Aldershot brought the biggest act of betrayal I have ever suffered.

We stayed in a nearby hotel and went to and from the camp each day by minibus. We trained exceptionally hard from Monday to Thursday – really, really hard. The last exercise on the Thursday was a 'combat relay' which was the most exhausting thing any of us had ever experienced. We were split into three teams and had to compete in three consecutive events. The first involved a trailer with a wheel off. We had to lift the trailer without jacks, secure the wheel and then push and pull this thing 200 metres. The second element of the race involved lifting barrels and other heavy lumps of kit over obstacles using planks and ropes and goodness knows what. Finally, we had to run carrying a telegraph pole. We did this for three miles over a cross-country course which included wading through water.

The Army trainers were so pleased with our attitude and our efforts over four gruelling days that they cancelled the Friday morning session and invited us to a barbecue in the sergeants' mess on the Thursday evening. We were told we could and should let our hair down. The Select Group officials were joined by three referees' managers – Joe Guest, Keren Barratt, and Ron Groves – and we all had a good time.

I had a very good time. Together with a few of the others, plus the army officer who had supervised the training programme, I took part in a 'port challenge'. By the end of the evening, I was seriously inebriated. In fact I was as inebriated as a newt.

In my defence, I had been on a diet and lost a stone during the summer. That, combined with severe dehydration from the intense training, probably meant that I could not hold my drink as well as I imagined. Another mitigating factor was that I was on private property, away from the eyes of the public, and knew I would be taken back to the hotel by minibus. I could also argue that drinking with colleagues after a tough few days is a worthwhile bonding exercise.

I could say a lot of things – but I did have too much to drink and I was blotto. I wasn't shouting, or aggressive or anything. I was ill. Uriah Rennie looked after me and guided me back to my hotel room but I was sick near reception and along one of the corridors – and then in a bucket by the side of my bed continually throughout the night.

The next morning, before anyone said anything to me, I got rid of the contents of the bucket, cleaned up the room completely and went down to reception to talk to the duty manager. I apologized for being ill the night before and said that I hoped I had not caused any problems or embarrassed anyone. I offered to pay for any cleaning bills. He said there had been no complaints and that, as far as he and his staff were concerned, there was no problem.

I got home eventually and telephoned Keith Hackett to apologize. He too said there was nothing for which to apologize. And so I went off on a family holiday the next day. I have felt better, but I thought the episode was over.

However, within hours of our arrival in Sardinia, Keith telephoned to say that he had received an anonymous, misspelled email. Copies had been sent to his secretary Kelly Wright, to Graham Noakes (Professional Games Match Officials Limited company secretary) and to Joe Guest, the Football Association's referees' officer. The email made allegations about my behaviour at Aldershot and, said Keith, the story was going to be in a newspaper.

My family deserved a holiday, but I had to spend it dealing with telephone calls about this story. Julia had always insisted that we had two weeks in the summer away from football, where I was just Graham and Dad and not a referee, but there was no escaping from football or from my refereeing life on that holiday. And I even felt I needed to take care where I put the family rubbish. I did not want a photographer taking a picture of empty wine bottles – that's the stage things had reached.

The email which wrecked the Poll family holiday had been sent from aldershot1234@hotmail.com and so it was clear that someone – one of my colleagues, one of my apparent friends – had gone to the trouble of setting up an untraceable hotmail account to remain anonymous. The email did not name me. It merely talked about 'Someone who lives in Tring and will be England's World Cup referee in Germany 2006' – which narrowed it down to a group of one.

The email alleged that I had consumed 'at least one and a half bottles of port plus a number of Jack Daniels and Coke'. If that were true, I would have needed an ambulance, not a minibus. The email made a series of other allegations about my behaviour, some of which were partially true. It said, 'If it was anyone else they would be dismissed but as he is your favourite he wont [*sic*] be sacked. He is representing England at the World Cup – is this the type of person we want representing us at the finals?'

The 'red top' tabloid newspaper which carried the story did so under a headline saying, 'Poll in booze shame'. The report exaggerated the account of my behaviour even more than the email had done.

Who sent the email? Who sold the story to the newspaper? I don't think they were the same person. I think the emailer was one of my colleagues who was present at Aldershot and I think he also told the person who sold the story to the newspaper. The email was sent to all the pertinent people and to their correct email addresses, so it was certainly done with inside knowledge. The informant could not go to the World Cup himself, but clearly wanted to damage my chances.

The Premier League press office announced that an investigation was being conducted 'in the wake of allegations concerning Graham Poll' but the truth was that the Premier League were really trying to discover the identity of the person or persons who sent the email. There was no investigation into my behaviour, because everyone knew what had happened and that I had apologized.

I made a special effort to get to Staverton after a European game for the first get-together of 2005/06, stood up in the meeting room in front of everyone and apologized. I said I was sorry about my behaviour and for any embarrassment I had caused. I said, 'I apologize to all but one of you.' I added, 'The person who sent the email should take it home and show his wife or child and tell them what he has done. But he won't do that of course, just as he didn't have the balls to put his name on his email.'

Peter Heard, the chairman of Colchester United, who was also chairman of Professional Group Match Officials Limited, stood up next. He said that I had made a mistake and admitted it, but that the email and leak to the press were divisive and seriously harmful to the entire group. He said that if he found out who sent the email, that person would be sacked. He then said, 'I want these people to leave the room' and started listing names. Mine was the first announced, because it was a fair bet that I had not sent the email. The other names on the list were people that I had eliminated – people that I knew would not do that to me – and men the Premier League had eliminated.

Eventually, only four people were left in the room, although they were not all 'suspects'. Of course, nobody owned up. The sneak just left the others smeared with the taint of suspicion.

The referees all think they know who it was and, months later, one of the refs said he thought three or four of us should have given the sneak a thumping to drum home the message that there should be a code of loyalty. I don't agree with the idea of a punishment beating – tempting though it is – but I do think there should be a code of loyalty. I could use this book to tell tales about lots of the refs – about drinking, womanizing, gambling – but I won't because those guys were colleagues of mine.

The Aldershot episode signalled an end for me: the end of my being able to relax at Staverton. After Aldershot, I was always on my guard in front of the other referees. The old days of a group of blokes sharing a common purpose and common experiences were gone. The 'good old days' had started to disappear when the Red Wine Club disbanded because Paul Durkin, Steve Dunn and Graham Barber retired. The days of being relaxed and trusting were gone for ever once that email was sent.

The board of Professional Group Match Officials Limited felt they needed to show the public that referees could not get drunk without being disciplined, so they announced that I was suspended for two games and even named the games. I believed that was wrong, because referees are taken off matches all the time without the public knowing. This time, they made a point of announcing publicly that I was being punished and that handed a victory to the emailer.

To soften the blow, I was allowed to choose the dates of my suspension. I selected weeks which enabled us to take another family holiday – the one in Sardinia had been wrecked by all the phone calls about Aldershot – and so I served my suspension in Jamaica. We stayed with Peter Prendergast, my mate the FIFA referee. As I was not banned by the Football Association, I refereed a Jamaican Premier League match. I took charge of a fixture between Tivoli Gardens and Rivoli, at a stadium known locally as The Hole, and had a wonderful time. The *Jamaican Gleaner* newspaper said the game was 'superbly controlled by British referee Graham Poll'.

Although the Aldershot episode was a vicious act of betrayal, I stopped feeling bitter about the sad emailer because the jealousy which ate away at him so much led to my having a lot of fun in the Caribbean.

There was a postscript to this episode when I started the 2005/06 season by refereeing Everton against Manchester United. In the tunnel, Roy Keane gave me what I think you would call 'an old-fashioned look' and said, 'If you can't take it, don't drink it.'

I said, 'Well, if anyone should know Roy, you should.'

Then he said, 'It said in the paper that you jumped on a car but didn't damage it. It must have been a f***ing Hummer, because you would have squashed anything else.'

Wayne Rooney asked, 'What happened, Pollie?'

I said, 'I got pissed.'

He just chuckled but seemed disappointed that there was not some more outrageous story. He said, 'Was that all?' Yep, that was all.

Then Phil Neville said, 'They only have a go at good players and it is the same with referees.'

So, although I do regret getting drunk at Aldershot, it did not damage my standing with footballers and the 2005/06 domestic season started well for me and continued to go well. That entire season was really always about the World Cup, however. Every match, every week, was a step closer to Germany. Every appointment I was given was an opportunity to impress – or to let myself down.

In the year 2000, when I learned that I was going to that year's European Championships, Graham Barber said to me, 'Pollie, there is now only one person who can stop you achieving what you want to in football. You have reached a level, and gained a level of recognition, which means that only one person can stop you now. That person is you.'

Now that we all know what happened in Germany, that sounds like an ominous warning, but that was not how Barbs meant it in 2000. He meant that my future was in my own hands. It was up to me to grasp every opportunity. So, throughout the 2005/06 season I was striving to seize the chance of going to the world's biggest football event.

Early in the previous season, FIFA had put me on their short list of forty-four and asked me to nominate three assistants, from whom two would go with me to the World Cup if I was selected. For the first time, teams of officials from the same country would officiate at World Cup matches. I chose Mike Tingey, Glenn Turner and Phil Sharp.

To prepare us for the World Cup, I had two of those three with me as assistants for nearly every domestic appointment but the most striking difference that season was the number of international games I was given. In a normal season, I would do eight or nine. In 2005/06 I did seventeen.

That was not a coincidence, of course. FIFA were appraising my performances and an early indication that they thought well of me came when Pierluigi Collina retired a year early. He had signed a deal to advertise Opel cars and the Italian FA thought that was a problem because Opel sponsored AC Milan. So Pierluigi stopped refereeing and I was given one of his fixtures: a World Cup qualifier between Spain and Serbia. Me! Taking over from Pierluigi!

The ultimate accolade for me, however, was to be given Bahrain against Uzbekistan. That might look like a surprising fixture of which to be so proud, but the circumstances were unique. The two teams were drawn together in the two-legged Asian Zone World Cup qualifying play-off. The first leg was played in Tashkent and Uzbekistan were leading 1–0 when they were awarded a penalty. It was converted by Server Djeparov, but the Japanese referee, Toshimitsu Yoshida, disallowed the goal because an Uzbek player had encroached into the area. The ref should have ordered the kick to be retaken. Instead, he gave Bahrain an indirect free-kick.

After the match, Uzbekistan lodged a complaint and eventually FIFA's World Cup organizing committee decided that the first leg would be replayed in its entirety. A Swiss referee was named for the first leg and there was symbolism in the appointment, because FIFA are based in Switzerland and the Swiss are famous for their neutrality.

Then FIFA asked me to take charge of the second leg – a match that they were desperate should not go wrong in any way. Again, I think there was symbolism involved. Just as Switzerland is the home of FIFA, so England is seen around the world as the home of football and English referees are considered incorruptible and beyond reproach. Well, they are seen that way outside the UK.

On the morning of my match, FIFA telephoned me five times to go through details. They were desperate to get everything absolutely right. I felt that to be selected for a World Cup qualifying play-off, outside Europe, and one which was so vitally important to FIFA, was a huge vote of confidence in G Poll (England).

The international matches kept coming and the season continued to surge towards a crescendo. In November I was given another World Cup qualification play-off match, between the Czech Republic and Norway. It went fantastically well and then I was told I was going to the World Club Championships in Japan at the turn of the year.

But before I went to Japan, there was a big disappointment. I refereed Manchester United against Chelsea on 6 November and when we got back to the hotel afterwards Mike Tingey said he had a fitness problem. Now, we all knew that the FIFA fitness test was going to be extremely rigorous. We also knew that if any member of a national 'team' of officials failed the fitness test, the entire team would be barred from the World Cup. In other words, if an assistant failed, then the ref would also be thrown out.

Therefore, with the help of Matt Weston, the Premier League's sports scientist, I set up a mock fitness test in Nottingham and made it as demanding as the FIFA trial. But in Manchester after that match at Old Trafford, Mike said to me that he had a virus which was sapping his strength and that he doubted he would be able to pass my test.

He was right. He couldn't do it. So I telephoned FIFA and told them that Mike would not be going to Japan. The selection of my team for Japan, for the rest of the season and for the World Cup if we went, had been done for me: the three-man 'A team' was Poll, Turner and Sharp.

It was not lost on us that the World Club Championships were a mini World Cup, a dress rehearsal for the real thing. There was a week's intensive training and then we took charge of the opening match between Al Ittihad of Saudi Arabia and Al Ahly from Egypt. That was a fixture that might have been a bit feisty, but it passed without any trouble, from a refereeing point of view – another successful stride towards the World Cup. I was also fourth official at Yokohama for the third–fourth final: it was Al Ittihad again, against Deportivo Saprissa of Costa Rica.

Once we were back home in England, we had a busy run of domestic games over the Christmas period and then I was invited to Saudi to take charge of a Prince's Cup semi-final – again, a unique experience for me and an indication, I felt, that I was gaining real recognition far outside Europe.

Next up, on what was beginning to feel like a world tour, was Juventus versus Werder Bremen in the European Champions League knockout stage. That was followed, nine days later, by a UEFA Cup match between Schalke 04, from Germany, and the Italians of Palermo. Mario van der Ende – the Dutchman who was an important man on FIFA's referees' committee – came to watch that match, which made me paranoid of course. The match was horrible. It was bitty and nasty and I was not as strong as I could have been but I sent someone off for a handball on the line which nobody else spotted – and TV showed I was right. It was another big stride towards Germany. The crescendo was continuing.

In fact, by then, I was as certain as anyone ever can be that I would be selected for the World Cup. The announcement was due on 31 March ... and on 29 March, my back went after 25 minutes of a match at Old Trafford.

It was a Wednesday night, Manchester United against West Ham. The pain was in my hamstring, but I suspected, correctly, that it was referred pain and that my back was in a bad way again. I took myself off and the fourth official went on. I was in the treatment room and Sir Alex Ferguson and Ryan Giggs popped in at halftime to give me some stick – and also to wish me well because they knew I was on the verge of World Cup selection.

I left the ground soon after half-time, was driven back to the hotel and lay flat out on my bed for the night. Of course it was my problematic sacroiliac joints playing up once more. Thankfully, I had learned since those injections in the summer that the joints could be put right by manipulation and massage. And so, although I was a bit sore, I was fit enough two days later to sit in my study waiting for the news from FIFA to appear on the internet.

Imagine what that was like, sitting there waiting for confirmation that twenty-six years of work would culminate in being named among the world's top officials for the world's biggest football tournament. I called up the FIFA site and kept hitting the refresh button. Nothing. I hit refresh, again and again – no sign of the announcement. After an impatient few minutes, I decided to distract myself by checking my emails – and there was one from FIFA. It said I had been selected for the 2006 World Cup in Germany.

How did that feel? Pretty good. Very few referees go to one World Cup, let alone two. The last Englishman to go to two before me was George Courtney, who had been my idol and had become my friend. He had introduced himself to me at my first Football League get-together, when I was a raw young linesman. Now I was going to emulate him. I had been sent home after one game in 2002, and yet I was going to 2006. How did it feel? Yep, pretty good.

I still had to finish the season, to drive myself on through important Premiership fixtures. And there was that Football League match between Sheffield United and Leeds in which I sent Neil Warnock off for shouting, 'Next time I hope he breaks his f***ing leg.' But not even the charmless Neil could undermine my feeling of achievement and fulfilment. I was going to my second World Cup.

Before Germany, however, I had one more extraordinary stop on my world tour. I was asked to take charge of the Emir Cup Final in Doha, the capital of Qatar – another very different experience in a very different culture. Before the kick-off, we all lined up as normal but were kept standing about. The giant screen suddenly showed a picture of a road, and then a limousine appeared on the road and we all watched as the limo drove to the stadium and the Emir emerged and made his way to a seat like a throne in the ground.

The match went to a penalty shootout, just like another game on that day – the 2006 FA Cup Final between Liverpool and West Ham. Apparently that was a terrific match, but I have never seen it. The other big event I missed because I went to Qatar was Rob Styles's stag night, but he understood – even though I was supposed to be organizing it.

I am very fortunate because my real friends always understood the commitment I had to make to refereeing, and so did my family. During that 2005/06 season, Julia and the children were my haven, as ever, and one of the downsides of going to big tournaments was the length of time I had to be away from my home in Tring. The 2006 World Cup in Germany was near enough for us to think it might be possible for the family to fly out and see me in some of my matches, which was a priceless bonus. But the long time away was still an issue for me because I knew it upset the children. So, before leaving for Germany I made a decision and told them. I said, 'This will be my last tournament. I won't go to Euro 2008. This will be my last long time away.'

It seemed to me then that my whole career had been leading to the 2006 World Cup. Thanks to the remarkable series of international matches in 2005/06, I knew that my reputation within FIFA could not be higher. I was on a pedestal. It seemed that I would be able to exorcize the 'failures' of 2000 and 2002, and the disappointment of 2004.

CHAPTER TWENTY-FOUR

Home Thoughts from Germany

And so we have reached the 2006 World Cup. At the beginning of this book I said that I did not want to be defined by what happened there, but I recognize that it is a hugely important part of my story. And it seems to me that the best way to start that part is to share extracts of the diary I wrote to email home to friends and family. I hope the diary will take you behind the walls of the grounds of the hotel outside Frankfurt, past the security guards and into the day-to-day life of a referee at the global event that is a World Cup.

It was certainly a strange existence. We were watched 24/7 and yet we were very much on our own in the sense that nobody else could understand the pressures we were under.

We needed to talk to each other and so we developed a code of signals involving the doors of our rooms. When the doors were closed, little white discs showed on the outside. If we double-locked our rooms, little red discs showed. According to our code of signals, if the door was wedged ajar, it meant, 'Come in, please!' If the disc was white it meant, 'Knock, and I'll probably welcome some company'. If the disc was red, it meant, 'Give me a bit of peace for a while'.

At the end of every day in Germany, last thing before bed, I sat down at my laptop and tapped in a diary entry – well, almost every day; if I missed one, I caught up the next day. I emailed those diary entries home to close family and close friends in England.

Of course, you know how this part of my story ends. Reading the diary again in order to write this book, I found that it included some prescient thoughts and some spooky coincidences before I got to that game in Stuttgart. It also included some comments which, with hindsight, look pretty daft. The good stuff and the bad stuff is all genuine – I haven't added anything later.

Reading the diaries has also made me realize that I need to explain the part played by Mars bars. No, they were not a staple of my diet, but in the April before the World Cup began, Mars started selling their eponymous chocolate bar in England with the packaging altered. The word 'Mars' was replaced by the word 'Believe' – to show support for the national football team.

In my emails, I used the Mars slogan – Believe – about England and, as you will see, I started to use it about myself; tentatively and with mocking self-awareness. I think, on reflection, that I was telling the close circle of mates and relatives who were receiving my emails to believe in me. But I was also instructing myself to believe because previous tournaments had ended so badly for me.

As I say, we all know how this part of my story ended. This is how it started ...

Friday, 26 May 2006
Arrived at the Kempinski hotel that will be our home for the next thirty-three to forty-six days. It was only a twenty-minute drive from Frankfurt airport. We'd been here for two courses and so felt at home. I have room 121, Phil is next door in 122 and Glenn is next in 123. Opposite us are my friend Peter Prendergast and his assistants.

All corridors have photographs of sports people and major matches. Franz Beckenbauer had signed his photo on top of the glass and a cleaner, obviously not a local, had tried to get it off!

One photo shows the England team from the 1966 Final. Next to them are the referee and one linesman – it has been cropped to cut off the Russian linesman who gave 'that goal'. Oh, the Germans and their humour!

Picked up all our kits. There are four different coloured match shirts, none of which is black. So let's hope the diet is successful.

There are five different training shirts. That doesn't augur well – lots of work. My boots do not fit but they have promised to change them in time for the tournament. In the meantime I have boots that are half a size too big. I'll put in extra inserts.

Before leaving England I had a meal out with Julia and it was a late night with a lot of alcohol. It will be my last alcohol until I have refereed my first World Cup 2006 match. That means none tonight and none for at least two weeks but my liver will appreciate the opportunity to recover.

I tried on all the kit before finally going to bed.

Saturday, 27 May 2006

Fitted for the official uniform – a very sharp pinstripe number, very dark blue with blue shirts and a black and grey tie. The trousers were clearly somebody else's (and not a referee, I hope, as they were massive on me). They found another pair.

There was a 'gentle warm-up' run at 11.30 am for all of us, through the woods which adjoin the hotel. It showed the scale of what we are involved in – 100 people running in identical clothing. Police had to stop traffic on roads as we crossed.

The pace was fairly quick, the terrain was rough and, because of the numbers, it was impossible to avoid tripping over stones. A few runners started dropping out with injuries and – disaster! – one of them was Peter Prendergast, the Jamaican referee who got me through the last World Cup with his wisdom and friendship.

He went over on a large stone and was clearly in distress. We had to finish the run but when it was over, about an hour later, I went to find him. His knee, which has been bothering him for the past month, had finally given way. FIFA will send him for a scan. He already knows that he has a meniscus problem and the scan will show that, so Prendy is really concerned.

After lunch, Phil, Glenn and I did our predictions for the tournament. We went through every match, made forecasts, worked out the tables and then made predictions for the knockout stages. Well, we were bored. Phil and Glenn went for the predictable Brazil win in the Final. I went for an England victory. IT'S COMING HOME. BELIEVE!

Sunday, 28 May 2006

Sunday is weigh-in day. Luckily it was before breakfast. First week and I was 95 kg (15 st) and have body fat of 16 per cent. Not too bad. It will be interesting to see how this changes now that I have given up alcohol.

Peter was told that it is unlikely he will be able to stay at the camp. The scan revealed two tears which will need an operation and then take at least four weeks to heal. The scan indicated that there was already a problem and FIFA feel he should have told them.

Lunch was followed by an appointment with the doctor who kindly removed two splinters from my fingers – a gardening injury from Tring.

We had training at 3.30. It proved that my boots were definitely too big for me. But luckily when I got back there was a pair of the right size waiting for me.

A massage and dinner was followed by a long chat with Peter. He'd had it confirmed that he and his team will be sent home. They will probably leave on Tuesday.

Monday, 29 May 2006

We started the day with a session on relaxation. Many people were still getting over jet lag, yet were woken at 7 am for breakfast in order to go to a relaxation technique session! We were told to sit comfortably, close our eyes, relax and not worry if we fell asleep – just as well for some of us.

Light training – no more than a warm-up – was followed by some practical refereeing exercises. Local boys' teams were drafted in and set up simulated match situations for us.

Lunch was followed by a visit to the indoor pool, and then the sauna, where no clothes are allowed. Iron that tee-shirt old German lady! Oh, it's not a tee-shirt.

Next came a massage which started well. But then honey was rubbed into my back and the skin was pulled upwards to 'invigorate the blood flow'. I had tears running down my face because the treatment was ten minutes of pure agony until the red-hot damp towel was placed on my back to remove any traces of honey, and my skin.

'You have beautifully soft skin on your back now', said Fritz, the masochistic masseur. That should make me referee better.

Spent the evening with Peter Prendergast. He has a 10 am flight to England where he and his assistants are going for a week to 'chill'. The assistants are then going home but Peter will return to Germany and meet up with his wife – who expected to be watching him referee. Now they will try to see games together.

I will try to organize tickets for him to see the England v Jamaica game at Old Trafford while he is in England and have offered him the use of my car. I wish I could do more for him. Overall, a depressing end to the day.

Wednesday, 31 May 2006

The fitness test. The European referees were together in the first run, which meant an 8.30 departure from the hotel. All were confident, but there was still apprehension in the air.

We all passed very competently.

Back to the hotel for a massage and bath. Phil and Glenn arrived back after passing their test but Phil reported a calf strain. The injury could prevent our getting an early game. It will be in the minds of the committee when they make the appointments tomorrow.

Phil stayed in his room to rest while Glenn and I went into the centre of Frankfurt. This is no tourist city and so we spent an hour in Starbucks having coffees and cake – but it was nice to get out of the hotel.

Day six ended with me itching to get into action. I was worried about Phil and acutely aware that a bad injury to any of us will mean no game.

Friday, 2 June 2006

Went running in the forest with the German trio – forty minutes at good pace to really blow out the cobwebs and get the blood pumping.

Phil seems to be improving slowly and we talked about him being more open about how he feels and how he is progressing. Clearly, we are getting worried about missing out on a match.

This afternoon we had another technical session, but I took no notes at all. Then off to an official dinner in our FIFA uniforms. The slight pinstripe makes us look like bankers. I said bankers. The dinner was at an old monastery. The champagne took a real bashing from the Australians but water was the order of the day for England. We were all presented with a watch and a World Cup commemorative coin. The coin is very nice but the watch is a Casio and looks like a five euros special from Frankfurt market.

Home by midnight, having left at 6 pm. Mark Shield, the Aussie ref, complained that the new, abstemious Graham Poll is boring. He'd like the old one back.

Late night after a chat with Julia. I am really missing her now.

Saturday, 3 June 2006

After a psychology session we set off for an eagerly anticipated high-intensity training session. Most referees and all the Europeans wanted some hard training (most had a good drink last night and wanted to run it off). But the session left the fitter guys wanting more. FIFA have to aim the training at the average and not the fittest. So it looks like another early-morning run tomorrow.

José Maria Garcia Aranda, Director of FIFA's Department of Refereeing, interrupted training to tell us about an extra meeting at 3 pm – to announce the first sixteen appointments. After lunch we were told we could collect an advance against the daily allowances to be paid at the end of the tournament. Some refs moved quicker than they ever did in training to join the queue for the $1000.

Before the appointment meeting, Phil, Glenn and I discussed the possibilities, like kids at the start of an adventure. We ruled out the matches we knew we would not get. We discounted the fixtures in England's group, and all of the matches in the group which should provide England's opposition in the first knockout round. We speculated about where we would go and what game we would get but, as the appointments were announced, the matches we considered possibilities all passed without our names. We began to fret that we would miss out. Then we got a game none of us had thought of – South Korea v Togo. I was disappointed initially but we eventually agreed it is the perfect game for us to ease our way into the tournament. It will need careful handling but is low profile.

Our trio had a personal meeting with the psychologist this afternoon – to allow us all to air how we are feeling and to give me feedback on some profiling done during the selection course. The profiling results exactly matched what they were looking for in a top referee – quite a relief. I've not been wasting my time for the past twenty-six years. They say I am confident, sociable and a leader of a group. They spent several thousand euros on what you could have told them for nothing!

We watched England beat Jamaica 6–0 in their last friendly before coming out here. That Peter Crouch hat-trick means anything is now possible. Crouch will probably win the Golden Boot and *Strictly Come Dancing*. It has been a good day.

Sunday, 4 June 2006

Some of us started the day with a run in the woods. Markus Merk and Mark Shield joined us and Shield decided to push the pace along. That made it a good session and ideal for me before the Sunday weigh-in. I have lost 1.5 kg. Maybe the alcohol ban is having some affect.

Another psychology session (more relaxation techniques for forty minutes) was followed by the official training session. It was the worst so far. The fitness coaches only spent thirty minutes with us and then came two hours of advice about training. You would not believe how basic it was.

In the afternoon we were offered an optional visit to a Zeppelin museum (!). Only a handful of takers for that. I spent the afternoon watching Holland against Australia, a friendly which was refereed by Mike Dean. He had a good game and it was a lot better than looking at old Zeppelins.

After dinner we took over the referees' lounge with its massive flat-screen TV and DVD player and watched *Gladiator*. We tried to put Spanish subtitles on for the South Americans but the only available subtitles were Hungarian, Icelandic and Norwegian – everything but Spanish. Still, the 'Kempinski Odeon' was better than another night doing Kakuro puzzles.

Monday, 5 June 2006

Chased up missing laundry and then got some excellent news from Phil. He had been for a run in the forest and felt absolutely fine.

There was a media 'open' event at 1.30, which made the tournament feel closer.

At dinner I got a few minutes with José Maria who resolved something that had been concerning me. My first match is to be in Frankfurt and there were plans for us just to go there from the refs' hotel. José Maria confirmed that we can have a different hotel for the evening before our game to develop a team ethos between the five officials and the match assessor.

And he said I will be able to have 'a few tickets'. So Julia can book a flight and hotel and be fairly certain it will not be in vain. What a great day. Who needs alcohol?

Tuesday, 6 June 2006

Following a rest day, it was back to the early starts and a bike ride. But it was only thirty-five minutes – hardly worth showering afterwards.

Summer has arrived and later we trained in beautiful sunshine. We started with another relaxation exercise; lying on the running track. They played crowd noises to see if we could relax amidst a baying crowd. The recording did not include the well-known English song about me, so I was perfectly relaxed.

In the afternoon I was interviewed by *Kicker* magazine, had a technical meeting with José Maria and a trip to a dentist. I had lost a filling. Just before the drilling started, the dentist asked, 'So, who vill vin da Vorld Cup?' I replied, 'Deutschland, naturlich.' Only when he had finished did I inform him that I was joking and that ENG-ER-LAND will win!

Still awaiting confirmation about tickets for our game but Julia has booked the flights anyway. My gang will experience the World Cup and will understand just what it's all about.

Wednesday, 7 June 2006

During a practical refereeing session, I was pulled up for my hand signal when giving a throw-in. My hand was ten degrees too low apparently. Then I was pulled up because my thumb was sticking up when I awarded a penalty.

After lunch we had an official visit to Frankfurt city hall, and the mayor said in her speech that the ball was not over the line in 1966. She made one very good point, saying, 'A decision that you are obliged to make in a split second could well be remembered for decades.' A sobering point – and she forgot to say that the only decision remembered for so long would be a wrong one!

In the evening, with considerable difficulty, I found a hotel for Julia and the kids to stay at. Everything is set. I was asleep by 9.30 and had my best night for two weeks.

Thursday, 8 June 2006

After two weeks of preparation, the tournament starts tomorrow.

Today began well with an excellent, high-intensity training session further enhanced by having to make refereeing decisions at the end of each run. We then refereed a four-a-side game in pairs to bring styles closer together and aid consistency.

I had salad for lunch. Alcohol abstinence is not having the desired affect. I still need to lose weight.

We had a short session on the Referee Communication System – the microphones and earpieces. We went around the grounds of the hotel testing the tiny mike and fitted earpieces and are all impressed with them.

Next up was a golf trip. I was paired with Kevin Stott, the American referee, and managed to win the first three holes with birdie, par, and par. Kevin weighed in with a couple of holes and we won seven of the nine holes and halved the other two.

It was a hot day and, as I played the eighth, I decided to give in and have a beer when I finished the ninth. One wouldn't hurt. But in the end I ordered a diet Coke – the ultimate sacrifice.

Dinner was excellent and afterwards the English and the Aussies 'borrowed' the DVD player and adjourned to my room to watch *The Shawshank Redemptio*n.

This was the best day so far. Now for the football.

Friday, 9 June 2006

We went for a 7 am bike ride only to discover, after breakfast, that our first official session of the day was to be – a bike ride. Then had a good game of football tennis. My team won 21–17 and Phil and Glenn were on the other team so the victory was sweet.

Glenn and I then had a quick set of tennis against a Canadian assistant and an American assistant. The English boys took one hell of a beating. We lost 6–0. Gemma, the family's ace tennis player, would have been ashamed of just how bad Glenn was. I wasn't much good either. Must have been the racket.

All this was the calm before the storm – because the World Cup finally got underway today with the first two games. *Da da daaa, dada dadada, dada dada da daaaa.* (Work it out. It's a football theme tune.)

Germany beat Costa Rica in Munich and the game went exceptionally well for the Argentine officials, who seem like a nice trio. I was impressed with the style and calmness of Horacio Elizondo and the way his assistants read the many tight offside situations. He will be one to watch as the tournament progresses.

In the second game Poland lost to Ecuador and, for me, Toru Kamikawa, the Japanese referee, let a little too much go.

I can't wait for my first game.

Saturday, 10 June 2006

This was MD minus three (three days to my match day) and so we had the final tough training session this morning. It was tiring but I felt very strong. In my group for the run was the Mexican, Archundia, who pushed us all the way, untroubled by the heat.

At 1.30 pm we left for the stadium to watch England play Paraguay. The number of England fans was incredible. They were only supposed to have 8 per cent of the tickets, about 3,500. There must have been nearly ten times more than that.

Security was tight. Even with VIP passes and all-areas accreditation, it still took the referees twenty minutes to get into the ground. In the VIP area I chatted with Alan Ball and Geoff Hurst and gave in to the champagne suppliers who were very insistent – really they were.

When we went out to look at the stadium – wow, England flags and banners were everywhere. But the heat was oppressive and I could not help thinking about my game, which will also kick off at 3 pm.

Prince William made an appearance in the VIP area and the Australians were most impressed. They say they don't want OUR Royal family any more but were in awe of the Prince.

The match started brilliantly for England, with Paraguay conceding an own goal. But not much else to talk about in the first half other than a complete poser of a referee who showed a lot of naivety in his decision-making.

At half-time we chatted to Freddie Flintoff and Steve Harmison. It seemed to me that FF had been at the lager for a long time.

'Hi, Pollie', said Freddie.

'All right, Fred,' I said. A standard reply. 'How do you see the first half, Fred?' Small talk.

FF said, 'Well, I reckon it's OK if we sit tight on the 1–0 lead.'

I said, 'We have to be careful, they could be like Sri Lanka!' A joke.

FF said, 'F*** off. You touched a f***ing nerve there, Pollie.'

'Well I'd best be careful. You look bigger in the flesh Fred!' Another joke.

'And I'm harder so take care!' Don't know if he was joking.

The second half of the match was absolutely dreadful, as no doubt you have all seen, and we were glad to get back to our hotel and settle down for the other two games. In between the two was the official debrief on the two Friday games. It was incredibly positive and clearly designed to bolster confidence. What a contrast to four years ago. Let's hope it continues.

Sunday, 11 June 2006

MD minus two. It was weigh-in day and once again my weight has come down – 0.1 kg or 100 g. That is insignificant – but better than going up.

After training, José Maria gave his final instructions to referees with imminent matches. He was pleased with the start referees have had but said that now we need to ensure consistency.

I usually communicate my decisions to the crowd. That is seen as strength in England but not here. Today's matches provide examples of this undemonstrative style and there is no communication with players. But that is a strength of my game and I will use it.

In today's debrief, the gloves came off for the Singapore referee who missed two red card tackles by a Trinidad and Tobago player. Luckily the same player was later sent off for two yellow cards. Nobody wanted to confirm that the ref got it wrong. José Maria was upset by what he perceived as a lack of honesty. He said, 'Our strength comes from inside this room. Everyone outside wants to kill us so within this room we MUST be honest and learn from each other's mistakes. This will be hard work from match one to match sixty-four but we must do it as WE will be the winners of this World Cup.' A passionate speech and one which made everyone BELIEVE again – well said José Maria.

I went to prepare my kit for packing tomorrow after training. I am getting really excited. Things are going well and I BELIEVE that my game will provide exactly the challenge I am looking for. No complacency but masses of desire.

Monday, 12 June 2006
MD minus one. I phoned Dad to wish him a happy seventy-third birthday.

The debrief meeting was once again positive but we were reminded that only eight games have been played of a total of sixty-four. That is the same as 12.5 minutes gone in a football match. We must keep up the good work. This was a timely comment as the Egyptian referee on the first match today had a poor game.

At 4 pm, we left for our city centre hotel, a fifteen-minute drive away, and our team of five were in high spirits. The relief to finally leave for OUR game was huge with a mixture of nerves, excitement and pure pleasure.

The new hotel is very nice although the bedrooms are inferior to those at our 'home', the Kempinski. Julia called to let me know they had arrived safely at their hotel, somewhere nearby in the same city. It was good to feel that she was close.

Thank you all for your messages of support. I hope to produce a strong performance. It might not be 100 per cent 'Pollie' because of the instructions not to mime offences etc, but I hope it is one that makes you all proud.

Tuesday, 13 June 2006
MD. Match Day. After four years of hard work the day had arrived for me to demonstrate to the World that I am a good referee. I could not help but think back to Japan and how bad I felt after the game there. I was absolutely determined not to let that happen again.

I'd had a dreadful night's sleep but still felt great physically and the family arrived to pick up their tickets. It was absolutely fantastic to see Julia, Gemma, Josie, Harry and

Laura. That was how to prepare for a game – being showered with love and affection after not seeing my family for nearly three weeks. We spent an hour together just chatting and catching up.

I had a meeting at 11.30 with my team to discuss tactics and instructions for the game and at 12.30 we left for the stadium. I had made a disc of lively tunes and we cranked up the volume.

I had to turn my phone off at midday to stop being affected by the huge number of good luck texts I was receiving. I wanted the game to be as normal as possible and having a 3 pm kick-off was a help.

Going out onto the pitch for the game, with the fantastic colours all around and the heat and noise hitting us, was a really emotional time. In the line-up I thought of all of my family, the early pitches I used to referee on and, finally, the job in hand.

Our concentration was broken by the PA system playing the Korean anthem twice, which delayed the kick-off.

Once we started, I was quickly into my stride and feeling good despite the heat. We were having problems with our communication system just before going out and sure enough within fifteen minutes of the start of the game we stopped using it.

A key moment was twenty-two to twenty-three minutes in: two cautions for Togo who were starting to flex their muscles.

The Koreans came from behind to win 2–1 and a really good game left me feeling immensely satisfied at a job well done. Fitness was excellent, detection of fouls was good and disciplinary action strong – four yellows and one red card. The only error was in issuing the second yellow card. For some inexplicable reason I showed the red card first – I had never done this before and am sure will never do it again. That should not be an issue in the debrief tomorrow but ...

Back in the dressing room, Justice Yeboah, who is a church minister at home in Ghana, gathered us together in a circle and gave a prayer of thanks – a moment of calmness and serenity and one which affected us all.

The assessor was delighted with the performance. He said it was the first of this World Cup to have personality shining through. That is my style and I wouldn't want to referee any other way.

We had dinner at a delightful restaurant which the German team use when they play in Frankfurt. Phil caused hilarity by ordering beef carpaccio and asking if it could be 'well done'. I had plenty to drink because there was plenty to celebrate. At last my tournament jinx was buried and I felt very confident in delivering a strong tournament.

Back in the hotel room by nine o'clock. An immensely satisfying day. My only doubt was that using the cards wrongly may have detracted from the overall performance.

Wednesday, 14 June 2006

Woke up with a slight hangover. I'd forgotten how good they feel!

Breakfast was sweet as José Maria congratulated me warmly on 'an excellent performance full of personality'. Of the error he said, 'Forget it. After all you English drive on the wrong side of the road, so we expect this kind of thing!'

So the morning passed in a semi-daze and I allowed myself the indulgence of looking forward to another game.

The debrief was good. The cards error was highlighted but it was certainly not a major issue.

Later there was a game of water volleyball. My team won 15–13. I am knackered but very, very satisfied and in danger of starting to BELIEVE this could be my World Cup.

Thursday, 15 June 2006

I was trapped in my room all morning with a badly upset tummy. I'll spare you the details but I was glad room service were not respecting the public holiday and turned up to replenish the loo rolls.

I had a massage and a little electric therapy for a bruised leg I picked up just before half-time in my game. I know none of you noticed, but a Togo player ran into me and his knee gave me a dead right leg for the second half. I performed despite a wound!

The bruising is coming out now so will be fine whenever I have my next match.

Went to the lounge to watch England. What a load of rubbish they were. Crouch had to foul an opponent just so that we could take the lead against Trinidad and Tobago. The referee, my friend from Japan, Toru Kamikawa, had a good game so at least the referee camp was happy.

Friday, 16 June 2006

Got up to learn some fantastic news. We are on the training board as MD minus three. That means we are to be given a game on Monday. We knew it wouldn't be France v Togo (because we've already refereed Togo). That left Saudi v Ukraine or Spain v Tunisia. Our feeling was the Spain game but we had to wait to find out.

I noted that a pattern of behaviour by referees has emerged. They go very quiet before getting an appointment, expectant when appointments are being announced and very happy again IF they get a match. Tension is beginning to build.

When our game was announced we learned that we are going to Hamburg for the Saudi Arabia v Ukraine game. Maybe my trips to Saudi, Bahrain and Qatar were time very well spent. Maybe there is planning somewhere up above? Maybe I look at things a little too deeply?

The group games are coming to an end and, because of the timetable of matches, we won't be able to do another group game after the fixture in Hamburg. But that means that if we do the Hamburg match well, we might get a knockout game.

I received further good news when I learned that Mum and Deborah, my sister, will be able to come to the match.

At dinner there were fortune cookies and in mine the message was short but simple; it said 'You might win'.

BELIEVE.

Saturday, 17 June 2006

MD minus two. Fresh as a daisy and off at 7 am for the forest run. The trainer accompanied us to ensure that we didn't go mad. They don't want us burning out, and Chris Strickland, USA assistant, Mark Shield and I are repeatedly told to slow down. On the run back we were allowed to go at our own, quicker pace – although a curry from the night before restricted Shieldsy.

In the technical session I was on fire. The players were sixteen-year-olds full of testosterone and attitude and some of the others refs were not up for it. They were hammered by José Maria.

When he finished with them he approached me. 'There is nothing I need to tell you Grahan.' (He can't quite say my name, but he's the gaffer.) 'Since you arrived you have displayed everything I want you to. This should be a very big tournament for you.'

Big breath. I daren't BELIEVE too much. But exactly how big did he mean?

Please nobody write to tell me to keep my feet on the ground; I have done, I am doing and I will continue to do so. But those who think I am full of confidence, BELIEVE me when I tell you I needed this encouragement from José Maria. It will motivate me even more. Complacency is not an option.

Sunday, 18 June 2006

MD minus one. We were flying to the match but took only carry-on bags and so packed the absolute minimum. We only had economy tickets and seats were not reserved. A twenty-minute delay meant that our Japanese fourth and fifth officials, Toru and Hiroshima (yes that is his name – now try not mentioning the war!) missed all of the Japan v Croatia game. Just before departure they got the news that the game finished 0–0. Japan must beat Brazil by three goals and hope that Australia draw with Croatia. Borrocks!

Hamburg was buzzing with fans who have been watching the game in the massive fan park. Approximately 50,000 people turn up for each game and there is a festival feeling. No hint of aggression, just happy faces.

Our meal was in a fish restaurant in the fish market area and we unsurprisingly chose fish. The mood was vastly more relaxed than before our first game; a good sign for things to come, I hope.

Final item for the day was to watch the end of France v Korea. We had some fun by trying to get Toru to tell us the name of the France player called Ribery. Yes, I know it was childish but it kept me happy!

Monday, 19 June 2006

Match day number two for me. I was really looking forward to my game.

There was a moment straight from John Cleese when the Referee Liaison Officer, Carsten, explained some details about the boat trip we went on. We were on the river Elbe and I said, 'Prague must be that way, as the Elbe goes to Prague.'

Carsten said, 'Ja, it goes via Dresden, vich you destroyed in ze Var!'

GP (shocked into defensive mode) replied, 'Well, you started it!'

Fortunately he didn't complete the *Fawlty Towers* sketch by denying starting the war and forcing me to deliver the line, 'Yes you did, you invaded Poland.'

In fact he just said, 'But now we are friends.'

I managed to squeeze in an hour with Mum and Deborah and had coffee with them in my hotel. It was great to share some time with family. They gave me my father's day present from home – a jigsaw puzzle with Gemma, Josie and Harry's picture on.

The game went extremely well and at the end both Rebrov and Shevchenko gave me their shirts along with a Saudi player who I had refereed in Japan last December and seemed to like me. Perhaps his parents are extremely rich and they will like me as well. Not even I BELIEVE that.

Aaron Schmidhuber was true to form in his debrief. He picked me up for allowing two free-kicks in the second half to be taken from the wrong place. 'How far from the correct place?' I asked, always keen to improve.

'Approximately 4.5 metres', he said. Well, send me straight home then!

Tuesday, 20 June 2006

Forgot to mention that after the game I had a pain in my back, but the physio sorted it out when we got back to the Kempinski. We hadn't realized that until the trip to Hamburg that the Kempinski has been 'home' for three-and-a-half weeks.

The debrief brought compliments all round and big praise for my caution of a Saudi who dived and for my body language. No mention of the free-kicks from the wrong place!

The eight final group match appointments were announced and when match forty-four came up, Australia v Croatia in Stuttgart, I was stunned to hear my name as referee. We will have to leave again tomorrow and will have had only two days between games, both of which will have involved travelling. This is a sign, nonetheless, that things are going very well and that FIFA are getting the message and are starting to BELIEVE!

The game has been identified as one with masses of potential for trouble: six Australians have Croat heritage and their behaviour has been less than exemplary with Harry Kewell only escaping a ban due to referee administrative error in their previous game against Brazil. Croatia are Croatia, known well to me from the last World Cup obviously and I am delighted to have them again. This match will provide the test I have been craving. Interestingly I have not been given a major team to referee – coincidence or planned?

We spent the late evening watching England disappoint again by drawing their final group game with Sweden. But things are going so well for England's officials that we are starting to BELIEVE!

Wednesday, 21 June 2006

What a great sleep: ten hours solid. It is both MD plus two and MD minus one for us. Less confusing was the fact that we had to be on the 4.15 train to Stuttgart which was scheduled to arrive at 17.48, very precise. I had one final treatment from the physio and my back was feeling great again.

Looking at our games it is great to think that we will have had three different stadia, kick-off times and referees' shirts to wear. Tomorrow is the worst shirt, a washed-out blue colour. That means there is only the fluorescent yellow to go. Mmmmm, nice.

When we got to our hotel in Stuttgart, another Maritim, it was vastly inferior to the other three we have stayed in since arrival almost four weeks ago. However, the food and service were excellent at dinner and I watched the Argentina v Holland game in my room before a (hopefully) good sleep to prepare for tomorrow's game.

The day ended with us feeling in very high spirits. We have recovered from the games and the travel and are really looking forward to another game on our quest.

Thursday, 22 June 2006

Match Day three for me. I woke a little earlier than I would have liked but still feeling good.

A nice breakfast was followed by a couple of hours in the city centre, walking around with Phil. Glenn had asked to look around the Mercedes museum as he really likes cars but as we need a haircut, PS and I set off to find a barber's.

Bought stamps for the Hamburg postcards, which I have not yet had the chance to post. After wandering around for two hours we finally found a hairdresser who looked OK, and a little later emerged looking the part as well as feeling good for the game …

CHAPTER TWENTY-FIVE

'Some Confusion' over Yellow Cards

It is necessary to interrupt my diary to fully tell the story of Stuttgart and that match; the match in which I made the mistake that has become an indelible tattoo I must wear forever.

When I have talked to people about that night, they are surprised that it took so long for the truth to dawn that something had gone horrifically wrong. In Britain, TV highlighted my error straight away. At home in Tring, Julia started to take telephone calls from friends and relatives who, loyally, were sure the television people were wrong and that I would explain it all later.

But I didn't even know there was a problem. German TV did not notice it and so nobody in the stadium in Stuttgart had it highlighted for them. Neither I, nor any of the other match officials, was aware of it as we started to wind down in the dressing room after the game.

Later, as people began to talk about 'some confusion', I still did not imagine there was anything really amiss ... until I picked up my mobile. After each of my first two World Cup games in Germany I received about thirty text messages saying, 'Well done' or indulging in jokey abuse. In Stuttgart, there was only one, brief message. It was from Peter Jones, the referee who had helped get me through the FIFA fitness assessment years earlier, and whose experience on the eve of the 1999 FA Cup Final served as a warning to me in 2000. Now, in 2006, his text message inadvertently warned me about something else. It said, 'Chin up mate.' At that moment, I knew there was bad news coming.

But let me start at the beginning. As soon as I arrived in Stuttgart I had sensed a different atmosphere. It was a group stage game, but one team would be eliminated. Australia needed a point to go through. Croatia needed to win. In effect, the knockout stage had come early for these two nations and, to ramp up the tension, there were Croatian-born players in the Australian team and Australian-born players in the Croatia side.

There is a large Croatian community in Australia and many footballers have to decide which country to represent. For instance, when Croatia played Australia in 1998, Anthony Seric was named in both squads. The defender lived in a Sydney suburb but opted to play for Croatia – and they thrashed Australia 7–0. I don't know how popular he was in Sydney after that.

Seric was a sub for Croatia in Stuttgart in 2006 and another of the Croatian defenders that night had been born in Australia and graduated from its Institute of Sport, funded by Australian taxpayers. His name was Josip Simunic; known to his mates as Aussie Joe and known to me forever.

The match started well for me and for Croatia. My first crucial decision, in the second minute, was to penalize a foul by Australia rather than play an advantage. Darijo Srna took the free-kick, struck it precisely and scored. To add to the good feeling about that decision, I also thought I did well to spot a handball in the area by Croatia's Stjepan Thomas. Penalty. Craig Moore drilled the spot-kick into the roof of the net. It was 1–1 at half-time. I had booked two players.

In the dressing room during the interval, one of the assistants congratulated me on seeing the handball. 'Brilliant penalty', he said, which was gratifying. We were halfway towards earning another match at the World Cup and I was feeling this could be my tournament. After the grievous hurt of the two previous major finals, things seemed to be going my way.

'Come on lads – re-focus,' I said to Turner and Sharp. 'First five and last five the most important.' We had to show the players that, although we had been away for fifteen minutes, we had picked up where we left off. Then we had to finish the job efficiently.

Croatia grabbed the lead again after fifty-six minutes. Nico Kovac's drive from thirty yards out was bobbling a bit but Australian goalkeeper Zeljko Kalac should have dealt with it easily enough. However, his dive was all wrong, the ball took a bad bounce in front of him, went over his prone body and rolled into the net. Croatian fans set off flares. The Aussie supporters, stunned into silence at first, roared back into life and urged their team to hunt for another equalizer.

My so-called three-card trick began in the sixty-first minute. Croatia's Simunic body-checked Australia's Harry Kewell, and I showed Simunic a yellow card. My system has always been to identify teams in my notebook by their colours and not the team name. It is a system which I had found prevents confusion, believe it or not. So in Suttgart I put 'Red/White' for Croatia at the top of my left hand column and listed the numbers of the players underneath. In the right hand column, I put 'Yellow' for Australia and listed their numbers. So when I cautioned Simunic that first time, I correctly put a 'C' for caution against Red/White number 3 in the left hand column and noted the time – '16/2' (which meant sixteen minutes of the second half).

The match continued. After seventy-eight minutes Liverpool's Kewell became an immortal hero in Australia with an outstanding equalizer. He chested down a pass, turned and scored with a right-footed volley. That guaranteed that the last moments of the match would be extremely tense for everybody as Croatia charged after a winning goal, Australia desperately defied them, supporters from both sides went through every possible emotion and I raised my own tempo to keep control.

Croatia's Dario Simic, whom I had cautioned in the first half, earned a second booking after eighty-five minutes and I sent him off. Brett Emerton, of Australia, collected cautions in the eighty-first and eighty-seventh minutes. I sent him off as well.

Then, in stoppage time, I cautioned Simunic again – but I didn't realize it was 'again'. He fouled Australia sub Joshua Kennedy and I showed him the yellow card – but, this time, as I now realize, I recorded it wrongly. I put the 'C' beside the Yellow 3, in line with the Red/White 3, which already had a 'C' against it. I didn't note a time or the offence. Although I have replayed the incident a thousand times in my head, I don't really know why I did what I did. I cannot fully understand why I got it wrong and why I failed to send off Simunic. Aussie Joe certainly speaks with a broad Australian accent. Maybe, just maybe, that is where the confusion set in.

Simunic began having a go at me. 'You're unbelievable,' he said. I told him, 'Any more of that and you'll be off ...' As he ran away he said, 'That IS unbelievable.' We all know now what he meant.

The match ended and the Aussies celebrated. I had given a total of eight cautions, two of which had led to sendings off. It had been mayhem, but it was not over. Simunic deliberately approached me and gave me another piece of his mind. Croatia had been knocked out by the country of his birth and he was massively disappointed. He vented his anger at me. I showed him the yellow card and then the red.

Then we all trooped off. As we did so, there was a man from the Croatian FA shaking his head, but his team had gone out, so I thought he was reacting to that. Australia had twice battled back from a goal down. They were on their way through to the next stage of the World Cup. Although I didn't know it, I was on my way home.

The referee's room in Stuttgart was unremarkable, with the usual whitewashed walls and bright lighting. It was not as big as the rooms at Hamburg and Frankfurt but it was not particularly small. It was a square room, with two shower rooms leading off from it, one on either side. As you looked in from the door, the main lockers area was opposite you, with a bench in front of the lockers.

It had been an incredibly tense, cracking game of football, with the added drama of the sendings-off near the end and after the game. I felt drained, unbelievably weary. Yet the only question in my mind was whether I should have awarded Australia a second penalty for another handball by Thomas. I was not 100 per cent certain it was a Croatian arm. Other than that, in our minds the game had gone well for us. We did the usual hugging, handshaking and saying 'Well done.'

Because of the havoc at the end of the match, there was a feeling in the room that we should get our paperwork done and dusted. Then we would be able to have a massage, go for a nice meal, relax, celebrate, and contemplate our next game.

So, to collate the match reports, I went through the notes in my book, calling out what I had recorded. I did the Red/White column first, the Croatians. Then I started on the Yellow column. The Australian 3 had the letter 'C' against him so I said, 'Australia 3, caution, no time.'

The fourth official said, 'No, you didn't caution him.' I checked with the two assistants, and they didn't have a caution down for him either. I thought to myself that, perhaps, for some reason, I had used 'C' to note that the number 3 was the Aussie captain. Perhaps that was what I'd done. That wasn't like me but I put it down to the fatigue.

We finished the reports. Everyone was happy. I went to another room for my massage. While I was having the weariness rubbed out of my muscles, Eugene Striegel, a senior guy in German refereeing, entered. He said that I needed to return to the referee's room as there was a problem. It did not cross my mind that it would be anything serious. Normally when I have made a mistake, or done something controversial, I have known. If I have awarded a dodgy penalty or something, I have said to myself, 'You prat.' Of course, players have a go at you about the incident and so, if your assessor mentions the controversy later, you are expecting it. This time, I did not have an inkling that anything was amiss.

Back in the ref's room, the two assistants were sitting in a state of shock. One – and I genuinely cannot remember which – had big tears ready to flow. The other was staring into nothingness. I thought someone's mother had died. I certainly did not think that the atmosphere in the room could be because of football.

Someone told me that there had been a mistake about one of the bookings. Momentarily I thought it was a joke, a wind-up, but then I thought about that rogue 'C' against the Yellow number 3. Was that it? With the first tendrils of panic beginning to grip my insides, I sat down on the bench in front of my locker and picked up my mobile to check the texts. The solitary message from Peter Jones flooded me with foreboding.

I was still clinging to the hope that the mistake, the confusion, was somebody else's. When I had sent off Simic, I had shown him his second yellow card and then the red. Simunic had run over to get involved. Perhaps people thought I'd shown Simic a straight red and Simunic a yellow. Perhaps everyone was confused about how many yellows Simunic had received. Perhaps.

I telephoned Christopher Davies, who was reporting the game for the *Daily Telegraph*, but he, too, was caught up in the uncertainty. I rang my wife. Julia could only say that 'they' must be wrong because 'I know you wouldn't make that kind of mistake.'

With alarm bells going off in my head, I decided that we should watch the DVD of the game. But, in one of those moments which always seem to happen when you are stressed, there was no remote control and no means for us to fast forward. We began watching the players warm up at the start of the game and thought we would have to watch it all at normal speed. But someone went and found a remote and we started to review the key moments. That was when I learned I had made the biggest mistake of my career.

In that instant, I knew I was going home – and I was going home in disgrace. I had let down England's 27,000 referees. I had embarrassed my family. Everything I had ever done in refereeing had been completely wasted. I had changed job six or seven times to help my refereeing. I had made sacrifices. It had all been an utter waste of time – all of it. I had squandered all the loving, unstinting support of Julia, my Mum and Dad and lots of friends and family. Every match I had ever done was rendered rubbish. My career was a complete joke. I was a joke – I was the biggest joke in any level of football. How could I face people? I needed to be alone.

The floodlights were still on and so, like a moth drawn to a flame, I was pulled out onto the pitch and stood in the centre circle. I just about had control of my emotions and could staunch the tears. Somewhere deep inside me, a lingering sense of pride demanded that I should not let others see how devastated I was.

But, later, as the car took me back to our city centre hotel, the woman driver looked at me with alarm and embarrassment. She did not know what had happened, but she could see I was wrecked.

The hotel was heaving full of partying Aussies. I concentrated on bulldozing my way to collect my key, get to the lift and disappear away to my room. But a woman in the golden shirt of her heroes spotted me. She said she was a friend of Mark Shield, the Australian referee, and insisted I joined the drinking. I think I was rude to her.

Once the door of my room was shut behind me, I sobbed. The tears flowed and flowed. All those clichés about living a nightmare and hoping to wake up seemed precise descriptions of my state of mind.

I rang Shieldsy and told him that I had just been horrible to a friend of his. I hoped he would apologize to her for me. I asked him what the mood was like among the other referees. 'Mate,' he said, 'everyone is gutted for you.'

I tried to get some sleep but none came. A few hours earlier, I had not been able to recall the sequence of bookings. Now I could not forget them. I kept shaking my head in disbelief. I still hoped I would wake from this nightmare.

At some time, in the small hours, I found myself sitting on the ledge of the open window of my room, with my legs sticking out into the hot summer night. I was not contemplating jumping or anything like that. I was just sitting there in my underwear, with the same thoughts going around and around in my head. Below, on the still noisy street, there was a marquee. Australians were going in and out and greeting each other with unrestrained enthusiasm. If they had looked up, they would have seen the man who made that massive mistake. My mood could not have been lower and theirs could not have been happier.

Later, to distract myself, I turned on my mobile. There was a text message from my daughter, Gemma. It said, 'HI DAD. JUST A QUICK TXT 2 LET U KNOW I'M THINKIN OF U AND HOPE U WERE RIGHT LIKE U NORMALLY R. LOVE U LOADS AND LOADS WHATEVER HAPPENS. X GEMMA X'. I still have that message. I have changed my mobile telephone more than once but always saved Gemma's message of unquestioned support and love.

The first person to get through on my mobile that morning in Stuttgart was Colin Paterson from BBC radio. He wondered if I would do an interview. I think I was rude to him as well. I listened to a voicemail from Rob Styles, who begged me not to make any hasty judgement about giving up. It was a kind, supportive message, and made me think for the first time that perhaps the decision about whether I would continue would be mine to make. I rang Rob back and said that, at the moment, my decision would be not to make a decision. That was my first meagre moment of positivity.

I had been mauled after the 2002 World Cup in Japan – the South American contingent of FIFA had ripped me apart – and so I expected a similarly brutal treatment by everybody in 2006. I was filled with paranoia and, in the morning, thought everyone was looking at me and sniggering.

That Friday morning, in the hotel in Stuttgart, I sent text messages to Neale Barry, head of refereeing at the FA, and Keith Hackett. I wrote a letter to José Maria Garcia Aranda, FIFA's head of refereeing. In the texts and the letter I apologized for bringing shame to the recipients.

The train journey back to Frankfurt was mostly silent, although inside my mind there was turmoil, and back at the referees' base I kept my head down, avoided eye contact and made straight for my room. I had not eaten since the game, but could not contemplate food and did not want to see anyone at lunch.

There was a knock on the door. It was José Maria and his assistant. They both hugged me and, in a phrase which I shall remember for ever, José Maria, who had every reason to believe I had let him down, said, 'We are not disappointed in you. We are disappointed for you.'

As we were talking, another well-wisher arrived at my door. It was Brazilian referee Carlos Simon, who, despite the presence of two of the most influential men in world refereeing said, 'Football's shit. Football's nothing. Your family is what matters.'

There was more support from Andreas Herren, FIFA's press secretary. I had prepared a media statement, apologizing, but Andreas said I had nothing for which to say sorry. FIFA would handle it, he said, although he could not do anything about the reporters and photographers who were apparently outside hiding in the bushes hoping to get a glimpse of me.

The day continued in a bit of a blur. It was Friday, one day after my calamity. I knew there was a debrief to get through at 6 pm, and that gave me something to think about. It was scheduled for the big room, with a big screen and a big crowd of referees to look at my big mistake.

In fact, most of the criticism was reserved for the assistants for missing an offside and that penalty which should have been awarded. There was a palpable sense of relief in the room. The other referees knew that the biggest mistake of the tournament had been made, and not by them.

After the debrief, some of the others went to another room to watch Switzerland versus South Korea – a nice, quiet game for referee Horacio Marcelo Elizondo, with nine bookings and a controversial goal when he overruled an assistant's flag.

I went to Mark Shield's room with his Aussie colleagues Nathan Gibson and Ben Wilson. Matt Weston, the Premier League's fitness guy, joined us and so did Glenn Turner and Greg Barkey, the fifth official from my Stuttgart match. Some of those present were there to celebrate Australia's success. I was there to drink myself to oblivion and after we had finished all the alcohol we could find, we decided to go to the hotel bar, which we had nicknamed 'The Far Post'.

I was reeling, which was not good news when my unsteady progress was interrupted by José Maria. He said, 'The chairman wants to see you.' So I went with him to see

Angel Maria Villar Llona, chairman of the referees committee. He showed me the statement FIFA would be releasing which he hoped would satisfy the press. I knew the media needed me to say something, rather than FIFA, but I did not want to make any more waves. So I said my thanks, and joined the Aussies and the others in The Far Post.

As a result of all the drink, I did get some sleep that Friday night, but alcohol is a depressant, and the following morning was the bleakest yet. There was no debrief to worry about, nothing to focus on and I was pitched into a very bad place.

Even now, when I think back, it frightens me to recall how depressed I was. From time to time I just curled up in a foetal position, hugging myself. I was in a state of intense despair. If you have been there, you have my profound sympathy. If you haven't, then I hope you never will be.

I know now that Graham Barber phoned me every hour and others were trying to get past the hotel switchboard. But I knew that my pain would hurt those who cared about me. I did not want anyone to know how bad it was. With that in mind, I managed to send one of my diary emails. This is what it said:

> June 24th – Well, the events of the past few days have kept me from my laptop and contacting you, so apologies but I guess you'll understand. Life is an incredible thing. Just when you think you've got it sorted – bang, something knocks you down.
>
> As for the 'situation', looking at the DVD it is clear I was absolutely exhausted in the final ten minutes and struggling. The game appears to have been too soon after the one in Hamburg and when I look in my notebook it's unbelievable that I didn't send 'Croatia 3' off.

> Everything that has preceded the incident was accurately recorded but I just blanked out. Why and how is irrelevant now. So for the next few days I'll have to train professionally and then return home to my wonderful family who will try to mend some very deep wounds.
>
> As for the future, time will tell. Now is not for decisions, it's merely for surviving and trying to regain some sanity. Thanks very much to all of you for your support. I know you will say otherwise but I feel I have let you down so very badly.

Thinking of my family and friends provided a pinprick of light in the black cave of my despair. Another came the following day when I summoned the remnants of my shattered spirit and persuaded myself to go on a refs' trip to the Fan Park on the banks of the river in Frankfurt to watch England's match against Ecuador in the first knockout stage.

We had VIP seats, which made us very visible, and I knew the trip would expose me to the sort of ridicule I was expecting for the rest of my life. However, I also knew I could not hide for ever.

With incredibly unhelpful timing, there was a power cut and the screens went dead at the precise moment that David Beckham won the game with a free-kick. We did not see the goal but its significance was obvious to me. If England reached the later stages of the World Cup, there was no way an English referee could also be involved. So perhaps I hadn't lost anything. Another ray of light, another positive thought.

Going to that Fan Park, where everyone could see me, was a big forward step for me, which I think took some inner strength. Perhaps that fortitude is what people see as arrogance in me. All I know is that, without it, I might still be in that black, black cave.

CHAPTER TWENTY-SIX

Don't Blame Anyone Else

I need to talk about the two assistants and the fourth official at that match in Stuttgart, because many people have blamed them for what happened – and the truth is that I blamed them at first.

Well, not as soon as I became aware of the mistake; not in that bleak moment in our changing room when it became apparent that I had shown Josip Simunic three yellow cards. Nor when I stood in stark solitude on the pitch afterwards.

But in the long, sleepless hours of that night in the hotel I started to blame them. On the painful journey back to Frankfurt by train, I said nothing, but inside, I blamed them. Back at the referees' base, the feeling that they were responsible festered – and the poison fed off hurtful little signs. The two assistants appeared to be joining the other officials for meals as normal. How could they eat? I certainly couldn't.

They didn't come to offer me their apologies or try to comfort me. Why not? Others were coming to my room, or telephoning or texting me with messages of support and sympathy. Finally, driven by despair and my increasing hurt,

I stomped to Phil Sharp's room. They were both there and I demanded an explanation for the apparent indifference. 'We just did not know what to say,' they both explained.

There is a saying in football that a referee can only commit suicide but an assistant referee can commit murder. In other words, a referee can only damage his own career but an assistant can wreck a referee's prospects. In the 2002 World Cup, mistakes by an assistant had led to my being sent home – and I had carried the can. I had taken the brunt of the criticism in the media. At the 2006 World Cup, the mistake was mine, but the other officials could have stopped me from committing professional suicide. That was what I believed.

My pre-match instructions to assistants about bookings and sendings-off had been the same for years. I always asked both assistants to keep a record of the cards I showed and to whom they were brandished. I told them, 'If you are not sure who I have booked, then ask the fourth official or ask me.' I even used to mention the ludicrously unlikely possibility of cautioning someone twice without sending him off. I used to say, 'Don't let me restart the match in those circumstances. Tell me my mistake so that I can send him off.'

But in the build-up to the World Cup I had worked with Phil Sharp and Glenn Turner as assistants for many, many games. We were a team in more than half of the games I refereed in the 2005/06 season, and they did not want me to repeatedly go through the same pre-match instructions. 'We know them backwards, Pollie,' they had said. So I stopped my usual pre-game talk. And I did not go through the instructions before the game in Stuttgart.

The fourth official should be the ultimate safety net. At the World Cup he sat next to the match coordinator who had a television monitor and who also listed cautions and send-offs. For the match in Stuttgart, the fourth official was Kevin Stott from the USA. He had been on the FIFA list for eleven years.

In Germany, all match officials had microphones and earpieces to talk to each other. The ref's mike was 'open' – it was on all the time. When I cautioned Simunic for the first time, I said into the microphone, 'Caution Croatia number 3, sixty-first minute, block.' The assistants and the fourth official must have heard that. In theory, they should all have noted the caution correctly, as I did.

Then, when I cautioned Simunic again, in stoppage time, I did not say anything into the microphone but neither of the assistants asked me who I had yellow-carded; nor did Kevin, the fourth official. As we now know, I recorded that caution wrongly – in the Australia column of my notebook. Did the assistants record it wrongly? Did they record it at all? I don't know. We have never discussed it.

It has been suggested to me by others that perhaps what the assistants and fourth official did – or did not do – was a compliment to me. Perhaps they just assumed that I would get it right, that I couldn't possibly make a mistake. Perhaps.

The point is, despite what I felt when I was in the 'cave' of my despair, they were not to blame for what happened in Stuttgart. I wanted to blame someone else, but the person who was culpable was me. I made the original mistake. I was the referee. It was my responsibility.

The fifth official, American Greg Barkey, had an internet blog during the World Cup. In it he likened the chain of events in Stuttgart to waking up in his bed at home, smelling smoke and going down to the kitchen to discover a fire. He ran to the tap but it was not working. The outside mains tap was working but his bucket had a hole in it. He could find no other receptacle so he went to the fire blanket but it was padlocked. He telephoned the fire brigade but they were on strike. Realizing the house was going to burn down, he ran inside to collect some valuable paperwork including his fire policy ... which expired the day before.

If I have interpreted his metaphor correctly, he felt that a chain of events, each of them unlikely and unlucky, combined to create a catastrophe. If just one link of that chain had not been there, then the catastrophe would have been averted. But that misses the point as well. In Greg's metaphor, what caused the fire? In Stuttgart, it was my mistake that was the discarded cigarette end.

British newspapers revelled in my misery. My mistake proved what many reporters and most of their readers believed – that referees are useless. And Graham Poll, the alleged best ref in England, was the biggest clown of the lot. Most writers thought it was utterly hilarious. Some were extremely critical of me – I was the braggart who had become a buffoon. Very few writers seemed to think it was a story about a man who had made a human mistake. One of the milder jokes at my expense was, 'Never mind new technology to help referees. Graham Poll needs an abacus.'

To make their fun complete, news organizations needed pictures of me looking miserable. A few shots of my family looking upset by my blunder would be good as well. So, while photographers lurked in the shrubs and trees outside the referees' base near Frankfurt, another large contingent of the media descended on Tring and camped outside my house.

Meanwhile, nicer people were visiting me in my black cave, or sending messages which demonstrated understanding and kindness. Every single person who took the trouble to reach out to me in the darkness did an important, valuable and humane deed and I thank them all.

They included David Beckham, as I have recounted previously in this book. They also included the top man in world football, FIFA president Sepp Blatter, and the head of our own FA, Brian Barwick, whom I have criticized in this book. I have to acknowledge that Brian was solicitous after Stuttgart. I was also contacted by the chief executive of the Premier League, Richard Scudamore. Countless referees got in touch. So did friends. So did family.

It would be self-indulgent to quote many of the messages, but I need to place on record my profound and lasting gratitude to my sister-in-law Tina. She sent the following email:

> Graham – I know that you have probably been flooded with messages but I felt I just had to send you one. I am completely overwhelmed with sadness that your amazing performances at the World Cup had to end like this. Your games have left us even more proud of you (if that's possible) and having read your last diary you have at last brought me to tears after all these years! I don't really know what to say because I'm sure nothing helped but I just wanted you to know we are so proud of you and just because of one mistake (my God, you are actually human) it doesn't change the fact that – Graham Poll IS one of the top referees in the world. We love you (get sick bag out!) and know that you will get through this because that's what makes you the amazing person you are. I think Charlotte's reaction to the events said it all. 'But Graham's done so well to get to the World Cup,' and that's age six. Shame the media aren't so bright. Take care Graham, our thoughts are with you. Lots of love, Tina.

What a shaft of light into my cave that was. But not everyone was so kind. One English referee, not good enough to make the FIFA list and not brave enough to put his name to his message, sent a puerile, vindictive and gleefully gloating text. And a couple of people I imagined would be supportive did not turn out to be that way. But my wife, children, family and real friends could not have done more to show me their affection and that was, and still is, a wonderful but humbling thing.

There was the little detail of FIFA announcing which referees would be kept on for the knockout stages of the World Cup, and which of us would be going home. I already knew which of those groups I would be in, but the process was still painful and prolonged.

I was going home, and was looking forward to it, but before I could make my way back to Julia, and the haven she would provide, she needed some help from me. The media were still laying siege to the Poll house in Tring and, in one of our many telephone conversations, Julia asked me to do something.

I knew that the only thing I could do was to give the news organizations what they wanted – an interview in which I admitted getting it hopelessly wrong. I was feeling raw and damaged but I knew that was what I had to do. I contacted Sky and they quickly arranged for me to face a camera in the grounds of the referees' base, and to face questions from Adam Craig of Sky Sports News. The interview was broadcast live in Britain and quotations from it were picked up by news organizations around the globe.

I took ownership of the mistake. I accepted the blame. I gave a shortened version of how I had found out about the mistake and detailed some of the support I had received subsequently. Then, near the end, came this exchange:

POLL: 'I've had three major championships – Euro 2000, the 2002 World Cup and this. None has gone right. None has worked for me for various reasons. If one thing goes wrong it's unlucky ... if two things go wrong maybe you're really unlucky ... if it's three you have to look at yourself and say something isn't quite right. I don't enjoy the amount of time away from home. I have young children. Therefore I won't be going to Euro 2008. That's a decision I've taken. It's not a knee-jerk reaction. I've discussed it with the FA already. It's time for someone else from England to have a go. I'll do whatever I can to help prepare him. But for me tournament football is over.'

CRAIG: 'So this is something you have thought about carefully ... as far as officiating in the 2008 European Championship is concerned it's a no-no?'

POLL: 'For me it's time. Tournament football ... it hasn't worked. You have to be honest with yourself and for the pain I've gone through ... I couldn't go through it again.'

CRAIG: 'Premiership fans aren't noted for their sympathy towards match officials. Are you expecting a bit of stick next season?'

POLL: 'You get stick whatever happens. I don't know what they'll come up with but it'll be witty and by then it'll probably be time to smile at it. I had 30,000 referees in England who clearly voiced their support for me and wanted me to achieve the ultimate ... to go out and maybe become the first [English referee] to do the World Cup final since Jack Taylor in 1974. A journalist wrote to me

> about the reaction in the media over what happened ... he said people have got to get a dose of reality ... they can move on after they've tried to destroy you but you can't. One day you'll hopefully sit there with a grandson on your lap and say, "Maybe I could have refereed the World Cup final ... and I haven't."'

The interview was screened repeatedly that day. Newspapers took screen-grabs of me looking tearful. They had the story and the pictures they wanted. The headlines were about me quitting international football. That wasn't what I had said. I had said I would not referee in any more major tournaments, but accuracy did not matter any more than my feelings.

The interview provoked another flood of messages. Most of them were extremely supportive. A few expressed surprise that I had turned out to be human. The broadcast also did what I had hoped it would: newsdesks called off the pack; the impromptu camp outside my house in Tring dispersed and there was no gang of reporters and photographers at the airport waiting to ambush me when I arrived back at Heathrow. Julia met me, but there was no media scrum. I'd given them what they wanted.

Yet, as I now know, although the journalists outside my house broke camp and went back to their offices, the media attention never really went away throughout the following season, my final as a professional referee.

CHAPTER TWENTY-SEVEN

The Referee's a Writer

So that is the story of my life as a top referee. It is certainly not the end of my story, however. Immediately after finishing my career at Wembley I began a third phase of my professional life. After careers in repping and reffing came writing. I joined the media – and enraged the football authorities straight away with a secret documentary and a series of critical interviews.

But before telling you how and why I upset the refereeing family, let me tidy up the end of my own refereeing. Although I resigned from the professional game at the end of the 2006/07 season, I did not stop refereeing entirely. In the summer of 2007, a year after pitching into that black cave of despair in Germany, I contacted the Hertfordshire FA and told them I'd like to do a few local games. My idea was to go back to refereeing on parks pitches, where it had all begun, and where I had enjoyed myself so much. The Herts FA could not have been more supportive. So I paid my fee and renewed my refereeing registration. I went from being an international referee to Level Five overnight, but that wasn't a problem for me.

I did wonder if my turning up to referee would be a problem for others, though. I feared that people would think I was Billy Big Boots, come to lord it over them. I thought that local nutters might want to make names for themselves by being sent off by Graham Poll. Perhaps one of the players would attack me. Parks refs do get assaulted, all too often, and there were plenty of people about who didn't like me – that much I knew.

I was entirely mistaken about how I would be received. I only refereed eight or so games in total, including charity matches, but at every fixture people seemed pleased that I turned up. For instance, when I took charge of a friendly match for a team of *Daily Mail* journalists, to a man they all came up and thanked me for doing so. Folk thanking me for refereeing and journalists saying nice things – I wasn't used to that!

It was very refreshing. But it wasn't a challenge. Without being disrespectful to the teams and players involved, the games I refereed in the 2007/08 season were all just a bit of fun. After what I'd been through in football, where I'd been and what I'd done, the parks matches were undemanding – and because of that I didn't really enjoy them. My life had always been about challenges and I hope it always will be.

So I decided not to renew my registration for the 2008/09 season. I wouldn't referee any more. It really was time to call it a day.

Perhaps I gave myself that extra season, when I thought it would be good to go back to my refereeing roots, because I was not sure I was right to walk away entirely. I could not bring myself to just stop refereeing abruptly at Wembley.

But in the days, then weeks and then months that followed that Wembley match, I never once missed my old life of a pro referee. Not once. There was not a single Saturday when I woke up and wished, even privately, that I would be putting on the shirt with the FIFA badge on it. As the months came and went, I grew more certain that I had been right to end my association with the professional game. I had told myself that would be the case, and it proved to be entirely true.

I did miss my referee mates. I missed the camaraderie. Refereeing is very much a lone way of life, but the advent of professional refereeing had brought us all together as a team. So I missed that feeling of blokes sharing the pressures, experiences and banter. I am fortunate to have a few really good mates, but they are a disparate lot – spread all over the place geographically and with very different life experiences. The people with whom I have a shared history, with whom so many things are remembered and understood without anything being said, are referees. But, although I missed the refs (or some of them!) I knew that the camaraderie I yearned for had gone. The team spirit no longer existed to the same extent among the elite refs. The Red Wine Club had been disbanded.

I really did understand, as well, that I had done my stint. It was time to move on, and I had already done so. After Wembley I had begun my third career, as a writer, broadcaster and after-dinner speaker.

By choosing a media career, I knew I would encourage the view that I am an egotist. And, sure enough, there have been many more doses of a very familiar criticism – that I love the limelight. Some of that criticism comes from people in newspapers. They write articles which appear under pictures of themselves, but they do not notice any paradox about haranguing me for enjoying exposure.

I concede that the new roles I took on were not those you'd expect a shrinking violet to select. But I am not wealthy enough to retire. I have to make a living to support my family and it makes sense to use the knowledge I acquired and the visibility I earned as a referee. So when television, radio and newspapers offered to pay me to put across some aspects of refereeing that I believe should be aired – well, yes, I grabbed the opportunity.

The BBC elected to use me on radio and television as a pundit and the *Daily Mail* signed me to write a weekly column for them. To launch those new adventures, I featured in a TV documentary for the BBC and gave a series of interviews to the *Mail*. Both projects enraged the football authorities.

The documentary was produced by Garry Richardson, a very well-respected broadcasting journalist. Soon after I had arrived back in England from the World Cup in Germany, he had approached me about making a TV film about my 2006/07 season and I had agreed. It was a sort of catharsis, I suppose, and I trusted Garry, who conducted several interviews with me during the season. He also gave me a small camcorder and asked me to make a video diary of the season. When Garry and I started the project, neither of us knew that we would be chronicling my last season as an elite ref. We just thought that getting on the Premier League treadmill after my mistake in the World Cup would make a good, human story – and I suppose I needed to show people that I was human.

I knew that if I asked permission to make the film, then there would be much debate and controversy, at the end of which permission would almost certainly be denied. Garry said that if he asked for BBC backing before making the documentary, then there would be dozens of meetings and scores of people involved in the process. So we decided to just get on with it without telling anyone and, when it was finished, Garry would take a look at what we had got and consider what to do with it.

As I have set out fully in this book, the 2006/07 season saw me at my lowest, at my most raw, and I used the camcorder to set down how I was feeling as events unfolded and as my love for refereeing was crushed by those events. But, as I pulled myself together sufficiently to keep going, I filmed some of those moments as well. And when that last Wembley fixture came around, I took the camcorder with me. Once the match was over, and with it my professional career, I got changed and then I took the camcorder out onto the pitch with me, stood in the centre circle, pointed the little machine at my own face and used it to help me say a private goodbye to Wembley and to elite refereeing.

The documentary that Garry made from his filming and my video diary was, I believe, a poignant record of an ordinary bloke struggling to cope with extraordinary events. One scene, for instance, showed me buying a paper on the morning after the match in which Jose Mourinho had shocked and appalled me with a horrible, foul tirade. You could see that I was still in shock, and I would like to think that viewers realized the impact of what had happened. I would like to think that it made some of them think that, when disgusting things are shouted at a ref, there is an ordinary, vulnerable human inside the referee's shirt.

Yet when the documentary was shown, on a special edition of the late Monday night BBC television programme *Inside Sport*, the FA and Premier League were furious that I had dared to record my own thoughts without seeking their consent. They were particularly purple-faced that I had taken a camera onto the Wembley pitch. You would think I had filmed some secret nuclear installation. There were dozens of TV cameras at the game, countless press photographers and most of the 74,993 spectators had taken pictures with their mobile phones. But that was not the point. I had done something without permission. I was a scoundrel and a rogue.

Before the start of the next season, the 2007/08 campaign, Richard Scudamore, the chief executive of the Premier League, said at a meeting of the refs that he did not want any 'celebrity refereeing' that season. Who did he have in mind, I wonder? His advice – and Scudamore's advice is holy writ – was that none of the referees should talk to the media all season. I found it all so sad. I had decided that my future was outside the refereeing family, so that family closed ranks against me. I had betrayed them. I was a traitor.

Of course, I believed I had been betrayed by the Football Association over their handling of the allegations made about me by Chelsea. So, when my *Daily Mail* interviews were conducted, I explained that anger and hurt. My interviews were very critical of the FA, because I felt then and now that by undermining me they had damaged the whole refereeing edifice – from the parks to the Premiership.

If you say, 'The FA let me down', it is as if you are criticizing a building, FA headquarters, instead of living, breathing people. So I talked about the chief executive of the FA, Brian Barwick, and said he had let me down. As I've explained in this book, I did have some issues with him, but my attack in the *Mail* was very personalized and, with hindsight, I got that wrong. It is something I regret.

In the days after the documentary and interviews, I was accused of damaging the recruitment and retainment of referees. Apparently, because I was quitting, and because I was critical of the lack of support given to refs by the FA, I was discouraging parks referees from persevering. Well, it would have been dishonest for me to walk away quietly and pretend that the world of refereeing was perfect. New referees would have discovered the reality soon enough anyway.

No, I wanted, and still want, to provoke a debate about the way the FA supports referees. Then perhaps, just perhaps, things might improve. It is too late for me to benefit from any improvement, but perhaps the circumstances might get better for the men and women at the grassroots, for those higher up the ladder and for those at the top. Then recruiting and retaining referees will become much easier.

Anyway, once my fledgling career as a pundit on radio and television and in the newspaper got properly under way, I upset the powers-that-be again. And again. I seemed to upset them most weeks, in fact.

I was very fortunate to make a fresh start in a new direction in my mid-forties. That is when lots of men and women have mid-life crises. In commerce, it is the stage when, probably, you have been promoted as far as you are going to get, but another decade and a half of working life is still stretching out ahead of you. For me, because of my notoriety as a referee, I was offered an opportunity to earn a few bob in the media. But I honestly saw it as a chance to do some good as well.

A major frustration felt by active referees is that much of the criticism they receive is ill-informed. When you make a mistake in a match, you accept that the media will point it out stridently. But when you get something right, and the media still say it was wrong, that is unfair and maddening.

Yet that is precisely what happens. Media people don't know the laws of the game, and it is profoundly aggravating. It is ignorance and it leads to the public being misinformed, so that the ignorance is perpetuated.

My media work has given me opportunity to redress the balance a bit, to explain laws and challenge some of the myths about them. Sadly, that is not how the football authorities view my contributions.

I knew when I began career number three that to have any credibility with comments on refereeing controversies, I would have to be honest. I would have to criticize my friends from time to time. If all I ever did was back them up, then nobody would take me seriously. The public would just think, 'There goes Poll, defending all the referees'. On the other hand, if I criticized referees when they were wrong, then it would carry more weight on the occasions when I told the public that, actually, the ref got it right this time. If I gave them stick sometimes, I could stick up for them when it was right to do so.

I did not, and do not, criticize match officials for the sake of controversy. Nor do I criticize destructively. If I think someone has made a mistake, I try to explain why the error has occurred. So, for instance, when Rob Styles wrongly awarded a penalty to Chelsea at Liverpool early in the 2007/08 season, I stressed the pressure Chelsea had placed him under all game and suggested that his positioning had compromised his view of the incident. I emphasized that he is human. One mistake didn't make him a bad referee, and certainly didn't make him a bad person.

But I did criticize Rob. He is a good mate of mine, and I value his friendship. Yet, if I am called on to give an opinion, then I believe I should give an honest answer. It is about credibility and because I have retained that credibility, a lot of people have responded positively to my new career.

As soon as I began speaking at sporting dinners and writing and broadcasting about refereeing matters, I came into contact with a lot of refs and started acting as an unofficial mentor to about a dozen of them. For instance, one guy came up to me at a dinner in Tiverton and asked me a question about his refereeing. I answered and a few days later he emailed me to thank me, and asked another interesting question. A dialogue developed and I tried to help and advise him.

One young lad wrote that his first game as a referee was approaching. 'What should I do?' he asked. It was a big question, but I tried to construct a helpful answer. Another lad, aged 16, wrote to me and said that he had a cup semi-final scheduled. It would be his first time with proper assistants, both of whom were sure to be older than he was. I wrote back, telling him of similar experiences when I was a teenaged ref. And so it went on and goes on. I am not making out that I am a hero, but I do care about refs and refereeing.

In my new, third career, I got an encouraging response from some of the public as well. When the first, hardback edition of this book was launched, at Corbetts bookshop in Tring (of course), I was very pleasantly taken aback to find myself signing copies all night. My mum was moved as well. It was the first time she'd seen a crowd that wasn't booing me. The owners of the bookshop said, 'This is better than Harry Potter', although they meant the size of the queue rather than my wizardry.

There was a second launch for the book at Waterstone's in Hemel Hempstead. There they told us that it was more successful than their previous 'celebrity' launch – by topless model Jodie Marsh. You can do your own jokes about her appendages and me.

Yet, even at that second launch, one chap said, as he stuck a book under my nose for a signature, 'You made some terrible decisions against my club'. He was wearing an Arsenal sweatshirt. Some people just cannot forgive me for being an ex-referee, and some of them are totally convinced that I had it in for their particular clubs.

I spoke at a dinner in Sheffield and afterwards a Sheffield United fan came up to me and said, 'Come on, you can admit it now. You were biased against the Blades, weren't you?' My answer was curt and included a swear word. Then I appeared on a BBC radio phone-in and one caller asked whether it was true, as his dad had told him for an absolutely certain fact, that I had once attended a function at some Arab bank or other and admitted that I was a Tottenham fan. Because I was on radio, I managed a less curt, less profane response.

Still it goes on. Even my media work has persuaded some people that I am definitely prejudiced. It is baffling. I suppose that when I write about something that I think is wrong, and if it involves a specific club, the fans think I am ill-disposed towards that club. I get that accusation from Everton, Chelsea and Manchester City.

The Chelsea thing I understand. It is because I dared to complain about John Terry's groundless accusations against me and dared to talk about Jose Mourinho spewing invective in my face. The Everton thing is probably partly because, in 2007/08, when Mark Clattenburg had a really difficult time in a Merseyside derby at Goodison Park, I empathized with him in print instead of merely condemning him. I did say he got things wrong, but I was one of the few men who knew what it was like to referee a pressure-cooker fixture at Goodison, and so tried to explain that. It didn't mean I don't like Everton.

Man City? I have no idea why I am supposed to have an antipathy towards them. I just know it is not true and I also know I am weary of all the arguments. Now, when I meet fans of a particular club, to avoid all the grief, I try to disarm them by confessing to some mistake involving their club years ago (even if I can't think of any). I won't and cannot admit to any bias, but I have had enough of all the conflict and the arguments. I don't want to keep enduring all the old rows. I don't need it.

I am pleased to report that very many people have been exceptionally friendly since I stopped giving free-kicks against their teams. I get lots of letters from supporters thanking me for what they perceive I did for football. It is very gratifying. As I have said, I get letters from referees as well, young and old at all levels of the game, and many say that what I did or said on some particular occasion encouraged them. That is a joy.

There was also a marvellous gesture by the FA, for which I owe my public thanks and deep gratitude. I was presented with an England cap, complete with the Three Lions badge. It was embroidered with my name and the relevant dates to commemorate my international refereeing career.

The idea of caps for referees had been discussed for quite a while, but I was still surprised and totally delighted to get an email in November 2007 from Neale Barry, Head of Senior Referee Development at the FA, inviting me to the annual lunch for international officials. The FA's referees committee meets every year to congratulate and recognize those officials who have been awarded their FIFA badge (it is awarded each year). Ray Lewis is chair of the committee. David Elleray is vice-chair. The commitee wished to mark my retirement from the international list by the presentation of a cap.

Bearing in mind that I had been so critical of the FA, and of chief executive Brian Barwick, I was apprehensive about what would happen when I pitched up at FA headquarters, in London's Soho Square, for the lunch. The worst case scenario, in my mind, was that while awarding me my cap, they would say, 'And Graham has let us all down by the way he has left the game and what he has said since'. Or perhaps they might just sit me down and say, 'Look, here is your cap. Now can you stop giving us stick?'

I wondered whether I should go. But I did, and I am very glad I did. To their credit, they did not let a few newspaper columns stop them doing what they believed was the proper thing. They proved themselves to be bigger men than that. I had represented England and English refereeing 100 times. They felt that I should be rewarded. They presented me with my cap, and it means more to me than I can express.

One organization that has not buried the hatchet is the Professional Game Match Officials Limited, which employs the elite referees. That is a source of disappointment to me.

I completed 14 years with PGMOL. I resigned, wasn't paid any notice period and did not even get a letter saying 'Thank you'. Nothing. I assume that in a cupboard in the Premier League office there is a piece of crystal with my name on it which was supposed to be given to me on my retirement. That is what people always get. But I had the audacity to film my own last season and subsequently criticize Keith Hackett, the boss.

I would love to name the referees who have responded well to pieces I have written, but I fear they might not be too popular for keeping in touch with me. That is how it is. Because Keith and his referees are attacked so often by the media, they pull the wagons round into a defensive circle and I am outside the circle now.

CHAPTER 28

Woolmer Green to Wembley

In this, the final chapter, I have something to tell you about my dad. As I write, he is not at all well. He has vascular dementia, a viciously cruel illness that has robbed him of his mind and taken the real Jim Poll away from us. The husk that is left is not my dad. To see such a robust man, who had such a big personality, stripped of his real self has been too much to bear. He is in a home, because he had to be sectioned under mental health legislation.

Then, within weeks of that happening, our family was devastated again by more truly terrible news. My brother-in-law John, Susan's husband, was diagnosed with cancer of the oesophagus. He was 54 when he was told. There are simply no adequate words to describe the impact of that news.

I promise you, the illnesses which struck Dad and John gave me a different perspective on life, and certainly about football.

My dad's condition is very common. Although that is no solace at all to us, it does drum home the fact that many families are forced to endure identical suffering. Vascular dementia happens when something damages the network of blood vessels feeding the brain. When the blood supply is restricted, brain cells die. So, for a fairly long period, my dad had been dying, cell by cell. His condition had been apparent for quite a long time, gradually worsening until it began affecting his every day life – and the lives of those who love him. By the time the curtain came down on my professional career at that game at Wembley, Dad was struggling. He was at the game, but the members of our family who there were with him spent a lot of the day worrying profoundly about him.

Soon after my retirement, the family helped Mum and Dad celebrate their 50th wedding anniversary, but there was a backdrop of sadness at that event was soon after that Dad was sectioned. He had become impossibly difficult to deal with and it needed nurses and other medical staff to cope with him. Watching them do so with infinite, caring patience is very humbling, and something else which puts football in perspective.

I hope this book has explained how my dad was a big influence on my life. What he instilled in me is very much part of who I am, and so his influence is still with me. But my real dad is not with me any more. He cannot see what I am doing with my life now, cannot share the joy I get from seeing my children grow and blossom, cannot listen to me on the radio or read my newspaper columns. I couldn't show him my international cap. It meant so much to me to receive that cap, and I know it would have meant an enormous amount to him, but I could not show him. It is at my home, with the handcrafted certificate he made so lovingly and with such pride for me in 1991, but he has never seen the cap and never will.

John's illness is brutal. Many of you reading this will know, because you have experienced something just as monstrous in your families. The rest of you cannot possibly begin to comprehend the savage impact on John and how utterly impotent the rest of us feel. We all want to do something, but there is precious little anyone can do.

His daughter, my lovely niece Laura, decided to run the London Marathon for a cancer charity. I decided to join her and I picked the Iain Rennie Hospice at Home, a quite outstanding local charity which I supported as best I could even before John's illness.

Now, I am a relatively fit bloke. Just a short while ago I was refereeing in the Premier League, trying to keep up with Thierry Henry. But, let me tell you, I found the amount of training necessary for the London Marathon incredibly daunting. I had no idea how tough it would be. Yet at least I was able to do my training runs during the day, and pick times when the weather was not too bad. Most people had to go out running in the evenings, after work, and because the race is in April, that meant they were training on dark, cold winter nights. I managed to finish in four hours and 19 minutes and raised more than £10,000.

If you watch the London Marathon in any year, you will see that most of the runners are raising money for good causes and that many of them have the names of people on their vests: slogans like 'For Jane'. They are running because someone they know is ill, or has died, and what kept them going during all those training sessions in all that shitty weather was love.

What is my point? Well, events in our family since I packed up professional refereeing have reinforced my understanding of what is important in life, and what is not. I now realize that, whatever Bill Shankly said, football is not more important than life and death. Of course it is not.

When something bad happens somebody will try to put it in perspective by saying, 'Nobody died'. And, without seeking for one moment to trivialize genuine suffering, I can now think back to what happened in Stuttgart and say, 'Nobody died'. That is the truth. That is the reality. What happened in Stuttgart did no physical harm to anybody. It only damaged my reputation. Nobody died.

Without getting too preachy, the moral for me from the illnesses that have devastated our family is that we should all make the most of our lives. We should relish our good health if and when we have it. And we should cherish our parents. We should not wait for the day when we say, 'I wish I'd spent more time with them'.

That thought has also helped me put my refereeing career in perspective, and to appreciate its benefits better, because that career enabled me to travel all over England and throughout Europe with Mum and Dad. They watched me do something that made them proud. That is priceless to me now.

Because I am no longer absorbed in my own little world of refereeing, I am more able to see things like that clearly now – and since retiring from professional refereeing, I have also formed a very different view of some big, refereeing issues. Specifically, I feel entirely differently about the offensive behaviour of players towards match officials and how I dealt with it. It is apparent to me now that I did not deal with it sufficiently strongly.

After I had been retired a few months, I started to become horrified by the level of abuse directed at match officials by players. So I got out DVD recordings of games I refereed in my last season in the Premier League and, of course, I received exactly the same sort of vile treatment, routinely, week after week. Yet at the time I did not realize. Of course, when something like the Mourinho incident occurred I was only too aware of it, but I did not acknowledge the persistent, casual but appalling abuse.

That will seem utterly incredible, I imagine, but sometimes you cannot see the wood for the trees. I was at the epicentre of it all and genuinely did not realize the level of the abuse, victimization and harassment that goes on week after week. I think that it had gradually become worse and worse over the years that I refereed. At the same time, the defensive shell I cultivated to cope with abuse was getting thicker and thicker. In the end I was tolerating grotesque behaviour – or rather, I was not even fully aware it was happening.

You will recall that in February 2005 I was accused of tolerating far too much foul language from Wayne Rooney. I now accept that the accusation was right. I was wrong. I did tolerate far too much that day but at the time I thought, 'I am managing this game of football well'. That was what I convinced myself about countless similar incidents. I was in there, involved with it, in the middle of it, and so I was empathizing with the players, understanding their passion, going along with the myth that I was serving the game by permitting the swearing and saying to myself, 'The critics just don't understand'.

I said that to myself a lot. In my years as a ref, people frequently complained that, by allowing Premier League players to berate us so horribly, the elite officials were letting down referees everywhere else in the country. I used to think, 'You don't understand.' But it was me who didn't understand what was happening. Now, when I talk to referees' societies, I begin with an apology. I tell them I let them down, because I did.

Of course, I could not have staged a one-man crusade to clean up the game. But it is important that I accept and acknowledge my own failing, even if it was part of a bigger problem.

And let's be clear about how difficult the problem has become. Imagine this scenario: a referee sends off Rooney. Everyone knows he swears, so that would be fine. But then, what if, say Rio Ferdinand loses his rag about the Rooney red card, and abuses the ref. Rio would have to go off as well, to ensure credibility for the Rooney dismissal. Next, Sir Alex Ferguson would be provoked into a frenzy on the touchline, use some choice Glaswegian and have to be sent to the stand.

In those circumstances, how do you think that match would be reported? I can tell you. The headlines would be about the ref spoiling the sporting spectacle. So the media need to change.

One insurmountable problem is that Premier League chairmen do not want to see their players – their expensive assets – sent off and suspended. In their short-sightedness, the chairmen care more about that than they do about respect for referees. They may say they want to cure football, but they certainly aren't prepared to take the medicine. And it is the chairmen who control the referees, because, unlike any other country, in England the Premier League is in charge of its own refs, instead of the national federation or Football Association.

Then, what about the fans? What about all the personalized abuse that is chanted and sung? How can we complain about players swearing and do nothing about foul-mouthed spectators?

Football at the top level is completely infected by the

routine use of profanities, and so I suppose I am calling for a sea change in the entire game and by almost everyone in it. And even as I make that plea, I know it cannot and will not happen. So, there will be no clean-up, and I will continue apologizing to referees' societies for my part in letting the situation become so dreadful.

As you can tell, I have definitely been taking stock – of my life and of football. To some extent, that is what I have been doing in this book as well. But I hope to have achieved more than that. I hope *Seeing Red* has introduced you to Graham Poll the man as well as Graham Poll the referee, because there is an important distinction between the two which is significant for football.

To illustrate what I mean, let me tell you about a Test match at Lord's, before I retired, when I sat with a friend and we struck up a conversation with a father and son sitting in front of us. They came from St Albans and we all got on very well. At the tea interval, I got the beers in. When I returned to our seats with the drinks, the father was chuckling to himself. He turned around to me and said, 'We were just saying – and you'll have to forgive this – how much you remind us of a bloke we both hate. We're both Arsenal supporters and you look a lot like a referee we detest.'

I could see exactly where that conversation was going, of course, so I reached into my pocket and pulled out my referee's ID card. I showed it to the father and son in front and said, 'Do you mean him?' They were embarrassed and shocked – shocked that Graham Poll was an ordinary, nice enough bloke. They thought they knew Graham Poll the referee. They were astonished to meet Graham Poll the man.

The point of that anecdote is not that I am a wonderful human being. It is just that I am a human being. I have failings and frailties and, perhaps, some qualities. They are human failings, frailties and qualities.

Now, to further explain the message I want to deliver, let's think about how referees were introduced into football. When the game first had proper rules, in the nineteenth century, there were no refs. The two teams used to decide issues among themselves but there were prolonged disputes, and so it was decreed that only the two captains should make decisions about whether goals had been scored legitimately, and so on. Unfortunately, the captains were often unable to agree, and so it was decided that each team should appoint an umpire. There were still arguments between the two umpires, hence it was decreed that an independent arbiter was needed. A neutral person used to stand on the side of the pitch, in a blazer and cap. If the umpires could not decide something between them, they would refer to this neutral chap. Because he was referred to, he was known as the referee.

Times changed and the game evolved, but from that moment on, it has always relied on an arbiter. It still does. So, one of several messages in this last chapter is that the referee is human and that he or she is simply an independent, neutral arbiter. Unless you want to go back to asking the rival captains to decide about fouls, offsides and so on, your game – the one you are watching or playing in – needs a ref. He or she is not someone who has turned up to ruin your weekend. He or she is just a person doing a very difficult job.

It must be one of the weirdest jobs in the world. Those who do it understand the appeal and yet those who have never done it will never understand why anyone would want to. Everyone assumes he or she knows everything about refereeing, everyone is prepared to give 'advice' about it, and yet very few people are prepared to do it.

And everyone who does take it on is accused of bias. It happened to me throughout my career, and it is still happening to me, although I have stopped ruining people's weekends.

Whenever a referee is accused of bias, I remind myself that the word 'fan' is short for 'fanatic'. Football fans are fanatics. Their passion is one of the things which makes football so engrossing and compelling. Unfortunately, however, that passion also means that fans see every refereeing decision through the prism of their own bias. Every time one of their players is sent crashing to the turf, they believe utterly that he has been fouled. Every time one of their players clatters into an opponent, they believe completely that it is a fair tackle. Their view of events might not be true, but they want it to be true so fervently that they convince themselves subconsciously. Then, if the referee does not agree with them – well, the referee must be useless or biased.

A similar thing happens with managers. They too are passionate and fanatical about their teams, and so their view of what happens during a game is distorted by that passion. I am sure that a manager believes it when he says something like, 'The ref didn't give us anything' or complains that 'If we were a big club, we'd have had a penalty.' They believe it – but that doesn't make it true.

If you doubt what I am saying, then go to a match when you don't care at all about either team. Then you will see how often players, managers and fans get worked up about perfectly accurate refereeing decisions. You will see how passion distorts their view of what has happened.

Yes, I understand why fans, managers and players, get so worked up. For instance, in my last game as a professional referee – that play-off final between Derby and West Brom –

I ignored West Brom's appeals for a penalty. I have no doubt that some West Brom supporters shouted 'Cheat!', but why on earth should I have wanted Derby to win? Was I party to some wicked, secret conspiracy against the Albion? Of course not, and to suggest so is a kind of madness. But it is a madness you hear repeated up and down the country every week.

Biased? No, I can categorically state that I never deliberately favoured any team or any player in any circumstance – not once in all the years in which I refereed. I never did it, and I was never even tempted. Nor have I ever met an English referee I suspected of bias. We love the game too much. The neutrality of the referee has been a central tenet of football from the moment teams started asking a chap in his cap and blazer to be the independent arbiter. That is why referees are so hurt and angered by any allegation that they are not impartial.

Now let's move on to the question of whether that referee you shouted at the other weekend really was useless. The important thing to remember about that is that there is a pyramid of refereeing just as there is a pyramid of teams. The very best teams are at the top of the pyramid and they get the top officials – those who have clambered up that ladder and survived and flourished under the sort of scrutiny and appraisal that is not matched in any other profession.

Lower down the pyramid, the teams are less good – and so are the referees. They are refs on their way up, on their way down, or at their natural level. And so it goes on, all the way down the football pyramid – the teams get a little worse and so do the referees. So if you think the referees you get are not very good, perhaps the club you play for or support isn't very good! If you are a Sunday morning footballer, you'll get a

Sunday morning ref. It's a bit much, if your centre-forward traps the ball further than he can kick it, to expect the referee to be magnificent. When I refereed in the Isthmian League, it was the correct level for me at that time. I was not as good a referee as I was when I was in the Premiership years later – but then the players on those Isthmian League pitches were not as good as the Premiership players, either.

One person doing the mad, weird job exceptionally well, at the time I write this, is Howard Webb, who has been selected for Euro 2008. He is the same age I was when I was picked for Euro 2000, so he might go to five major championships. I hope he does. I hope he excels at those championships. I hope he has an outstanding career, and that it ends a lot better for him than it did for me.

If he referees a European Champions League Final, I will be delighted. If he goes all the way, and referees a World Cup Final, I will say, 'Fantastic!' I want an English referee to be successful. When I packed up, I had set certain benchmarks, such as refereeing more Premier League matches than anyone else, but those benchmarks are there to be surpassed. I hope Howard is the man to set new records.

I am not envious. I've had my time. I came to that conclusion on an aeroplane in the February of my last season as a pro. I was flying to Rome for a UEFA referees' course. I had made my decision to retire, but I was still mulling it over a little because I was still having sequences of matches that I really enjoyed. So, like a salesperson trying to figure out how to attain his next target, I made a list as I sat on that plane. No, I made two lists: one was the reasons to remain as a referee; the other was a list of reasons to give up.

The 'Reasons to Carry On' list was very short. The most persuasive item appeared to be 'financial security'. It would be a safe option to continue refereeing, but actually that was not very convincing at all, because I don't believe you can referee honestly and fearlessly if you are worried about the impact a decision might have on your future income.

The 'Reasons to Stop' list was a lot longer. Very near the top was 'family'. My family had endured enough.

People say that, for a man, being present at the birth of his first child is the best day of his life. Well, I was there when Gemma arrived in the world. I remember that the sun was streaming in through the window of the delivery room at the Royal Berkshire Hospital in Reading. But I cannot pretend I enjoyed the experience. I found it very difficult. My wife, Julia, was going through agony and I was powerless to do anything other than hold her hand and tell her I loved her.

I think that for Julia, supporting my refereeing became a little like that in the end. She saw me reviled and ridiculed and understood that I was no longer invulnerable to that treatment. She saw that I was suffering, but she could do nothing to stop that suffering. She never once asked me to stop refereeing, but I knew, without words, that she would be happier when I did.

With my mum, the situation was similar. My dad, as I have explained, was already too ill to comprehend what was happening to him, let alone me, but my mum understood only too well what I was going through. I have written about how I understand her pride in my achievements, but I cannot begin to comprehend what it must have been like for a loving parent to watch me unravel in Stuttgart and witness my anguish later.

Since I have retired from the Premier League, I have been much more relaxed about the house. I have been a better person to live with, I am sure. But the family are not seeing all that much more of me. Because of my after-dinner speaking, I have fallen back into a routine that is very much like my refereeing schedule. I drive off somewhere, deliver my speech, stay the night, then probably go straight to another venue and stay the night again. It is similar to going to Staverton for a ref's get-together, going on to a match and being away from Tring for days at a time.

Anyway, when I compiled my list on that plan, 'family' was prominent on the list of reasons to pack up. Another entry was 'injury'. My back would not have let me go on for much longer. But, as I sat there on that aeroplane making my lists, I knew that the real reason I had continued refereeing after Stuttgart was that I did not want to be beaten. And on that flight I came to the happy conclusion that I had not been beaten. I could keep going for another season if I wanted but I did not have to keep going to prove anything. If I stopped, it would not be because I was running away from anything.

That was a liberating moment. I concluded that, if I kept going I would be doing so for the sake of it, out of habit. There were no more refereeing targets for me to aim at – just more of the same. So, alongside the 'Reasons to Stop' list, I wrote a four word summary of my thoughts. It said, 'The race is run'.

And, for the most part, I thoroughly enjoyed the race. That may seem an unlikely conclusion in a book which includes accounts of hurtful experiences and which is critical of some individuals and organizations and some aspects of the way the game is run. Those accounts and those criticisms are in this book because I have tried to be truthful, but I also want to state with all the conviction I can muster that there are far, far more good things about football than there are problems. Whenever I refereed a top match, I knew for certain that of the twenty-two players on the pitch at any one time, at least sixteen of them, and perhaps as many as nineteen or twenty, had never dived and would never do so. The same proportion would never abuse or belittle referees, or do anything deliberate to damage the game.

When Arsenal moved from a ground holding 38,000 to one with a capacity of more than 60,000, they still sold out every week. There is a frantic clamour for tickets for matches at the new Wembley. These are just two examples of many that convince me that football is a vibrant, successful game, and at the top it is played by sensational athletes who are mostly very decent men. I know it, and it needs saying more often. In my new career in the media, I try to do so.

So here comes yet another message. I would say to anyone who loves football, or whose son or daughter loves football, that refereeing is a great option. Despite all the negativity I felt in my final professional season, and despite my sermons in this book about the terrible behaviour of some players and managers in the Premier League, I certainly believe refereeing is worthwhile and rewarding. It is an involvement in football. It will mature you as a person. It will make you a much more rounded individual. It will make you more capable, more self-reliant and more resilient.

I fell into refereeing, but within four games I loved it. It was not as good as playing. I didn't get the dressing room camaraderie or all the crack of having a beer later with team-mates. But I did enjoy something of the latter with the excellent North Herts Referees' Society. And I was a lot better as a ref than I was as a player. So I embarked on a career which I now look back on with pride – and a sense of appreciative wonder.

Refereeing gave me countless remarkable experiences that money could not buy. As I tell people when I speak at dinners, Roman Abramovich is rich enough to have bought Chelsea and, if he wanted, he could select himself to play at centre-forward. But he could not referee a Premier League match, because that is something you can't buy.

Refereeing also gave me some weird but memorable adventures. I have eaten things I could not identify. I have seen some of the hairiest belly dancers I never wanted to see. I have visited countries which I had not even heard of before. And I didn't visit them as a tourist – I was there as a participant in a big event. I have had experiences I could not have imagined.

For instance, as just one of countless examples, I never dreamed that I would be in a car with a police escort in the middle of Moscow, driving on the wrong side of road and playing chicken with cars coming the other way. The attitude of the Moscow police was that the cars coming in the opposite direction would just have to pull over. It was not an entirely relaxing way for a referee to prepare for a match, and it is not something you should try over here if you take up refereeing and are in a hurry to get to a game in the Welwyn and Hatfield Sunday League.

For the most part, my refereeing journey was a huge amount of fun. Think about it: if I offered you the chance now to do a job for twenty-seven years with the promise that you would enjoy almost all of it, you'd take it. Of course you would. Even in the last of my twenty-seven seasons, when things became difficult, I did enjoy many games and relish many aspects of refereeing.

Am I a vain thing from Tring? Well, I never wanted to be famous. I certainly never wanted to be infamous. I just wanted to referee football matches because I love football and, for most of the twenty-seven seasons as a ref, I loved refereeing. When I started to clamber up the refereeing ladder – well, then yes, I wanted to get as high as I could. But not for fame or celebrity. I relished the physical and mental challenges of refereeing, and wallowed in the feeling of success I earned by dealing well with those challenges.

I wanted the toughest challenges, and that meant the biggest games. The recognition that came with succeeding in those matches – when people said I was a good ref and when I continued to get top matches – was pleasurable. Of course it was. But I never wanted to use that recognition as a door to becoming 'a celebrity'. I did not want to walk the red carpet at premieres, hang about in fashionable clubs or move to somewhere trendy. Whenever I came home after refereeing, I was more than content that home was an ordinary house in Tring.

When I was selected for the 2002 World Cup, Paul Durkin telephoned me and said, 'Nobody can take that away from you. You will always be Graham Poll, World Cup referee'. But I am not sure that was and is a good thing. I would quite like to be Nicky Normal with a group of mates who like me for being me, and not because I might have a good story about David Beckham.

That is how I feel now, but I'll admit this: my life could have taken one of two paths from 2006 and, given my personality, I am not sure I would have handled success as well as I dealt with failure. From comments passed by several people, including the incomparable Jack Taylor, it seems now that if I had refereed completely competently in Stuttgart then I would have had a chance of emulating Jack by refereeing the World Cup Final. Jack told me he thought I would have done it. That would have been the ultimate achievement for me and I am not sure how I would have reacted. There is a danger that my personality – all right, if you've got this far in my book I am prepared to admit it to you – can veer towards arrogance. Certainly, if I had refereed the World Cup Final my veneer of confidence would have been pretty thick.

Some players struggle to deal appropriately with success. It was said, for instance, that Frank Leboeuf, the ex-Chelsea defender, used to tell people too often about how he had won the World Cup with France. Would I have been like that if I had refereed the World Cup Final? I would have known that my reputation (and future income from commercial opportunities) was secure. Would I have struggled to remember the advice of Fred Reid and his wife – to keep my feet on the ground and 'my cloth cap on'? I would like to think I'd have remembered their advice and stuck to it, but I am not sure.

We'll never know. That is not the path my life took from Stuttgart. Instead, I came home with my head down in shame. I was battered and very nearly broken. Yet I believe I became a better person.

Craig Mahoney, the referees' sports psychologist, borrows a phrase from the philosopher Friedrich Nietzsche. He says, 'If it doesn't kill you, it will make you stronger.' And because I didn't shrivel up and retreat into my shell after Stuttgart, because I refused to let my career die at Stuttgart, I do think it made me stronger. Instead of revelling in success after the 2006 World Cup, I had to work very hard to re-establish myself – to rebuild my self-esteem and my credibility with others. I think that taught me some humility.

It definitely taught me some other lessons. For a start, I was left in no doubt about the deep love of my family and the supportive friendship of real mates. Some people go through their entire lives without experiencing either – or without realizing them or understanding their importance.

So, although as I say, I am not sure how I would have dealt with real success, I am happy with how I dealt with failure.

That is not to say I am glad Stuttgart happened in the way it did. Of course I can't pretend it was a good thing to have made my mistake in front of a worldwide television audience. And I think it is grossly unfair that I will always be remembered for one, human mistake after a career of more than 1,500 games. But that's life – that's my life – and perhaps my story might give heart to others who suffer setbacks because I think it shows that the human spirit is remarkably resilient.

This book started in the centre-circle at Stuttgart. The stadium was almost deserted and I was desolate. I was taking a private moment to try to compose myself. I was truly frightened about the future.

But I faced that future and dealt with it, and so the book can end in the centre-circle of another almost empty stadium. After my last professional game, after that play-off final, I walked out into the middle of the pitch at Wembley. I took my secret camcorder with me for the documentary I was making, but the fundamental reason for going back out onto the pitch was that I wanted another moment on my own. It was 340 days after Stuttgart, and of course I thought back to that day, but as I stood there at Wembley, alone again, I knew that I had coped with the aftermath of Stuttgart. I had not let my career finish in failure. Instead, I had battled back and finished on my own terms. I had completed an incredible journey, with some diversions on the way, from Woolmer Green to Wembley.

That last time, as I stood there in the middle of a vast stadium and took it all in, I was content.

APPENDIX

My Top Ten Frequently Asked Questions

1) SHOULD FOOTBALL USE TECHNOLOGY TO HELP REFEREES?

The short answer is 'Yes'. Referees have said for years that they would welcome any system which helps them on matters of fact. So if a foolproof system can be developed that tells you when the ball has crossed the goal-line (or any line, come to that) then we should use it. For me, that is a no-brainer.

But, when I look a little deeper at the question of technology I have lots of questions myself.

I would have welcomed any technology that gave me the opportunity to immediately put right any decisions I got wrong – but when would I have consulted it?

And if a player goes down in the box, does the referee stop play immediately and consult someone who is watching TV monitors? Or should he allow play to go up the other end and then ask someone? Neither of those answers is satisfactory.

People say, 'Only consult technology for major decisions' but what constitutes a major decision? In my last season, a free-kick given to Fulham over by the sideline proved a major decision, because it led to the goal with which they earned a point at Charlton. So should the referee consult technology for every free-kick?

I'd hope not. But that is the danger with technology. It's a Pandora's Box. Once you've opened it, it's open for ever and for everything.

As I say, for straightforward matters of fact – has the ball crossed the goal-line? – then I'd introduce technology as soon as a robust, reliable system exists. But for other issues during a game, the biggest and unanswered question about technology is when to apply it without detrimentally affecting the game.

2) WHY DON'T ASSISTANT REFEREES SIGNAL FOR MORE FOULS?

The two key jobs for an assistant are to say when the ball has gone out of play and to get offside decisions right. Believe me, those tasks are hard enough, because they involve looking in two different directions, ninety degrees apart, and making judgments about moving people and a moving ball. Talk about multi-tasking.

Because the assistant is concentrating on those tasks, and on getting his position correct for those judgments, sometimes he doesn't see an additional occurrence, such as a foul. And don't forget that a 'linesman' is not sufficiently experienced to referee at the level at which he is assisting. Premiership assistants referee in the Conference or a 'feeder' league.

And, any way, an assistant should not signal for every foul he sees. If he thinks the referee has a good, clear view of the incident, he should leave it to the referee – because the referee might want to play-on.

I always said to my assistants that they should flag for infringements if they saw them clearly and thought I had no view of them. But, frankly, if they got the ball-out-of-play decisions and most of the offsides right, I was more than happy.

3) SHOULD EX-FOOTBALLERS BECOME REFEREES?

The assumption behind this question is that someone who has played a lot of football at a good standard understands the game better than someone who hasn't. That assumption is right, as far as it goes. So if you take two guys who have never refereed before, one of whom is an ex-footballer and one who isn't, then the ex-footballer should be better at refereeing to start with, no question.

But neither of them will be as good as someone who has refereed for 15 seasons. Again, no question.

During 15 seasons, a referee will have been mentored, assessed, analysed and scrutinized. He or she will have taken charge of 750 games or so, and will have learned so much about managing situations, not making decisions too hurriedly, positioning himself or herself to get a clear view, how to calm a game down by refereeing robustly for a while, how not to react to all the abuse … and so on and so on. And during those 15 seasons and 750 games he or she will have learned a lot about football – about why and how teams commit fouls at specific times and for specific reasons, for instance.

Refereeing requires a different, additional set of skills to those of a footballer. It would be good for the game if good ex-footballers wanted to learn those additional skills and become referees, and perhaps they could be fast-tracked in some way.

But they would have to start at a level appropriate to their lack of experience, otherwise they would just not be able to cope.

4) ARE PROFESSIONAL REFEREES A GOOD IDEA?
The introduction of professional referees in England led to an increase in fitness: that much is definite.

Yet, the economics of the situation dictates that only a small number of referees can be paid enough to be full-time professionals. It is difficult for other referees to gain promotion to that group and it is a big deal if one of the pros is 'relegated' from the top, professional group.

That means that a small band of referees get all the top games and that can be counter-productive. It means, for instance, that one referee might referee the same club six times or so a season – and that can lead to conflicts with that club. At the same time there is a temptation, for some, to referee safely: to avoid controversy, avoid being kicked out of the group and maintain a nice income.

Yet I would solve the problem by making the elite group smaller. Because of the amount of time and commitment involved, I do believe that international referees need to be full-time professionals. But that group need only be of ten or so refs.

Below that there should be a bigger group of refs, paid enough to make it worth their while and to compensate them for the career sacrifices they'd have to make, but not necessarily full-time. That group should cover the Premiership and the Football League and there should be fluidity within that group, so that more get a chance of refereeing big matches and, at the same time, good referees officiate in the Football League.

The advances that have been made in preparation (better diet, Pro-Zone analysis of performances, good advice from a sports psychologist and so on) should be available to the whole group but you don't have to be full-time to benefit from things like that.

5) HOW CAN FOOTBALL STOP THE DIVERS?

Diving is done by footballers. That statement might be blindingly obvious, but it is important because it is footballers who have to stop the diving.

I remember the very honest answer given by Harry Redknapp when his Portsmouth team were beaten by a penalty won for Arsenal by a Robert Pires dive. Harry was bitterly upset but when asked whether he would discipline one of his own players for diving, he admitted that he probably would not.

So that is the problem. When players are successful because of their diving, their managers, team-mates and fans do not complain.

It is tough for referees to spot diving, because players have become very proficient at it. And those who say divers should be red-carded do not understand the mentality of referees. It is difficult enough making a decision when you know that only a yellow card is at stake, but if you had to send someone off for diving, you'd be even more reluctant to make the decision.

I'd introduce an 'honesty' system, and link it to retrospective punishments.

If a player goes down in the box and the opposition claim it was a dive, then the referee should ask the player concerned, 'Were you fouled?'

If he says 'Yes', and the referee agrees, then give the penalty. But if after the game the study of several, slow-motion camera angles shows that no foul has been committed then the diver should be suspended. He should be treated as if he had been sent off for serious foul play and banned for three games.

Asking him the question avoids the risk of banning players who have just slipped. If a player has simply fallen over, he can say, 'No, I was not fouled.'

Club chairmen would not be happy about paying the wages of someone who kept getting banned, managers would not be best pleased about not being able to select him, and the player would soon get the message.

6) WHY ARE REFEREES NOT MORE CONSISTENT? WHY DON'T THEY SHOW MORE COMMONSENSE?

You hear both these questions asked, but they contradict each other. 'Consistency' suggests applying the law the same way all the time. 'Commonsense' implies having leeway to apply the law differently in some circumstances.

If a referee shows 'commonsense' in one situation – for instance, if he makes an allowance for a young player kicking the ball away in the heat of the moment when he has been pulled up for a foul – then you could argue he is not being consistent if he books another player for doing the same thing in a pre-meditated, cynical way to waste time.

FIFA have made a number of law changes which say certain things are mandatory. Those changes should aid consistency, but they leave no leeway for not taking action, even if that is what 'commonsense' dictates.

At the highest level, lots of work is done on trying to get referees to react in the same way – to show consistency. But no two situations are exactly the same. And, of course, because referees are human, different referees will interpret events differently.

So, sorry, but these two questions probably remain irreconcilable to some extent.

7) HOW CAN WE STOP SPECTATORS ABUSING REFEREES?

It's not really a problem when 30,000 people chant, '*The referee's a banker*' or whatever it is they sing. That's part of the game and part of life. But when one person yells foul abuse, full of hatred, then I think it is a problem. Why should that be acceptable? Why should my wife and children have to hear that? And, because nothing is done, it makes people think it is OK and makes them more inclined to abuse parks referees and referees in youth football. I'd like it to be stopped at the top matches. I'd like CCTV used to identify the culprit and for stewards or police to eject him (or her!). In every Premiership programme there is a warning that swearing is an offence and yet you never see any action taken.

8) HOW CAN WE STOP PLAYERS ABUSING REFEREES?

In Chapter 28 I explain how my perspective about swearing at referees has changed since I retired but people have to remember that using foul language is not an offence. The law prohibits using 'offensive or insulting or abusive language and/or gestures'. And, sadly, foul language is commonplace in society. Words which were unacceptable in my parents' day now appear on t-shirts. Football reflects society. So a certain amount of swearing is to be expected during a football match. But, just as the fan who stands and shouts something vile is not acceptable, so it is not acceptable for players to scream abuse in a ref's face, or to call him a cheat. How can we stop it? By backing refs who take action against it and by punishing the offenders and their clubs.

9) WHY NOT HAVE ZERO-TOLERANCE TOWARDS DISSENT?

It would not be credible, sensible or workable to have a policy of zero tolerance in football. It is a passionate, physical, all-action game. And if every time someone said something in the heat of the moment he was booked or sent off, then every game would have to be abandoned for lack of players. But referees do have to be a bit braver and not put up with unacceptable levels of dissent. And to encourage referees to be braver, the FA needs to back them. Read Chapter Three, and you'll understand my point.

There needs to be a change in the attitude of the media as well. If a high-profile player is sent off for abusing a referee, then, instead of assuming that the referee has been too sensitive (or worse, believing allegations of bias) it would help the entire game if newspapers, radio and television condemned the abusive player instead of criticizing the official.

10) WHAT CHANGES WOULD I MAKE TO THE GAME OR THE LAWS?

I get asked this a lot when I speak at dinners. And I've mentioned already in this section that I'd like to see retrospective punishments introduced for cheats.

It won't surprise you to read that I also want the disciplinary procedures to be much tougher against managers who make personal comments about referees. It is OK to say, 'That should have been a penalty.' It is not OK at all to say, 'The ref didn't give a penalty because he doesn't like us.'

That questions the referee's integrity and undermines the whole basis on which the game is played. So the penalties for managers who make personal comments have to be sufficient to act as deterrents – and that means the deduction of points.

I have two other ideas. The first is that I would like to see an experiment with 'sin bins'. If a player has lost his cool he is likely to either abuse the referee or go and kick an opponent. Yet, at present, a referee can only talk to him or show him a card. I'd like to see whether giving the player five minutes in a 'sin bin' to calm down would work. I'd like to see referees given that extra tool. I don't know whether it would work, but I'd like to see an experiment to find out.

The other change I favour is taking time-keeping away from the referee, to avoid arguments and to make it more accurate. And I'd like to specify a minimum amount of time that the ball must be in play. In Champions League matches, for example, there is only about 46 minutes of play in the entire game. The rest of the time is eaten up by delays when the ball is out of play or waiting for free-kicks and so on. I'd set a minimum of thirty minutes active play for each half and have someone in the stand timing it. When the time is up, a hooter should sound and the ref should stop play.

Career Statistics

MY FIRST SEASON

Date	Competition		Home team
6 Sep	North Herts League Div 5	Referee	Woolmer Green Rangers Res
7 Sep	Stevenage Minor League 2	Referee	Colwell Youth
13 Sep	Herts County Junior Cup	Referee	Cam Gears
20 Sep	North Herts League Div 4	Referee	Ickleford Res
21 Sep	Herts County Sun Junior Cup	Referee	Great Wymondley
21 Sep	Stevenage Minor League 4b	Referee	Woodland
28 Sep	Stevenage Minor League 7	Referee	Stevenage Colts
10 Oct	Representative Game	Line	Buntingford Minor League
11 Oct	North Herts League Div 3	Referee	Provident Mutual
12 Oct	Herts County Cup U12	Referee	Stevenage Colts
25 Oct	North Herts League Div 5	Referee	Sandon Res
26 Oct	Stevenage Minor League 5	Referee	Bedwell Rangers
1 Nov	North Herts League Div 4	Referee	Shephall Athletic Res
2 Nov	SML U12 Cup	Referee	Longmeadow Athletic
9 Nov	SML 2	Referee	Derby Way Wanderers
15 Nov	NHL Div 2	Referee	Jackdaw
16 Nov	Herts County Cup U14	Referee	Fairlands Youth
22 Nov	Herts Intermediate Cup	Line	Knebworth
23 Nov	SML 2	Referee	Colwell Youth
6 Dec	NHL Div 3	Referee	Ashwell Res
7 Dec	SML U14 Cup	Referee	Ripon Rangers
14 Dec	SML 4a	Referee	Longmeadow Athletic
20 Dec	NHL Div 1	Referee	Letchworth United
3 Jan	Herts County League Prem	Line	Sandridge Rovers
17 Jan	Friendly	Line	Letchworth Town
18 Jan	SML 4a	Referee	Bedwell Rangers
24 Jan	NHL Div 2	Referee	S.B.M.
25 Jan	SML 2	Referee	Fairlands Youth
31 Jan	NHL Div 1	Referee	Walkern Res
1 Feb	SML U16 Cup	Referee	Longmeadow Athletic
7 Feb	Nat Ass Boys Clubs - Nat Cup	Line	Herts & Beds
14 Feb	NHL Div 4	Referee	Forest Res
15 Feb	SML 2	Referee	Fairlands Youth
21 Feb	Herts County League Div 1	Line	Sandridge Rovers Res
22 Feb	SML 4b	Referee	Shephall Athletic
28 Feb	NHL Div 5	Referee	Cottered Res
1 Mar	SML 2	Referee	Cygnet Athletic
14 Mar	NHL Div 4	Referee	Wymondley United
21 Mar	Herts County League Div 3	Referee	Whitwell Res
22 Mar	SML 4	Referee	Welwyn Pegasus
28 Mar	NHL 1	Referee	Dynamics
29 Mar	SML U10 Cup Final	Line	Westmill
4 Apr	Herts County League Prem.	Line	Knebworth
5 Apr	Stevenage Sunday League 4	Referee	H.B.T.
10 Apr	Adult Training Centre Cup Final	Line	Luton
11 Apr	NHL Premier Div	Referee	Ashwell
12 Apr	Herts County Cup U16	Line	Cygnet Athletic
14 Apr	NHL Premier Div	Line	Albion
16 Apr	NHL Div 4 Cup Final	Line	Borg Warner Res
18 Apr	Herts County League Div 3	Referee	Radlett Res
25 Apr	NHL Div 2	Referee	Benington
26 Apr	SML 7	Referee	Cygnet Athletic

MATCHES: 52 (40 Referee, 12 Assistant); REFEREED: 21 Non-league, 19 Youth league.

The first of my twenty-seven seasons and the start of the journey from parks to the Premiership. The four columns on the right before the result were when I received and then confirmed details from the fixture secretary and then the home club. I did not include a column for crowds because there weren't any. I did not have a column for cautions, either, because there were not many of those. Challenges which would

Away team	R	C	R	C	Result
Anchor	–	–	–	–	6–0
Bedwell Rangers	–	–	–	–	3–7
Taylors	–	–	–	–	18–0
Wymondley United	–	–	–	–	3–3
Stevenage Post Office Res	–	–	–	–	4–1
Fairlands Youth	–	–	–	–	2–11
Derby Way Wanderers	–	–	–	–	0–5
Stevenage Minor League	–	–	–	–	0–4
City Hearts	–	–	–	–	4–2
Goffs Oak	–	–	–	–	6–0
Lister Hospital	–	–	–	–	1–7
Fairlands Youth	–	–	–	–	0–4
Fold United	–	–	–	–	1–2
Fairlands Youth	–	–	–	–	0–11
Whitehill	–	–	–	–	1–2
Borg Warner	–	–	–	–	0–1
Southfields	–	–	–	–	5–0
Elliot Sports	–	–	–	–	7–2
Cygnet Athletic	–	–	–	–	6–0
Weston United	–	–	–	–	3–1
Austen Arrowheads	–	–	–	–	6–0
Bedwell Rangers	–	–	–	–	4–1
Argonauts	–	–	–	–	1–5
St Margaretsbury	–	–	–	–	3–0
Wycombe Wanderers	–	–	–	–	1–6
Longmeadow Athletic	–	–	–	–	4–5
St Ippolyts Res	–	–	–	–	0–0
Bedwell Rangers	–	–	–	–	0–3
Wilbury Wanderers	–	–	–	–	0–3
Westmill United	–	–	–	–	0–5
Suffolk	–	–	–	–	1–4
Henlow Res	–	–	–	–	5–1
Derby Way Wanderers	–	–	–	–	4–2
Mount Grace O.S.	–	–	–	–	4–1
Austen Arrowheads	–	–	–	–	8–0
Kings	–	–	–	–	3–3
Whitehill	–	–	–	–	1–8
Kalstan	–	–	–	–	1–1
Bovingdon Res	–	–	–	–	0–0
Shephall Athletic	–	–	–	–	2–4
Hitchin Clublanders	–	–	–	–	3–0
Woodland	–	–	–	–	4–0
Sandridge Rovers	–	–	–	–	2–1
White Lion	–	–	–	–	10–0
Stevenage	–	–	–	–	1–7
Codicote	–	–	–	–	10–0
Panshanger	–	–	–	–	4–2
Cotterod	–	–	–	–	2–1
Royal Oak	–	–	–	–	0–1 aet
ICI Plastics Res	–	–	–	–	1–1
Sandon	–		–	–	2–1
Westmill United	–	–	–	–	3–2

be illegal now were commonplace and bookings were a rarity. In that entire first season, I remember that I only took five names. You can see that, almost straight away, I was doing three games a weekend. I was seventeen and yet I did more men's matches than youth games. At the end of the season I was appointed linesman at three cup finals – more than I appeared in during my entire playing career.

MY FINAL SEASON

Date	Competition		Home team
8 Aug	Friendly	Other 1	Tring Athletic
9 Aug	Friendly	Other 2	Chelsea
12 Aug	Championship	FL 1	Colchester United
19 Aug	FA Premier League	PL 1	Arsenal
23 Aug	UEFA Ch. Lge. 3rd Qual, 2nd leg	UEFA 1	Steaua Bucharest
26 Aug	FA Premier League	PL 2	Fulham
6 Sep	EURO 08 Qualifier	UEFA 2	Poland
9 Sep	FA Premier League	PL 3	Everton
13 Sep	Coca Cola League One	FL 2	Brentford
17 Sep	FA Premier League	PL 4	Manchester United
23 Sep	FA Premier League	PL 5	Middlesbrough
27 Sep	UEFA Ch. League Group Day 2	UEFA 3	Real Madrid
30 Sep	FA Premier League	PL 6	Chelsea
2 Oct	FA Premier League	4th 1	Watford
14 Oct	FA Premier League	PL 7	Portsmouth
18 Oct	UEFA Ch. League Group Day 3	UEFA 4	Olympiakos
22 Oct	FA Premier League	PL 8	Manchester United
28 Oct	FA Premier League	PL 9	Fulham
5 Nov	FA Premier League	PL 10	Tottenham Hotspur
8 Nov	Carling Cup 4th Round	FL 3	Everton
11 Nov	FA Premier League	PL 11	Manchester City
18 Nov	FA Premier League	PL 12	Reading
2 Dec	FA Premier League	PL 13	Arsenal
6 Dec	UEFA Ch. League Group Day 6	UEFA 5	AC Milan
9 Dec	FA Premier League	PL 14	Manchester United
16 Dec	FA Premier League	PL 15	Reading
23 Dec	FA Premier League	PL 16	Portsmouth
27 Dec	FA Premier League	PL 17	Charlton Athletic
30 Dec	FA Premier League	4th 2	Watford
1 Jan	FA Premier League	PL 18	Liverpool
6 Jan	FA Cup, 3rd Round	FA 1	Sheffield Wednesday
13 Jan	FA Premier League	PL 19	West Ham United
24 Jan	Carling Cup Semi-final 1	FL 4	Tottenham Hotspur
27 Jan	FA Cup, 4th Round	FA 2	Bristol City
31 Jan	FA Premier League	PL 20	Chelsea
3 Feb	FA Premier League	PL 21	Wigan Athletic
10 Feb	Coca Cola Championship	FL 5	Coventry City
17 Feb	FA Cup, 5th Round	FA 3	Manchester United
25 Feb	FA Premier League	PL 22	Tottenham Hotspur
28 Feb	FA Cup, 5th Round Replay	FA 4	Blackburn Rovers
8 Mar	UEFA Cup Round of 16 1st leg	UEFA 6	Paris St Germain
31 Mar	FA Premier League	PL 23	Newcastle
7 Apr	FA Premier League	PL 24	Arsenal
9 Apr	FA Premier League	PL 25	Charlton Athletic
15 Apr	FA Premier League	PL 26	Wigan Athletic
18 Apr	FA Premier League	PL 27	Liverpool
21 Apr	FA Premier League	PL 28	Fulham
28 Apr	FA Premier League	PL 29	Wigan Athletic
3 May	UEFA Cup semi final, 2nd leg	UEFA 7	Sevilla
6 May	Friendly	Other 3	Tring Tornadoes Managers
9 May	FA Premier League	PL 30	Chelsea
13 May	FA Premier League	PL 31	Portsmouth
18 May	CC League One Play-off semi	FL 6	Nottingham Forest
28 May	Championship Play-off Final	FL 7	Derby County

MATCHES: 54 (52 Referee, 2 4th); REFEREED: 7 FIFA/UEFA, 4 FA, 31 Premier league, 7 Football league, 3 other.

My last season, and a very different set of statistics from a very different world. I no longer had to worry about getting confirmation of the kick-off time and venue, but the number of cautions had risen to an average of just over four a game and 1.8 million spectators paid to watch matches with which I was entrusted. This last set of

Away team		Result		C	S/0	Attendance
Bedmond Social		5–0		0	0	50
Celtic		1–1		2	0	21,000
Barnsley		0–2		3	0	5,000
Aston Villa		1–1		3	0	60,000
Standard Liege		2–1		9	1	50,000
Sheffield United		1–0		6	0	22,000
Serbia		1–1		7	0	15,000
Liverpool		3–0		4	0	40,000
Swansea		0–2		4	0	4,000
Arsenal		0–1		4	0	75,500
Blackburn Rovers		0–1		4	0	26,000
Dynamo Kiev		5–1		2	1	80,000
Aston Villa		1–1		2	0	41,000
Fulham		3–3	4th	–	–	–
West Ham United		2–0		8	0	21,000
AS Roma		0–1		1	0	32,000
Liverpool		2–0		4	0	75,800
Wigan Athletic		0–1		3	0	21,000
Chelsea		2–1		9	1	36,000
Arsenal		0–1		3	1	32,000
Newcastle United		0–0		4	0	42,000
Charlton Athletic		2–0		4	0	25,000
Tottenham Hotspur		3–0		3	0	60,000
Lille OSC		0–2		1	0	40,000
Manchester City		3–1		4	1	75,000
Blackburn Rovers		1–2		3	0	23,000
Sheffield United		3–1		2	0	24,000
Fulham		2–2		0	0	25,000
Wigan Athletic	Abandoned 56'	1–1	4th	–	–	–
Bolton Wanderers		3–0		3	0	40,000
Manchester City		1–1		5	0	30,000
Fulham		3–3		10	1	30,000
Arsenal		2–2		5	0	36,000
Middlesbrough		2–2		2	0	19,000
Blackburn Rovers		3–0		1	0	38,000
Portsmouth		1–0		1	0	15,000
Cardiff City		2–2		5	1	17,000
Reading		1–1		3	0	70,000
Bolton Wanderers		4–1		4	1	35,000
Arsenal		1–0		6	0	19,000
Benfica		2–1		4	0	35,000
Manchester City		0–1		4	0	52,004
West Ham United		0–1		1	0	60,053
Reading		0–0		1	0	27,000
Tottenham Hotspur		3–3		3	0	16,000
Middlesbrough		2–0		1	0	43,000
Blackburn Rovers		1–1		2	0	23,000
West Ham United		0–3		3	0	22,000
Osasuna		2–0		5	0	45,000
Tring Tornadoes U-16		2–1		0	0	350
Manchester United		0–0		7	0	42,000
Arsenal		0–0		0	0	20,000
Yeovil		2–5 aet		8	1	26,000
West Bromwich Albion		1–0		8	0	75,000
						1,806,757

statistics gives me a sense of satisfaction because by the turn of the year I knew that my career was reaching its conclusion and yet my performances remained good enough for me to get some terrific fixtures and to finish my refereeing journey at Wembley.

MY FULL CAREER

Year	Season	Games	Referee	Line	4th	Premier League
1	1980–1981	52	40	12	–	–
2	1981–1982	73	62	11	–	–
3	1982–1983	54	40	14	–	–
4	1983–1984	64	47	17	–	–
5	1984–1985	62	38	24	–	–
6	1985–1986	57	49	8	–	–
7	1986–1987	81	61	19	1	–
8	1987–1988	77	51	25	1	–
9	1988–1989	71	49	22	0	–
10	1989–1990	67	44	23	0	–
11	1990–1991	76	52	24	0	–
12	1991–1992	59	58	1	0	–
13	1992–1993	60	58	0	2	–
14	1993–1994	47	44	1	2	11
15	1994–1995	36	32	1	3	22
16	1995–1996	48	38	4	6	21
17	1996–1997	42	37	2	3	22
18	1997–1998	45	42	–	3	22
19	1998–1999	48	43	–	5	25
20	1999–2000	58	48	–	10	21
21	2000–2001	55	49	–	6	23
22	2001–2002	53	45	–	8	24
23	2002–2003	53	45	–	8	23
24	2003–2004	55	46	–	9	24
25	2004–2005	50	48	–	2	31
26	2005–2006	57	55	–	2	29
27	2006–2007	54	52	–	2	31
		1554	**1273**	**208**	**73**	**329**

A career in numbers. Here is a spreadsheet of all twenty-seven seasons which demonstrates how much time I gave to refereeing – because I loved it. My seventh season, 1986/87, when I became a Football League linesman, I was also refereeing in the Isthmian League and still doing Sunday matches. To clock up 81 games that season, I was doing as many as ten matches a month some of the time, while holding down a job. I only did two seasons in youth football, because there were too many abusive parents.

Football League	Football Association	FIFA UEFA	Non League	Other	Youth League	Attendance
–	–	–	21	–	19	–
–	–	–	45	0	17	–
–	–	–	40	0	0	–
–	–	–	47	0	0	–
–	1	–	37	0	0	–
–	3	–	46	0	0	–
–	3	–	55	3	0	–
–	3	–	48	0	0	–
–	6	–	42	0	1	–
–	7	–	36	0	1	–
–	2	–	49	1	0	–
22	7	–	26	3	–	–
19	9	–	28	2	–	–
25	5	–	3	0	–	458,692
3	6	–	1	0	–	589,050
2	11	2	2	0	–	748,550
3	8	4	0	0	–	847,438
2	6	6	0	6	–	894,750
3	4	8	0	3	–	1,175,022
9	6	10	0	2	–	1,238,054
13	5	6	0	2	–	1,298,507
6	4	11	0	0	–	1,463,352
7	4	10	0	1	–	1,385,411
7	4	9	0	2	–	1,151,667
3	3	10	0	1	–	1,561,791
4	5	17	0	0	–	1,107,000
7	4	7	0	3	–	1,806,757
135	**116**	**100**	**526**	**29**	**38**	**15,726,041**

Look at the international matches, and how the number jumped in my penultimate season – because FIFA were preparing me for the World Cup.

In my last three seasons in the Premiership, the number of games I refereed in that competition increased substantially. I was not the only guy doing so many but it was certainly true that a few men were getting a lot of games. Most of mine were high-profile, potentially volatile matches and, because I refereed them honestly without fear, I had more than my share of controversies.

MY PREMIERSHIP RECORD

		Home				Away			
		P	W	D	L	P	W	D	L
1	Manchester United	27	18	7	2	30	18	5	7
2	Wimbledon	12	10	1	1	12	4	4	4
3	Chelsea	30	15	12	3	24	11	6	7
4	Nottingham Forest	7	3	2	2	4	2	2	0
5	Leeds United	16	9	2	5	20	9	5	6
6	Southampton	19	9	7	3	4	1	1	2
7	Arsenal	25	11	8	6	24	11	5	8
8	Blackburn Rovers	13	8	2	3	19	6	7	6
9	Liverpool	23	13	4	6	24	9	3	12
10	Aston Villa	18	7	6	5	17	5	9	3
11	Reading	6	3	2	1	5	0	5	0
12	Fulham	26	11	8	7	10	2	5	3
13	Newcastle United	19	11	2	6	19	4	7	8
14	Derby County	14	7	5	2	5	0	1	4
15	Portsmouth	12	7	2	3	5	0	1	4
16	West Bromich Albion	8	4	1	3	7	2	2	3
17	Charlton Athletic	12	8	4	0	12	1	2	9
18	West Ham United	14	6	3	5	21	6	9	6
19	Middlesbrough	11	5	2	4	14	4	5	5
20	Wolves	3	2	1	0	6	1	2	3
21	Queens Park Rangers	7	3	0	4	2	1	0	1
22	Bolton Wanderers	11	5	3	3	10	3	1	6
23	Wigan Athletic	5	1	2	2	3	1	2	0
24	Ipswich Town	7	3	2	2	7	1	2	4
25	Leicester City	13	6	3	4	15	3	2	10
26	Norwich City	3	1	0	2	6	2	1	3
27	Sunderland	9	3	2	4	12	3	3	6
28	Birmingham City	8	2	3	3	9	2	3	4
29	Tottenham Hotspur	15	5	5	5	23	5	4	14
30	Manchester City	12	2	6	4	18	4	4	10
31	Everton	12	3	4	5	18	4	3	11
32	Coventry City	8	3	2	3	12	1	4	7
33	Crystal Palace	8	2	4	2	4	0	0	4
34	Sheffield United	4	1	1	2	6	1	1	4
35	Sheffield Wednesday	8	1	3	4	7	0	2	5
36	Watford	3	0	2	1	1	0	0	1

This table shows all the teams who spent any time in the Premier League while I was refereeing in that competition (between 1993/94 and 2006/07). This is the analysis of their games which I refereed. I included cup games, but awarded points for those matches as if they had been in the League. So Manchester United averaged the most points from the games I refereed – but that is because they were the best team during that period and won eight titles. It surprised me that Wimbledon were the second most successful team in games I refereed. But I only really took charge of them during their very successful spell. Nottingham Forest and Leeds are right up there for the same reason, and yet, as I write, they are both in the third tier of English

	Total				Goals		Av
P	W	D	L	F	A	Diff	Points
57	36	12	9	102	56	46	2.105
24	14	5	5	41	30	11	1.958
54	26	18	10	88	54	34	1.778
11	5	4	2	18	15	3	1.727
36	18	7	11	51	37	14	1.694
23	10	8	5	48	36	12	1.652
49	22	13	14	68	49	19	1.612
32	14	9	9	38	30	8	1.594
47	22	7	18	70	59	11	1.553
35	12	15	8	44	39	5	1.457
11	3	7	1	14	10	4	1.455
36	13	13	10	50	46	4	1.444
38	15	9	14	61	49	12	1.421
19	7	6	6	27	25	2	1.421
17	7	3	7	23	20	3	1.412
15	6	3	6	16	19	-3	1.400
24	9	6	9	29	32	-3	1.375
35	12	12	11	47	41	6	1.371
25	9	7	9	37	35	2	1.360
9	3	3	3	13	8	5	1.333
9	4	0	5	15	17	-2	1.333
21	8	4	9	24	29	-5	1.333
8	2	4	2	11	13	-2	1.250
14	4	4	6	17	30	-13	1.143
28	9	5	14	36	53	-17	1.143
9	3	1	5	12	20	-8	1.111
21	6	5	10	18	27	-9	1.095
17	4	6	7	23	26	-3	1.059
38	10	9	19	47	59	-12	1.026
30	6	10	14	32	45	-13	0.933
30	7	7	16	31	51	-20	0.933
20	4	6	10	24	29	-5	0.900
12	2	4	6	15	21	-6	0.833
10	2	2	6	10	15	-5	0.800
15	1	5	9	14	23	-9	0.533
4	0	2	2	3	7	-4	0.500

football. I am sure Neil Warnock will draw some conclusion about the fact that when I refereed Sheffield United when he was manager, they averaged less than a point a game – but at least they are above Sheffield Wednesday.

There are some apparent anomalies. Spurs, for instance, are lower in the table than I expected, but that is partly explained by the statistical quirk that I refereed them in a lot of away games, and most of those away games were tough London derbies. So when you look at any club, bear in mind that I often refereed their toughest games.

Full career statistics at www.grahampoll.co.uk

Acknowledgments

This book is dedicated to my wife and children. My wife, Julia, has had to tolerate a lot of intrusions into the family life which we cherish so much, but her love has been steadfast and has provided my safe haven. Our children, Gemma, Josie and Harry supported their dad – and now they can support their favourite football teams with more gusto and less worry.

Special gratitude is also owed to my mum and dad, Beryl and Jim, whose role in my career is touched on in this book but whose importance in my life can never be adequately expressed. I must record my special thanks as well to other family members who have shared my adventures and been there when I needed them. In particular, I want to state my appreciation of Julia's parents, Malcolm and Gill, who were not football people and yet responded supportively when both their daughters married referees! Julia's sister Tina, and her husband Tony Conn, must get a special mention, as must my sisters who followed my career closely, Deborah and Susan, and Susan's husband John and children Laura and James.

Special thanks as well go to Graham Barber, my best mate

in refereeing, who has proved a true and priceless friend, and to two journalists who collaborated with me on this book. Christopher Davies painstakingly compiled much of the information over the course of eight years and then Mick Dennis took up the writing baton and captured my 'voice'.

Let me also acknowledge my 'back-up team'. Matt Weston, the referees' fitness instructor, somehow made me quick enough to keep up with Premiership players, and my local physio, Ros Needham, will probably have arthritic thumbs after all the work she did on my thighs over the years. Dr Panikos Sissou kept me supplied with painkillers and sleeping tablets when I needed them and, in later years, Gary Lewin performed miracles on my back.

While that lot were trying to sort out my body, sports psychologist Craig Mahoney went to work on my head. He helped me become strong enough to get over the bad times and also helped me appreciate the many good times.

Keith Hackett and Richard Scudamore believed in me and supported me one hundred per cent. Thank you, gentlemen.

I would also like to acknowledge the support of two friends in the media, Garry Richardson and Paul Hayward, and to recognize the long-term backing of the North Herts Referees Association and the Herts FA.

All my previous employers showed considerable understanding, especially Coty UK Limited, whose managing director, Ian Williamson, deserves my gratitude.

My friendship with David Allan, Jeremy Bingham and Alan Crompton has endured the years and, finally, I would like to thank the people of Tring for their quiet solidarity.

I have been very lucky with my friends and family and with my choice of home town and I acknowledge that now with heartfelt thanks.

Index